Music
All Around Me

Antony Hopkins

Travis & Emery

First Published, Leslie Frewin, 1967.

Republished Travis & Emery, 2011.

©Antony Hopkins 1967.

Hardback: 978-1-84955-006-2 Paperback: 978-1-84955-007-9

Published by
Travis & Emery Music Bookshop
17 Cecil Court, London, WC2N 4EZ, United Kingdom.
(+44) 20 7240 2129
neworders@travis-and-emery.com

Contents

Prelude   13

Overture   21

The Child Mozart Plays for an English Connoisseur   26
The Playing of Maria Anna Stein, *by Mozart*   28
Liszt as Pupil   29
Liszt Visits Beethoven   29
The Prize-giving Concert, *by Berlioz*   30
A Few Words from Stanford   33
Mendelssohn, at 14, Gives Criticism   33
'So You Play Organ . . .'   34
André Gide Describes Some Early Piano Lessons   37
'Hats off Here Likewise, Gentlemen'   40
Questions to a Prodigy   41
Benjamin Britten as a Young Composer   42

Étude   45

Rules for Practising the Piano   48
Chopin's Teaching Methods   49
Paderewski and the Spider   52
Ten Seconds of Bliss   53

Aria   55

My Career as a Singer, *by Neville Cardus*   58
How to Become a Prima Donna, *by Geraldine Farrar*   59
by Anna Case   60
by Ursula Greville   60
by Anna Case   62
The Cinderella Syndrome   62
The Star-spangled Manner   63

Sonata — 67

- The Dramatic Situation — 71
- 'A Vista of Joys Unknown' — 71
- The Language of Programmes — 73
- On Playing Hamlet and Beethoven — 74

Theme & Variations — 77

- Music and Memory-Images — 82
- The Goblins of the Fifth — 86
- A Letter from Mendelssohn — 88
- Stravinsky as Inventor — 89
- Tippett's Inception of Creation — 91

Interlude I — 92

- Mendelssohn Goes to Buckingham Palace — 92

Images I — 95

Composers, Conductors and Singers
Photographs by Zoë Dominic, Stephen Fry, Godfrey Macdomnic, Lotte Meitner-Graf and Roger Wood

Scherzo — 113

- Musical Intelligence Among the Animals — 118
- Oneupmanship — 119
- Tetrazzini Awash — 119
- The Piano that Played Itself — 121
- An Orange at the Opera — 123
- Friedman Interrogated — 124
- Cadenza — 125
- Paderewski's Awful Moment — 126
- Too Good for J Walter Thompson — 127
- Schoenberg Asks a Girl to Play... — 127

Blues — 129

- Mozart's Letter to the Municipal Council of Vienna — 134
- Mozart to Michael Puchberg — 134 & 136

Schubert: 'My Peace is Gone'	136
Schubert's Last Letter	137
Beethoven in Death	137
A Letter to Clara, from Schumann	138
Chopin's Chronicle of Despair	139
Brahms Visits Schumann in the Asylum	141
Puccini on Poverty	144
Delius: A Simple Little Tune	144
An Acknowledgement from Schoenberg	146
Letters from Alban Berg	146
Gustav Holst: The Last Days	147

Romance   149

Mozart to his Wife	152
Berlioz to Ferdinand Hiller	153
Beethoven to his Beloved	154
Robert Schumann to Clara	156
Enrico Caruso to Dorothy	156

Images II   159

Players
Photographs by Zoë Dominic, Guy Gravett, Godfrey Macdomnic, Lotte Meitner-Graf and Axel Poignant

Danse Macabre   177

Paganini Takes the Stage	179
Paganini: the Long, Last Journeys	180
Berlioz in the Charnel House	182
Berlioz's Mission of Vengeance	182

Interlude II   187

Parthenia	190
Thomas Bateson	190
Samuel Danyel	190
Henry VIII, Act III, Scene I	191
On Orpheus Going to Hell for a Wife	191
On Lute-strings Catt-eaten	192

Charles Lamb	194
Ode Written for a Concert	195

Oratorio & Anthem   199

Psalm 150	202
On Mendelssohn's Preparation of the *St Matthew Passion*	202
The Charity Children Sing in St Paul's	210
The Village Choir Practice	212
Young Cardus alters the score	214

On Conductors   215

Bach's One-Man Band	219
Mozart Whips Them Up	219
Beethoven's Tragi-comic Concert	220
The Conducting of Hector Berlioz	222
Ten Golden Rules Inscribed in the Album of a Young Conductor	224
Nikisch and the Sparrows	225
Richter Omnipotent	226
The Orchestra Speaks	226

Opera   233

Opera in Paris, 1760	236
Mozart on Opera, to his Father	237
Tolstoy Witnesses a Rehearsal	238
Chaliapin the Perfectionist	240
Caruso the Irreverent	241
The Magnificent Mullings	242

Pot-pourri   245

A Classic of Criticism	249
All Right on the Night	251
Mozart Improvises	251
Plus ça change. . . .	252
Paderewski's Parrot	252
Mendelssohn's Scottish Lament	253
Don't Shoot the Pianist	254

Requiem 257
   Bach 260
   Mozart 260
   Beethoven 262
   Schubert 265
   Schumann 266

Acknowledgements 269

Prelude

(*From Latin praeludium.*) An introductory piece played, for example, before a church service or a musical performance, or forming the first movement of a suite or other sectional work; also one paired with a fugue, to which it forms an introduction; from the nineteenth century onwards sometimes a separate concert work especially for pianoforte (Chopin, etc) or orchestra; and from Wagner onwards the orchestral introduction to an opera where it does not take the form of a detached overture and leads straight into the first act.

Prelude

MY STUDY is overflowing with books as never before; they lean drunkenly in the shelves where random volumes have been removed, they trip me as I cross the room to answer the telephone, they totally cover a divan bed which is supposedly for guests but which is never used. I am faced with a choice that is almost too dismaying – what to keep, what to leave out. It is a procedure to which a composer is accustomed; I have always maintained that composition is seventy per cent rejection and thirty per cent acceptance, and even there, the mathematical proportion is probably quite wrong. Say 'ninety-nine per cent rejection' and I would not argue, for at each individual moment of a composition it seems that there is one sound and one alone that is the right and logical solution. Only *this* harmony, *this* instrumental timbre, *this* sonority will suffice; the composer senses what it is by a combination of instinct, taste and craftsmanship. Nobody else realises how many alternatives were rejected before he made the final choice; in all probability, he is not consciously aware of them himself. I once defined the act of composition as 'the identification of sounds half-heard', and I have yet to think of a better definition.

But what instinct do I, a musician, have when I must choose not notes but books? Even within my own house there are hundreds of books that I have never really read; they are there as friends, to fall back on in time of need. I have an extraordinarily unretentive mind, capable of being forcefully fed for a brief period, but singularly empty of solid facts. Nearly all of my professional work as a lecturer and broadcaster is based on musical intuition and deduction. I start from the notes and then think out loud, and I find it easy enough, for there is always so much to say. Faced with the prospect of compiling an anthology of writings on music, my first instinct was to run away. Gradually, with a strange mixture of reluctance and fascination I started to dip into books, looking for likely material. It was a process remarkably akin to searching for some theme for a composition, although that is a misleading analogy if misinterpreted.

Musical instinct came to the rescue over one of the hardest problems – how to organise the mass of material which was obviously available. I hit upon the idea of using the forms of music as categories; Prelude, Romance, Rhapsody, Caprice, Intermezzo, all seemed to have literary possibilities. I toyed with False Relations, a term that has a special harmonic significance, and looked (vainly as it happened) for sufficient instances of treachery in composers' families to fill a section. I soon became involved in a game not unlike a vast jigsaw puzzle; into which slot would this chosen passage fit? Then came the search for the missing pieces needed to make up a section, to balance serious thought with frivolity or simply to provide a reasonable sense of proportion.

To a certain extent, any anthology is bound to reflect the personal tastes of the compiler, and this, of course, is by no means detrimental. I had to decide, however, if there was to be any educational content in the book, or whether it was to be pure entertainment. In the event, I found the various categories helped me to resolve this problem; if I included a section called Sonata, it provided a justification for some reasonably serious matter. But however serious the content there is no excuse for really obscure writing. There are many ways of writing about music from the high-flown rhapsodic style of Thomas Mann or Sacheverell Sitwell to the unbelievably prosaic approach of the teach-yourself harmony textbook. My pet abomination is the polysyllabic, baffle-them-with-science type.

> The succession of axis tones in each series of these verticalised set-segments proceeds in a direction that is exactly contrary to that of the immediately adjacent elements and in a direction that is exactly parallel to that of the next adjacent elements. . . . The foregoing description must be understood to refer exclusively to the *precompositional* formulation of a systematically arranged series of verticalised set-segments . . . etc.

You may think that I invented those chiselled gems of prose as a parody, but I assure you that they are taken from a book whose intentions and content are wholly admirable. (*Serial composition and atonality;* George Perle.) All it needs is an English translation.

Perhaps the first requisite for a writer on music, more important than literary style or even clarity of expression, is a manifest love for his subject. Present-day scholarship has tended to become a shade clinical in its quest for the truth; I still have a great fondness for Grove's book on Beethoven's symphonies precisely because it reveals not only a deep affection for the music but a real sense of joy in discovery. Tovey has the same quality, and his *Essays in Musical Analysis* remain the yardstick by which any subsequent attempts to reveal music must be judged.

I suppose it is inevitable that to a musician, descriptions of music in novels often seem rather wide of the mark. I have tried to select some of the better examples for inclusion in this volume, but one notable omission should be mentioned, Thomas Mann's *Doctor Faustus*. This novel, whose hero is fairly clearly based on Schoenberg, contains a number of passages on music which show a genuine perception. The canvas is so vast however that it does not readily lend itself to the selective knife of the anthologist. One needs to be drawn fully into the book not to be put off by the intense concentration of ideas which Mann imposes on his reader. For instance:

> In art, at least, the subjective and the objective intertwine to the point of being indistinguishable, one proceeds from the other and takes the character of the other, the subjective precipitates as objective and by genius is again awakened to spontaneity, 'dynamised', as we say; it speaks all at once the language of the subjective.

At first glance this is almost as forbidding as the text-book jargon of George Perle and his 'verticalised set-segments'. But Mann has given himself the inestimable advantage of establishing characters within the scope of a novel, characters who can talk in this way without offence since it is part of their nature to do so. All the same, I felt that to abstract even a substantial section such as the immensely long speech of Saul Fitelberg, the impresario, would be an injustice; if an anthology is to give any satisfaction at all, the extracts of which it is comprised must be reasonably complete in themselves.

A temptation which I have resisted is to include the many notorious examples of wrong judgements that critics have been prone to in the past. These have already been garnered into one of the most entertaining anthologies of all time, Nicolas Slonimsky's *Lexicon of Musical Invective*. There is no book more calculated to make us regard the judgements of present-day critics with scepticism. What is one to make of this, written in all seriousness by the music critic of the *Boston Journal* on 6th October 1893?

> The musicians are in a forest. The forest is dark. No birds are in this forest save birds that do not sing. . . . The players wander. They grope as though they were eyeless. Alarmed, they call to each other; frightened, they shout together. It seems that obscene, winged things listen and mock the lost. . . . Suddenly the players are in a clearing. They see close to them a canal. The water of the canal is green, and diseased purple and yellow plants grow on the banks of the canal. . . . A swan with filthy plumage and twisted neck bobs up and down in the green water of the canal.

The work under discussion? – Brahms's First Symphony in C minor. Slonimsky's book is full of such treasures, and I recommend it as ideal bedside reading. In all fairness, one must admit that it is only too easy to make wrong judgements, especially when one is called upon to give an opinion under pressure; it is the critic's hazard. Cecil Gray made an eloquent plea on his fellow-critics' behalf in his *Survey of Contemporary Music*. In a book which has its fair share of miscalculations, he argues:

> Why should one be afraid of being wrong? Only fools are always right. All positive and constructive criticism is of value, even when it is wholly wrong-headed. The most preposterous assertions of a Ruskin, Tolstoy or Nietzsche have ultimately done more for the true appreciation of art than all the colourless non-committal timidities of ordinary art critics. Although his judgements were invariably wrong, William Blake is a better art critic than Mr Bernhard Berenson, who is always drearily and monotonously right.

It is a point of view that I often reflect in my teaching; I like to provoke my pupils at times, in order to establish a positive resistance on their part. If they feel that something I say is sufficiently disturbing, they are more likely to develop a coherent defence of their own opinions. I have to be prepared to take the risk of losing their respect if they are not sufficiently intelligent to become aware of my purpose.

It may seem surprising that I have not devoted more space to contemporary music. It is precisely because it is contemporary, and therefore constantly changing, that I feel it does not really belong within these covers. As John Cage says:

> Contemporary music is not so much art as it is life and anyone making it no sooner finishes one of it than he begins another just as people keep on washing dishes, brushing their teeth, getting sleepy and so on. Very frequently no one knows that contemporary music is or could be art. He simply thinks it is irritating. Irritating one way or another, that is to say keeping us from ossifying.
> (*Silence* – lectures and writings by John Cage.)

A great deal of value has been written about the approach to modern music; Aaron Copland is particularly clear-headed about it, both in his Norton lectures of 1951–2 on Music and Imagination and in various articles such as the one he wrote for the *New York Times* in 1949, which has been reprinted in Morgenstern's immense anthology, *Composers on Music*.

Unavoidably, this book is partly an anthology of other anthologies. So many collections have already been made that to discover something genuinely new would be extraordinary. What I hope is new is the formula. Each section has a preface in which I justify my selection where necessary; the definitions of the musical forms which make up the various portions are taken from Eric Blom's *Everyman's Dictionary of Music*. It is the most concise and accurate dictionary, and I enjoy the challenge which its liberal use of abbreviations offers to one's commonsense. The so-called Interludes are complete in themselves and need no introduction. The comparative lack of good poetry about music led me to play with the idea of scattering it about the book in a random fashion, but eventually I decided that the poems I have chosen could constitute an Interlude in themselves.

I could never have explored the enormous mass of potential material without some assistance, and I must here pay tribute to Adrian Jack, a former student of mine at the Royal College, who has been tireless in dredging libraries of their contents; although a large percentage of this book is culled from my own shelves, there are many choice passages which I would never have known if it had not been for his guidance. I am grateful to him in two ways – for doing a lot of research (and taking it in good heart when I often rejected what he had found), and for the pleasure which some of his discoveries gave. I should also like to thank

Helen Cooper for typing what must have seemed at the time a very disorganised pile of unrelated oddments.

There remains but one thing – the dedication. I feel the book should be dedicated to somebody, but it is always a little tricky to single out an individual. I propose therefore to make some small amends to a group of people whom I have often criticised. I frequently rail against systems of education, about the inadequacy of musical institutions in England, about being badly taught as a child, and so on. I stand by all my criticisms, but I also acknowledge that the fault most probably lay in me. I dedicate this book to all who had a hand in educating me, to my first piano teachers, to the staff at school who inculcated a vague conception of history, geography, Latin, English and a host of other subjects into my mind, to my adopted father who taught me much, to my adopted mother who gave me a good seat on a horse, to the writers of the books I have read, to musicians with whom I have worked, to pupils from whom I have learnt many things, to producers who have tactfully tried to curb my excesses, to those even who have hurt me, for pain can teach one a lot; here, all of you, is a present that I hope will show you that I have not stopped learning, for the day that I do that will really be

THE END

Overture

(*From French Ouverture=opening.*) An instrumental introductory composition preceding some other large work, especially an opera or oratorio in modern times; but also sometimes an independent composition for concert use, though that use at first arose from the insertion of overtures to larger works into concert programmes.

Mendelssohn at eleven years old

Overture

A CHILD is born musical; no amount of teaching, however patient and devoted, can create musicianship if the seed has not been planted in the first place. Good teaching develops what is already there. Certainly it can widen the range of knowledge, instil disciplines, encourage a sense of adventure, arm the pupil against technical hazards, pass on the benefits of experience, nurture sensitivity, extend physical skills, raise the standard of self-criticism. Yet all this is not much more than tilling the soil and nursing the tender shoot; if the seed was not good in the first place, you will wait in vain for the flowers. But just as trees and plants take varying times to mature, so do musical talents. Sometimes the bud takes a long time to open; occasionally, as with Mozart or Mendelssohn, it bursts into flower with an unbelievable luxuriance.

Unbelievable? By the standards of normal human behaviour it would seem so, but we must believe, for the evidence is there. We can experience for ourselves the perfection of the Mendelssohn Octet, written when he was sixteen years old; we can read of Mozart's extraordinary childhood; there are many of us who heard Menuhin play when he was a boy. To belittle the prodigy, to regard the child pianist as someone who belongs more to the circus than the concert-hall is a natural enough reaction, for inevitably we tend to be discomfited at this evidence of what seems to be a supernatural power. What is this gift that so lavishly endows a chosen few?

As yet, I have never seen a satisfactory explanation of musical precocity. It seems that these remarkable children are given the key to a door that for some of us never opens, while for others, it only reveals what lies behind after we have painstakingly picked the lock. When I listen to the recording of the Elgar violin concerto that Menuhin made when he was fifteen, I am aware that I am in the presence of something that is virtually miraculous. No child of fifteen could possibly comprehend through experience the emotions that the music conveys; nor could any teacher project such emotional power into a child. The performance can only be explained as a short cut by which the player attains a state of maturity through the music itself; Elgar's soul is made manifest through the young Menuhin's body; the child is literally 'possessed'. It is in this respect that music can most justly be compared to a religious experience.

My own belief, although I can only convey it in the vaguest terms, is that what the orthodox Christian would call the Divine Spirit is a condition of greater awareness which can be reached by divers routes. Each one of us is receptive to a greater or lesser degree, though what we are receptive *to* varies with the individual; for one it is art, for another music, for someone else it may be the consciously assumed habit of religion. The creative artist is able to pierce the veil that normally conceals this higher state from ordinary mortals, and in his work he gives us tangible proof of the journey that he has made. Like Lucifer, he brings down the fire from Heaven, and we who watch or listen can share its warmth. By this analogy, the composer is one who actually steals a part of this 'divinity', and re-creates it in musical terms; the inspired performer is in touch with the higher sphere, but only through the medium of the composer; the prodigy has sneaked under the veil to have a look before he has any right to do so.

In cold print this may seem like muddle-headed mysticism of the sort of which, intellectually, I would profoundly disapprove. The belief is there, however, even though it may be badly expressed. I only dare to put it down in order to justify part of my selection for the first section of this anthology. I have taken the word Overture to mean a beginning – the beginning of a career, whether as composer or performer. The description of Mozart as a child is included because I shall never lose a sense of wonder that such a person as Mozart could ever be born. He was, of course, well taught by his father; the admirable precepts of Couperin show that the education of children was taken very seriously in those days, and although Leopold Mozart may not have brought up his little son exactly according to these rules, I doubt if he departed from their principles to any degree. Other children were not so well taught, as Mozart's own description of the playing of an eight-year-old girl reveals. Her name was Maria Anna Stein, and her father, who made excellent pianofortes, had high hopes of her as a pianist. Mozart could not resist a pun on her name, which, in German, means 'stone'.

From the nineteenth century I have chosen two brief descriptions of

Liszt, one as a boy of eight, and the other describing a visit to Beethoven three years later. Not every eleven-year-old is capable of transposing Bach fugues and I like the way in which this accomplishment is mentioned but not over-emphasised.

The grand set-piece of this opening section is Berlioz's classic description of the prize-giving concert at the Conservatoire in Paris. I consider the Berlioz autobiography to be far and away the most entertaining book ever written by a composer, and I make no apology for including several substantial excerpts. But in comparison to Mozart or Liszt, Berlioz was a late starter; this extract then is a useful way of raising the age group under perusal.

The first two 'lessons' that I have quoted, the one by Stanford and the other by Mendelssohn, show rather different approaches to the art of teaching. I am fascinated by the Mendelssohn letter, since he was only fourteen when he wrote it; such seriously detailed criticism would seem unpleasantly precocious, did it not have a very convincing air of authority behind it. I am sure that every point he made was perfectly valid. I wonder what sort of a music-master Mendelssohn would have made had he been put into the philistine atmosphere of an English public school. Things are getting better nowadays, but certainly the teaching of music at Marlborough as described by Siegfried Sassoon seems to have been singularly amateurish. Private lessons appear to have been little better if we are to judge by the experience of André Gide.

A brief glance at prodigies, not wholly serious, brings us to Benjamin Britten and the present day. Because the past is littered with legendary figures, we must not assume that we live in times when new legends cannot be made. There will always be prodigies, though the true child genius of the order of Mozart or Schubert is admittedly a very rare and special creature.

At least the prodigies themselves are usually self-deprecatory to a fault when they look back upon their early years; illusion or sentiment do not exist for them, toughened as they are by the gruelling competition of professional life. As a final chord to this Overture I quote an anecdote told by Mischa Elman.

> 'For an urchin of seven, I flatter myself I rattled off Beethoven's Kreutzer sonata finely. This sonata, you know, has in it several long and impressive rests. Well, in one of these rests, a motherly old

lady leant forward, patted my shoulder and said, "Play something you know, dear." '

Elman never lost a sense of humour, for even at the very end of his life he would say, 'You know, the critics never change; I'm still getting the same notices I used to get as a child. They tell me I play very well for my age . . .'

The child Mozart plays for an English connoisseur

As during this time I was witness of his most extraordinary abilities as a musician, both at some public concerts, and likewise at his father's house; I send you the following account, amazing and incredible almost as it may appear.

I carried to him a manuscript duet, which was composed by an English gentleman to some favourite words in Metastasio's opera of Demofoonte.

The whole score was in five parts, viz accompaniments for a first and second violin, the two vocal parts, and a base.

I shall here likewise mention, that the parts for the first and second voice were written in what the Italians style the Contralto cleff; the reason for taking notice of which particular will appear hereafter. . . .

The score was no sooner put upon his desk, than he began to play the symphony in a most masterly manner, as well as in the time and style which corresponded with the intention of the composer.

The symphony ended, he took the upper part, leaving the under one to his father.

His voice in the tone of it was thin and infantine, but nothing could exceed the masterly manner in which he sung.

His father, who took the under part in this duet, was once or twice out, though the passages were not more difficult than those in the upper one; on which occasions the son looked back with some anger, pointing out to him his mistakes, and setting him right.

He not only however did complete justice to the duet, by singing his own part in the truest taste, and with the greatest precision: he also threw in the accompaniments of the two violins, wherever they were most necessary, and produced the best of effects. . . .

When he had finished the duet, he expressed himself highly in its approbation, asking with some eagerness whether I had brought any more such music.

Having been informed, however, that he was often visited with musical ideas, to which, even in the midst of the night, he would give utterance on his harpsichord, I told his father that I should be glad to hear some of his extemporary compositions.

The father shook his head at this, saying, that it depended entirely upon his being as it were musically inspired, but that I might ask him whether he was in humour for such a composition.

Happening to know that little Mozart was much taken notice of by Manzoli, the famous singer, who came over to England in 1764, I said to the boy, that I should be glad to hear an extemporary Love Song, such as his friend Manzoli might choose in an opera.

The boy on this (who continued to sit at his harpsichord) looked back with much archness, and immediately began five or six lines of a jargon recitative proper to introduce a love song.

He then played a symphony which might correspond with an air composed to the single word, *Affetto*.

It had a first and second part, which, together with the symphonies, was of the length that opera songs generally last: if this extemporary composition was not amazingly capital, yet it was really above mediocrity, and shewed most extraordinary readiness of invention.

Finding that he was in humour, and as it were inspired, I then desired him to compose a Song of Rage, such as might be proper for the opera stage.

The boy again looked back with much archness, and began five or six lines of a jargon recitative proper to precede a Song of Anger.

This lasted also about the same time with the Song of Love; and in the middle of it, he had worked himself up to such a pitch, that he beat his harpsichord like a person possessed, rising sometimes in his chair.

The word he pitched upon for this second extemporary composition was, *Perfido*.

After this he played a difficult lesson, which he had finished a day or two before: his execution was amazing, considering that his little fingers could scarcely reach a fifth on the harpsichord.

His astonishing readiness, however, did not arise merely from great practice; he had a thorough knowledge of the fundamental principles of composition, as, upon producing a treble, he immediately wrote a base under it, which, when tried, had a very good effect.

He was also a great master of modulation, and his transitions from one key to another were excessively natural and judicious; he practised in this manner for a considerable time with an handkerchief over the keys of the harpsichord.

The facts which I have been mentioning I was myself an eye witness of; to which I must add, that I have been informed by two or three able musicians, when (Johann Christian) Bach, the celebrated composer, had begun a fugue and left off abruptly, that little Mozart hath immediately taken it up, and worked it after a most masterly manner.

Witness as I was myself of most of these extraordinary facts, I must own that I could not help suspecting his father imposed with regard to the real age of the boy, though he had not only a most childish appearance, but likewise had all the actions of that stage of life.

For example, whilst he was playing to me, a favourite cat came in, upon which he immediately left his harpsichord, nor could we bring him back for a considerable time.

He would also sometimes run about the room with a stick between his legs by way of horse.

I found likewise that most of the London musicians were of the same opinion with regard to his age, not believing it possible that a child of so tender years could surpass most of the masters in that science.

I have therefore for a considerable time made the best inquiries I was able from some of the German musicians resident in London, but could never receive any further information than that he was born near Salzbourg, till I was so fortunate as to procure an extract from the register of that place, through his excellence Count Haslang.

It appears from this extract, that Mozart's father did not impose with regard to his age when he was in England, for it was in June, 1765, that I was witness to what I have above related, when the boy was only eight years and five months old.

MOZART AND HIS TIMES: *Erich Schenk*

The playing of Maria Anna Stein, by Mozart

ANYONE who sees and hears her play and can keep from laughing must, like her father, be made of stone. For instead of sitting in the middle of the clavier, she sits right up opposite the treble, as it gives her more chance of flopping about and making grimaces. She rolls her eyes and smirks. When a passage is repeated, she plays it more slowly the second time. If it has to be played a third time, then she plays it even more slowly. When a passage is being played, the arm must be raised as high as possible, and according as the notes in the passage are stressed, the arm, not the fingers, must therefore do this, and that too, with great emphasis and clumsy manner. But the best joke of all is that when she comes to a passage that ought to flow like oil and which necessitates a change of finger, she does not bother her head about it, but when the moment arrives, she just leaves out the notes, raises her hand and starts off again quite comfortably – a method by which she is much more likely to strike a wrong note. . . . She may succeed, for she has great talent for music. But she will not make progress by this method, for she will never acquire great rapidity, since she definitely does all she can to make her hands heavy. Further, she will never acquire the most essential, the most difficult and chief requisite in music, which is rhythm, because from her earliest years she had done her utmost not to play in time.

THE GREAT PIANISTS (*Mozart*): Harold C Schonberg

Liszt as pupil

HE WAS A PALE, delicate-looking child and while playing swayed in the chair as if drunk, so that I often thought he would fall to the floor. Moreover his playing was completely irregular, careless and confused, and he had so little knowledge of correct fingering that he threw his fingers all over the keyboard in an altogether arbitrary fashion. Nevertheless, I was amazed by the talent with which Nature had equipped him. I gave him a few things to sight-read, which he did, purely by instinct, but for that very reason in a manner that revealed that Nature herself had here created a pianist. . . . Never before had I so eager, talented or industrious a student. Since I knew from numerous experiences that geniuses whose mental gifts are ahead of their physical strength tend to neglect solid technique, it seemed necessary above all to use the first months to regulate and strengthen his mechanical dexterity in such a way that he could not possibly slide into bad habits in later years. . . . Since I made him learn each piece very rapidly, he finally became such a great sight-reader that he was publicly capable of sight-reading even compositions of considerable difficulty; and so perfectly as though he had been studying them for a long time. Likewise I tried to equip him with skill in improvising by frequently giving him themes to improvise on.

THE GREAT PIANISTS (*Czerny on Liszt*): Harold C Schonberg

Liszt visits Beethoven

I WAS ABOUT ELEVEN years old when my respected teacher, Czerny, took me to see Beethoven. Already a long time before, he had told Beethoven about me and asked him to give me a hearing some day. However, Beethoven had such an aversion to infant prodigies that he persistently refused to see me. At last Czerny, indefatigable, persuaded him, so that, impatiently, he said: 'Well, bring the rascal to me, in God's name!' It was about ten o'clock in the morning when we entered the two small rooms in the Schwarzspanierhaus, where Beethoven was living at the time, myself very shy, Czerny, kind and encouraging. Beethoven was sitting at a long, narrow table near the window, working. For a time he scrutinised us grimly, exchanged a few hurried words with Czerny and remained silent when my good teacher called me to the piano.

The first thing I played was a short piece by Ries. When I had finished, Beethoven asked me whether I could play a fugue by Bach. I chose the Fugue in C minor from the Well-Tempered Clavier.

'Could you also transpose this fugue at once into another key?' Beethoven asked me. Fortunately, I could. After the final chord, I looked up.

The Master's darkly glowing gaze was fixed upon me penetratingly. Yet suddenly a benevolent smile broke up his gloomy features; Beethoven came quite close, bent over me, laid his hand on my head and repeatedly stroked my hair. 'Devil of a fellow,' he whispered, 'such a young rascal!'

I suddenly plucked up courage. 'May I play something of yours now?' I asked cheekily. Beethoven nodded with a smile. I played the first movement of the C major Concerto. When I had ended, Beethoven seized both my hands, kissed me on the forehead and said gently: 'Off with you! You're a happy fellow, for you'll give happiness and joy to many other people. There is nothing better or greater than that!'

This event in my life has remained my greatest pride, the palladium for my whole artistic career. I speak of it only very rarely and only to my intimate friends.

BEETHOVEN: LETTERS, JOURNALS AND CONVERSATIONS: *Michael Hamburger*

The prize-giving concert, by Berlioz

TWO MONTHS afterwards the prizes were distributed, and the successful cantata was performed. The ceremony was precisely the same then as it is now. Year by year the same musicians play works which are almost always the same, and the prizes, which are awarded with the same amount of discrimination, are bestowed with the same solemnities. Every year, on the same day, at the same hour, the same academician, standing on the same step of the same staircase, repeats the same sentence to the successful candidate. The day is the first Saturday in October, the hour four in the afternoon, the step the third; everyone knows who the academician is, and here is the sentence:

'Now, young man, *macte animo*; you are going on a delightful journey ... the classic home of the Fine Arts ... the country of Pergolesi and Piccinni ... inspired by those blue skies ... you will return with some splendid work ... the world is at your feet.'

In honour of the great event the academicians don their green-embroidered uniforms; they are radiant, dazzling. They are about to crown a painter, a sculptor, an architect, an engraver, and a musician. There is great joy in the abode of the muses.

On the first Saturday in October, then, their radiant mother 'flaps her wings', and the successful cantata is at last fully performed. An *entire* orchestra is brought together, complete in all its parts. There are stringed instruments, two flutes, two oboes, two clarinets. (To tell the truth this important section has only been completed recently. When the grand prix rose above my horizon, there was only one clarinet and a half, for the old man who had played the first clarinet from time immemorial, having but one tooth left, was only able to produce about half the notes from his asthmatic instrument.) There are four horns, three trombones, and even so modern an instrument as the cornet-à-pistons. Do you call that nothing? It is all true. The Academy on this day is completely transformed; it is off its head; it is guilty of actual extravagance. We are all at our posts, and the conductor raises his baton.

The sun rises; violoncello solo, slightly *crescendo*
The little birds awake; flute solo, violin *tremolo*
The little brooks murmur; viola *solo*
The little lambs bleat; oboe *solo*

And as the *crescendo* increases, it comes to pass that by the time the little birds, little streams, and little lambs have each had their say it must be at least midday. Then comes the recitative:

'Already dawning day' ... etc ...

Then follow the first aria, the second recitative, the second aria, the third recitative, the third aria, which generally kills the hero but revives the singer and the audience. The perpetual secretary then gives out the name of the composer in sonorous tones, holding in the one hand the wreath of artificial laurels with which to crown the victor's brow, and in the other the real gold medal (which will enable him to pay his bills before he leaves Rome – it is worth a hundred and sixty francs, I know this for certain).

The laureate rises:

'*Son front nouveau tondu, symbole de candeur,*
Rougit, en approchant, d'une honnête pudeur.'

He embraces the perpetual secretary (slight applause). He sees his august master standing close by; pupil and master embrace, as it is right they should (more applause). The laureate's parents are on a bench behind the academicians, shedding silent tears of joy; he vaults over the intervening benches, crushes the toes of one man, treads on the coat of another, and casts himself into the arms of his sobbing parents; nothing could be more natural. But instead of applauding the public is beginning to smile. On the right of this touching group stands a young girl, making desperate signs to the hero of the hour; he dashes towards her, tearing a lady's gauze dress to shreds in his haste, and crushing in a dandy's hat; she is his cousin, and he clasps her in his arms. He sometimes even embraces his cousin's neighbour (much laughter). Another woman, standing in a dim, remote corner, makes sympathetic signals, which the hero is careful not to observe. But he flies to embrace his sweetheart – his betrothed, who is to share his good fortune. He is careless of other women in his anxiety to reach her; knocks one down, gets caught in the foot-stool of another, and comes down with a heavy fall; he renounces his purpose, and returns to his seat humiliated and bathed in perspiration (loud applause and roars of laughter). How delightful! How charming! This is the crowning moment of the academic séance, and I know a great many people who go there solely on purpose to enjoy it. I bear the jesters no ill-will, for it happened that in my case there was neither father nor mother, cousin, fiancée, master nor mistress to embrace. ... My master was ill, my parents absent or angry, and as for my mistress ... So I merely embraced the perpetual secretary, and as for my blushes, they were hidden beneath a shock of red hair, which, combined with certain other peculiarities, placed me undeniably in the category of owls.

Besides, I was in anything but an embracing mood that day; in fact, I don't think I ever was in such a passion in my life, and this was the reason for it. The subject of the cantata was *The Last Night of Sardanapalus*. The poem closes at the point where Sardanapalus, feeling himself vanquished, calls for his prettiest slaves, and mounts his funeral pyre with them. I had at first intended to write a sort of symphony descriptive of the conflagration, the shrieks of the reluctant women, the defiant words of the proud voluptuary in the midst of the devouring flames, and the crash of the falling palace. But when I recollected how limited were the means at my disposal I refrained. A glance at this orchestral finale would have caused the academicians to condemn the whole piece; while played on the piano it would have sounded perfectly unintelligible. So I bided my time, and when I had secured the prize, and knew that my work would be performed by a full orchestra, I wrote my conflagration scene.

It produced such an effect when rehearsed that some of the academicians, quite taken by surprise, came up and congratulated me, not at all resenting the trap into which I had led them. The hall was full of artistes and amateurs, curious to hear the work of the youth of whom such strange tales were told. Many of them too had heard such glowing reports of the sensation produced by the conflagration scene at rehearsal that an unusual amount of interest was excited.

Before the concert began I placed myself, score in hand, beside Grasset, the ex-conductor of the Théâtre-Italien, for I had my misgivings as to his powers. Mdme Malibran, whose curiosity had been aroused by the reports of the rehearsal, could not find a seat in the hall, so we got a stool for her near myself, between two double-basses. I have never seen her since.

The *decrescendo* begins.

(The cantata opens with the words, 'Night has already drawn her veil across the day', so that I had to describe a sunset instead of the usual dawn which looks as if I had been predestined to take life and the Academy against the grain from the beginning.)

The cantata proceeds in due course. Sardanapalus hears of his defeat, resolves on death, sends for his women; the conflagration begins. Those who were present at the rehearsal whisper to their neighbours, 'Now the crash is coming; it is wonderful – astounding!'

A hundred thousand curses on musicians who do not count their bars! In the score, the horn gives the cue to the kettledrums, the kettledrums to the cymbals, the cymbals to the big drum, and the first sound of the big drum brings in the final explosion. But the damned horn makes no sign, the kettledrums are afraid to enter, and of course the cymbals and big drums also remain silent; nothing is heard! nothing!!! And all the time the violins and basses carry on their impotent *tremolo*, and there is no explosion, a conflagration that goes out before it has begun; a fiasco instead of the talked-of end of all things. *Ridiculus mus!* No one who has not been through a similar experience can conceive what a fury I was in! With a cry of horror, I flung my score right across the middle of the orchestra, dashing down two of the music-desks. Mdme Malibran started back as though a shell had burst at her feet. There was a general uproar at once in the orchestra, among the scandalised academicians, the mystified musicians, and the enraged friends of the composer. This was the most disastrous of all my musical catastrophes up to then; would that it had been also the last!

MEMOIRS OF HECTOR BERLIOZ: Edited by Ernest Newman

A few words from Stanford

HIS CRITICISMS were expressed in various ways, mostly unpremeditated, and many of them are delightedly quoted by the recipients to this day. He was devoted to C S Lang, who was later to become Director of Music at Christ's Hospital. It was Stanford's custom when his work was over at the RCM to take a taxi to the Savile Club in Piccadilly, but one day he received orders from his doctor to walk the distance for the sake of exercise. Lang having heard of this, used to wait for him on the steps to see that he obeyed instructions. One morning he turned up at his lesson with a superb (as he thought) six-part Motet, a setting of Dominus Illuminatio Mea. Stanford looked at it for a minute or two, threw it on top of the piano and started in on the Dorian mode or some other remote subject; he never mentioned the masterpiece. In the afternoon they walked together to the Savile. There is an undertaker's shop in Knightsbridge and as they passed the door Stanford gave him a shove and said:

'Take it in there, me boy.'

That was the only reference he ever made to it.

CHARLES VILLIERS STANFORD: Harry Plunket Greene

Mendelssohn, at 14, gives criticism

TO WILHELM VON BOGUSLAVSKI

Your letter has given me very great pleasure because I see that you have not yet forgotten me. Do not be cross with me because of my tardy answer. You wish to have my conscientious judgment on your symphony. But the score came into my hands six weeks later than the letter; the post office did not deliver it in time. That is why I could not write earlier. As you really want me to give a verdict, I must do it. Well:

In general, I must first say that I very much like all the themes of the first movement, that I thoroughly like the *adagio* with the exception of the *forte* theme in the middle, and that to me the minuet seems pretty and gay, all but a protraction at the end that delays it. The theme of the last piece with the first *forte* and the development up to the piano are not bad either, but from there on it seems to me just a little weak, and I do not at all care for the end with its trumpeting.

Secondly, in detail and more precisely: you find fault with the introduction with its single violin, which, I presume, must be played as a solo. I like it quite well, and also the successive entrances of the four instruments. But the *adagio* as a whole is much too long. It is meant to be an introduction, but you have made an independent movement of it, with modulations and development, so that the listener is tired before he gets to the *allegro*. But I have not cut out anything and await your order to do it. The theme and the way you draw it out in the *allegro* is very pretty; but later, when you ought to conclude in A major (the dominant of D major) you close, instead, in D major and start again in G major. As a result the modulation becomes very monotonous. Then again you modulate quite cleverly into D major and begin a good, new theme and develop it regularly, but just as one expects this part to draw to a close, you move again into F-sharp major and through several successive sevenths into A major, and only from there back to D major. This is quite unnecessary. The introduction of the return to the theme at the end of the first part is pleasant, clear, brief and very well distributed among the instruments. The beginning of the development is good and appropriate. But I do not at all like the end because of the modulations into A-flat major and A-flat minor in a piece in G major. The coda is pretty and not too long.

In the *adagio* the part for two violins and viola is too long. The entry of the violoncelli relieves it. You must cut out something in the middle part.

I have already given you my opinion about the minuet and the last movement.

As a whole, the symphony has given me great pleasure, and I know how to appreciate the fact that you are abandoning your Pandects and the Corpus Juris in order to devote your time to counterpoint. Farewell, thanks again for letter and music.

MENDELSSOHN LETTERS: *G Selden-Goth*

'So you play organ . . .'

ONE AFTERNOON during my first week at Marlborough, I went to see 'old Bam' about my music lessons. 'Bam' was Mr W S Bambridge, the organist, who for many years had been an affectionately regarded institution both in the college chapel and outside it.

With my music under my arm I made my way to his house, which was at the edge of the town, just beyond the little Kennet. Leaning over the bridge to give my mind a few minutes' rest by listening to the river, I wondered how much water would gurgle under the arch before I had acquired control of the organ. It seemed a very large instrument for me to tackle, considering how poorly I played the *Venetian Gondola* piece in Mendelssohn's *Songs Without Words*. But if I couldn't make a piano sound eloquent and spirited (as the piano-tuner did in between the dull parts of his work) how could I hope to produce magnificent noises from an organ? It must feel fine to be able to do that, I thought, as I stared vacantly at Savernake Forest up the hill – and then just saved *Songs Without Words* from falling out of my 'kishe' into the Kennet. (For the benefit of non-Marlburians I must explain that a 'kishe' is the flat cushion which the boys fold around their books and sit on when at their work.)

Before ringing the bell I put my tie straight and thought what a relief it had been when I discovered the correct way to get it inside my collar. Mr Bambridge, whose lean figure and bearded face I had already caught glimpses of in chapel, greeted me with bluff geniality. More than that, he looked at me as though I was an object of interest, which no one else at Marlborough had hitherto done. A spectacled lady was standing by the piano, and she, too, eyed me with what seemed like expectant curiosity. A slight wave of uneasiness passed through my system. Could it be that they believed me to possess musical ability? My apprehensive feeling increased when 'Bam' produced a letter which I recognised as being on Weirleigh notepaper. 'Well, my boy,' he remarked in his bass voice, 'your mother writes that you have a real love of music. Let's hear what you can do.'

The sequel needs no elaboration. Too nervous and flurried to play it even tolerably well, I created an immediate fiasco with the *Venetian Gondola Song*, and was thankful when they stopped me halfway down the first page. Real though my love of music was, I had been unable to give them any audible proof of it. With a twinkle in his eye Mr Bambridge laid aside my mother's letter and arranged the time of my first organ lesson.

On the day after my interview with Mr Bambridge, while dubiously consuming some beef which was rather a queer colour ('College meat' in those distant days was notoriously bad and often had magenta blotches on it) Mr Gould astonished me by giving one of these choleric performances of his. Flabbergasted me, in fact, since it was upon me that he swooped. The combination of my affluent surname with my mother's solicitude for my health had imbued him with an idea that I was one of the pampered rich and rather a soft sort of boy into the bargain. I became overwhelmingly aware of this when he seized me by the shoulder and shook me violently, exclaiming, in a voice which was somewhere between a bay and a bleat, 'So you play organ, do you, you wretched fellow, you play organ! I know why you play organ. You play organ to get out of playing games, you wretched brute!'

Considering that I'd got a nasty bruise on the shin playing hockey on the previous afternoon, this onslaught seemed jolly unfair; so I replied, with tremulous resolution: 'No, sir, I don't. I want to learn the organ, but I don't want to get out of playing games.'

This somewhat appeased him, and he moved on, amid the suppressed merriment of those sitting around me. But for the remainder of the day I felt aggrieved and indignant at his ungenerous imputation that I was the sort of boy who would rather play *The Lost Chord* than get his house colours.

Mr Gould's annoyance about the organ lessons turned out to have been a blessing in disguise, for it had created quite a new Gould joke. So far I hadn't learnt half the members of my house by name and had only got to know a few of the younger ones to talk to. Nobody else had done more than give me a casual or incurious stare, except when some lordly youth shouted 'Fag' and told me to fetch something for him. During the next few days, however, several of the Olympians took notice of me, though their attentions consisted only in gazing at me with mock solemnity and then saying in sepulchral tones, 'You play organ.' No reply was expected; but it made me feel less lonely and inferior.

Soon afterwards I had a further opportunity of being modestly conspicuous.

Late one afternoon the rather pudgy-faced lad who played the piano at evening prayers entered my study to tell me that as he'd cut his finger badly I'd got to play the hymn tune that night. I protested that I wasn't nearly good enough to do it, but he assured me that no one would mind a bit if I made a few mistakes, and I was unwillingly persuaded to experiment with the piano. After hearing my rendering of *Lead, Kindly Light* he decided that I was quite capable of acting as accompanist, and, having chosen what he considered an easy tune, left me to rehearse it at my leisure on the ancient upright. 'You needn't worry about the words. The loud and soft bits don't matter,' he remarked, adding: 'It's Saturday, and Gould always has an extra glass or two of port that evening, so he won't be particular.' I observed with relief that the hymn had only five short verses, and after playing the tune through about a dozen times I seemed to have mastered it, though I still felt that I should break down owing to nervousness.

Anyhow, at nine o'clock I was duly seated at the instrument with my back to the audience, which included, of course, the matron, who always sang the hymn as if her genteel voice had been looking forward all day to its bit of exercise.

Like one in a dream I waited. Then Mr Gould came through the door of the library which was between his part of the house and ours. After reading out one or two routine notices, the head of the house handed him the usual slip of paper with the number of the hymn on it, and we amen'd our way onward towards my part of the proceedings. After *Lighten our darkness, we beseech Thee, O Lord*, Mr Gould, rather as though he were thinking of something else, gave out 'Hymn number four hundred and fifty-seven'. With fingers which felt as if they belonged to someone else I executed my solo, unconvincingly, but, at any rate, correctly. The worst was over, it seemed, for I should now have the support of some sixty throats, including Mr Gould's husky baritone and the matron's pious alto. Almost without waiting for my timid accompaniment the house came to my aid in wholehearted harmony. In fact, they surprised me by the hosanna-like loudness of their singing.

> 'How blest the matron who endued
> With holy zeal and fortitude,
> Has won through grace a saintly fame,
> And owns a dear and honoured name.'

Preoccupied as I had been by my responsibilities as a musician, I had altogether overlooked the facetious interpretation of the words. And even now, as I struck the first chord for Verse 2 (which began 'Such holy love inflames her breast') I could only confusedly suppose that I had somehow blundered when Mr Gould practically bellowed 'Let the music cease!' After an irreverent silence, our housemaster, since it was his duty to do so, asked the Almighty to grant us in this world knowledge of His truth and in the world to come life everlasting. When all was over and we had risen from our knees, he made a beeline for me and was evidently about to shake me till my teeth rattled. But my horrified countenance must have made him think again and realise that the forbidden hymn had been chosen for me. So he changed his course and merely stopped on his way out to exclaim from the library door to those who had not already made themselves scarce: 'You brutes! You wretched brutes!'

THE OLD CENTURY AND SEVEN MORE YEARS: *Siegfried Sassoon*

André Gide describes some early piano lessons

MADEMOISELLE DE GOECKLIN's lessons now being considered inadequate, I was handed over to a male professor, who, unfortunately, was very little better. Monsieur Merriman showed pianos in Pleyel's shop: he had adopted the profession of pianist without having the smallest vocation for it; nevertheless, by dint of hard work, he had succeeded, if I remember right, in carrying off a first prize at the Conservatoire. His playing was correct, polished, icy, and more like arithmetic than art; when he sat down to the piano, it was like a cashier sitting down to his desk; his fingers added up the notes – the minims and crotchets and quavers – as if they were figures; he proved the piece as if it were a sum. He might certainly have given me some mechanical training; but he took no pleasure in teaching. Music with him became the driest of tasks; his favourite composers were Cramer, Steibelt, Dussek – at any rate, it was under their rod of iron he thought fit to place me. He considered Beethoven libidinous. Twice a week, he made his appearance, punctual to the minute; the lessons consisted in the monotonous repetition of a few exercises (and even these were not really useful for finger work, but just dull routine), a few scales, a few arpeggios; then I would drum out 'the eight last bars' of the piece I was learning, that is to say the last bars I had practised; after that, he made a pencil mark – a kind of large V – eight bars further on, to show the next piece of work that had to be got through, much as one marks the trees that have to come down when a wood is being thinned; then, getting up as the clock struck the hour:

'For the next time, practise the eight following bars,' he would say.

Never the smallest explanation. Never the slightest appeal, I will not say to my musical taste or feeling (how could there be any question of such things?) but to my memory or judgment. At that age, when a child is all growth and pliability and receptiveness, what progress I might have made, if my mother had confided me in the beginning to Monsieur de la Nux, the incomparable master I had later on – too late, alas! But no! after two years' mortal droning, I was only delivered from Merriman to fall into the hands of Schifmacker.

It was not, I admit, as easy then as it is now, to find good music-masters; the Schola had not yet begun to turn them out, and the musical education of the whole of France was still far to seek; moreover the people in my mother's set knew practically nothing about music. My mother unquestionably made great efforts to educate herself as well as me; but her efforts were ill-directed. Schifmacker had been warmly recommended to her by a lady-friend.

'Would you believe it?' she said to my mother; 'he has actually made me take a liking to it – to music! An extraordinary man! Try him.'

The first day he came to the house he expounded his system. He was a stout, fiery, old man who puffed and panted, who was as red as a furnace, who whistled and stuttered and spluttered as he spoke like a locomotive letting off steam. He had white hair, cut *en brosse*, and white whiskers, and it all looked like a mass of driven snow melting on his face, which he was continually mopping.

'What do most music-masters tell you?' said he. 'You must do exercises! Exercises here! And exercises there! But look at me! Do you suppose I ever did exercises? Never in the world! One learns by playing. Like speaking. Come, Madame, a sensible lady like you, what would you say if your son was to do tongue exercises every morning, because, forsooth, he will have to use his tongue during the day: ra, ra, ra, ra, gla, gla, gla gla.' (Here, my mother, positively out of her wits with terror at Schifmacker's moist explosiveness, drew back her armchair, while he pulled his so much the nearer.) 'However fast or slow your tongue wags, you can only say what you have to say, and at the piano you always have fingers enough to express what you feel. Ah! if you feel nothing, you might have ten fingers on each hand and be none the better for it!' Then he went off into a loud laugh, caught his breath, coughed, choked for a few moments, turned up the whites of his eyes, then mopped himself, then fanned himself with his handkerchief. My mother offered to fetch him a glass of water, but he made a sign that it was nothing, fluttered his little arms and short legs in a final spasm, explained he had wanted to laugh and cough at the same moment, gave a resounding 'H-h-m' and turned to me:

'So, my boy, that's an understood thing, eh? No more exercises. Look, ma'am. Look how pleased the little rascal is! He's thinking "We shall have fun with old Schifmacker." And he's quite right too.'

My mother, completely overwhelmed and bewildered by all these tomfooleries, and amused by them too, no doubt, was still more alarmed; for she, who never spared herself pains and brought unrelaxing diligence to all she did, could not altogether approve of a method that did away with all compulsion and effort; she tried in vain, however, to get in a completed sentence through all this spattering of words and saliva.

'Yes, provided he . . .' 'But he doesn't want . . .' 'Evidently . . .' 'On condition you . . .'

And suddenly Schifmacker got up:

'Now I'll play you something, so that you mayn't think I can do nothing but talk.'

He opened the piano, struck a chord or two, and then dashed with a triumphant flourish into a little study of Stephen Heller's which he played diabolically fast and with amazing brio. He had little short red hands with which he seemed positively to knead the piano almost without moving his fingers. His playing was like nothing I have ever heard before or since; he was totally lacking in what is called 'mechanism', and I think he would have come to grief over a simple scale; it was never in fact the actual piece as it was written that he played, but an approximation, full of spirit, flavour and strangeness.

I was not particularly delighted at having my exercises cut off; I was already fond of practising; if I changed masters, it was in order to get on and I wondered whether this devil of a fellow . . . ? He had peculiar theories; as, for instance, that the finger on the note should never be motionless; his idea was that the finger should continue dealing with the note like the finger or bow of a violinist which is directly applied to the vibrating string itself; in this way he fancied himself able to increase or lessen the sound, and mould it as he pleased, according as he weighed with his finger on the key, or lightened his pressure on it. This is what gave his playing the strange, swaying motion which made him really look as if he were kneading the melody.

His lessons came to an abrupt end with a frightful scene. This is what happened. Schifmacker, as I have said, was corpulent. My mother, fearing that the delicate constitution of the little drawing-room chairs would be incapable of supporting such a weight, had fetched in out of the hall a stout and hideous seat covered with American cloth and strangely at odds with the drawing-room furniture. She put this seat by the piano and moved the others some distance away, 'so that he should understand where he was to sit', said she. At the first lesson, all went well; the chair bore up under the oppression and agitation of his ponderous bulk. But the next time something appalling happened – the American cloth, which had no doubt been softened during the previous lesson, began to stick to the seat of his trousers. We didn't notice it, alas! till the end of the hour, when he tried to get up! In vain! He stuck to the chair and the chair stuck to him. His trousers were thin (it was in summer) and if the stuff had been ever so little worn, it would have given way to a certainty; there were a few moments of agonising suspense . . . But no! One last effort and it was the American cloth that yielded, very, very gently, and not without relinquishing something of its own, as if in a spirit of conciliation. I was holding the chair down, not as yet daring to laugh, so great was my consternation, while he kept exclaiming as he pulled:

'Good God! Good God! What's this hellish invention?' while all the time he was trying to look over his shoulder backwards at the unsticking process, so that his face grew redder than ever.

Fortunately, however, it was managed without any serious damage being done except to the American cloth, which was left limp and draggled, with an effigy of Monsieur Schifmacker's voluminous behind imprinted on it.

The curious thing is that it was not till the following lesson that his wrath broke out. I don't know what upset him that day, but when I went with him into the hall to see him out, he suddenly burst into the most violent invective, declared that he saw quite clearly what I was up to, that I was a sly, deceitful little wretch, and that he would never again set foot inside a house where he was treated with such ignominy.

And as a matter of fact, he never came back; we learnt from the papers a little later that he had been drowned in a boating party.

IF IT DIE: *André Gide*

'Hats off here likewise, gentlemen'

YESTERDAY MORNING I sat in a reverie, throwing my mind back over what now seem countless years, trying to recall even so much as the names of all the young violinist prodigies I had heard during nearly two generations. Kochalski, Von Vecsey, Chartres, Kubelik, Heifetz, Elman, Von Reuter – and so forth – were names that leapt quickly to the eye of the memory.

They were all 'geniuses' then, that is why the word has depreciated in meaning. And now, after many days and much experience, one is less disposed to prophesy about the newcomer, be he who he may.

As one looks back on these and similar 'prodigies' one cannot but wonder if one's original judgement was justified. Indeed, most of them played, or so it seemed, in the glamour of the réclame which surrounded their first appearance, much as Yehudi Menuhin played in the Albert Hall yesterday afternoon. They were all swans until, by a strange freak of nature, they became, on examination, geese – most of them that is, not all. In the course of a brief year or two they won a few golden eggs. But very soon fecundity ceased, usually from over-exploitation, and oblivion followed. From force of habit some of us came to measure all prodigies with the same kind of yardstick.

Now, after being one of the four or five or even more thousands of enthusiastic listeners to Yehudi Menuhin in the Albert Hall yesterday afternoon, one is compelled to acknowledge that the old yardstick must be used as firewood, that an entirely new standard must be set up. I do not hesitate to say that in this twelve-year-old robust, healthy-looking boy we have a prodigy whose like has not been heard among violinists in the last five and fifty years, and quite probably has not been heard, as Fritz Kreisler has laid it down, since Mozart. I think I have heard them all, here or elsewhere, and I am convinced.

It is easy enough to say that he plays as his master taught him to play. What more can you ask of a lad not yet thirteen years of age? But a boy who can even be taught to play the prodigious programme essayed yesterday –

the César Franck *Sonata*, Bach's *Chaconne*, Bruch's tedious and dated old *Scottish Fantasy*, and other things – is fantastic.

Many 'old stagers' (most of whom are younger than I) will possibly repudiate such enthusiasm when I say that I have rarely heard the *Chaconne* (which now might be pensioned off a while) played more smoothly or sound more simple and 'violinistic'. The chords no less than the passage-work flowed from the wonderful bow of this Heaven-gifted lad with consummate ease, and most of us know the heart-breaking efforts of the multitude of violinists to do more than play the mere notes.

What matter if there is more in some of the real music played than was vouchsafed yesterday? That is no fault of the boy. Heaven alone can say what so enormous a talent may open into. Far be it from me to try. Remember the boy's Brahms last Monday in Queen's Hall and his Bach yesterday! 'Hats off, gentlemen – a genius', said Schumann on Brahms's coming. 'Hats off here likewise, gentlemen', and keep them off, lest in removing them later when another prodigy arrives you may be taken in by geese which you thought were swans.

The audience somewhat felt its way with the boy. He had a very good but not very enthusiastic reception. But enthusiasm grew so warm with the afternoon's development that very soon all ice had melted, and so much was the audience enthralled that it completely forgot its usual habit of applauding when the violinist stopped in his playing of the *Chaconne* to tune up his strings, which had slightly dropped.

At present his tone is rather thin, but it is very sweet, if small; his finger technique is quite immaculate, as well in chord playing as in passage work, and his bow is marvellously flexible.

Why, incidentally, does Menuhin stand sideways while playing? He was very finely and most sympathetically assisted by M Hubert Giessen at the piano.

The close was as usual on such occasions. After a truly remarkable technical exhibition in music of the pure virtuoso type, the crowd swarmed to the platform and obtained the encores upon which their hearts were set. The lights were extinguished, Menuhin appeared in his overcoat, and all was over.

THE DAILY TELEGRAPH, 11th November 1929: *Robin H Legge*

Questions to a prodigy

LIKE MOST great pianists, Rosenthal resented the importunities of proud mothers who begged him to listen to their children; experience had taught him to be sceptical of their talent. Once he was forced to listen to a prodigy. The conversation is said to have run something like this:

'How old are you?'

'Seven, sir.'

'And what would you like to play for me?'
'Please, sir, the Tchaikovsky concerto, sir.'
'Too old!'

THE GREAT PIANISTS (Rosenthal): *Harold C Schonberg*

Benjamin Britten as a young composer

HE WAS FIVE when he began composing. Many years later, when *Peter Grimes* was being performed in opera houses throughout Europe, he gave a broadcast talk to schools, describing his earliest attempts to write music. 'I remember the first time I tried,' he said, 'the result looked rather like the Forth Bridge ... hundreds of dots all over the page connected by long lines all joined together in beautiful curves. I am afraid it was the pattern on the paper which I was interested in and when I asked my mother to play it, her look of horror upset me considerably. My next efforts were much more conscious of *sound*. I had started playing the piano and wrote elaborate tone poems usually lasting about twenty seconds, inspired by terrific events in my home life such as the departure of my father for (a day in) London, the appearance in my life of a new girl friend, or even a week at sea. My later efforts luckily got away from these (purely) emotional inspirations.'

And now Britten continues the story in his own words:

'As a child I heard little music outside my own home. There were the local choral society concerts and the very occasional chamber concert, but the main event was the Norwich Triennial Festival. There in 1924, when I was ten, I heard Frank Bridge conduct his suite *The Sea*, and was knocked sideways.

'It turned out that my viola teacher, Audrey Alston, was an old friend of Bridge's. He always stayed with her, and when the success of *The Sea* brought him to Norwich again in 1927 with a specially written work called *Enter Spring*, I was taken to meet him.

'We got on splendidly, and I spent the next morning with him going over some of my music. From that moment I used to go regularly to him, staying with him in Eastbourne or in London, in the holidays from my prep school.

'Even though I was barely in my teens, this was immensely serious and professional study; and the lessons were mammoth. I remember one that started at half past ten, and at teatime Mrs Bridge came in and said, "Really, Frank, you must give the boy a break." Often I used to end these marathons in tears; not that he was beastly to me, but the concentrated strain was too much for me. I was perhaps too young to take in so much at the time, but I found later that a good deal of it had stuck firmly.

'This strictness was the product of nothing but professionalism. Bridge insisted on the absolutely clear relationship of what was in my mind to what was on the paper. I used to get sent to the other side of the room; Bridge would play what I'd written and demand if it was what I'd really meant. He taught me to think and feel through the instruments I was writing for; he was most naturally an instrumental composer, and as a superb viola player he thought instrumentally.

'For instance, by the time I was thirteen or fourteen I was beginning to get more adventurous. Before then, what I had been writing had been sort of early nineteenth century in style; and then I heard Holst's *Planets* and Ravel's string quartet and was excited by them. I started writing in a much freer harmonic idiom, and at one point came up with a series of major sevenths on the violin. Bridge was against this, saying that the instrument didn't vibrate properly with this interval; it should be divided between the instruments. He fought against anything anti-instrumental, which is why his own music is grateful to play.

'The holiday teaching continued right through my schooldays (at my public school my musical education was practically non-existent, though I continued with the viola) until I left in 1930 to go to the Royal College of Music. At about eighteen or nineteen, perhaps naturally, I began to rebel. When Bridge played questionable chords across the room at me and asked if that was what I had meant, I would retort, "Yes it is", and he'd grunt back, "Well, it oughtn't to be." '

An extract from an article that first appeared in the 'Sunday Telegraph' in 1964, the year of Britten's fiftieth birthday. It was then translated into a broadcast talk and recorded in this form by Benjamin Britten for BBC 'Music Magazine' of January 9th, 1966, as a tribute to his teacher, Frank Bridge, who died twenty-five years ago on January 10th, 1941.

Étude

(*French=study.*) Strictly speaking an étude is a technical exercise for an instrumental (more rarely a vocal) performer, but, in practice, it takes the form of a composition of greater or lesser musical value. Études may be as much exercises in expression as in technique, and at their best (eg Chopin's) they will combine both purposes.

Liszt at the piano, wearing his Hungarian sword of honour, 1855

Étude

IF AT ANY TIME there happen to be workmen in the house – decorators painting the staircase, the gasmen repairing the cooker, or even the window-cleaner on his too infrequent visits, I always feel acutely self-conscious about practising the piano. How idle I must seem to them, tinkling away at the keyboard when I could be doing something useful. I adopt a defensive attitude when I meet them in the hall, dropping silly remarks about 'having a day off for once', or claiming that I didn't get back from the studios till 2 am. Yet how unnecessary this is; perhaps only a professional musician can really appreciate the amount of work involved in perfecting technical skills, but the sheer number of hours involved makes an impressive total, even to the man in the street. 'Practice makes perfect' is a trite saying, but for all its triteness it is eternally true.

Since amateur pianists often waste a great deal of the time that they spend practising I felt that it would be to their advantage to include in this anthology some maxims about how to work productively, as well as some indication of the self-discipline involved.

The rules for practising the piano which Busoni formulated in a letter to Wottersdorf, written on 20th July 1898, are an example of inspired common-sense. Seldom can so much practical advice have been concentrated into so small a space; they should be copied and pinned in a prominent place above every teacher's piano as a constant reminder. The description of Chopin's teaching methods I have included since the Mikuli edition in which it appears is now difficult to obtain; it is too valuable to lose, and every Chopin-player should study it. I do not guarantee, however, that practising the G♯-minor study, Op 25, will always produce the same reaction in spiders as it did in Paderewski's hands. This episode is by way of being light relief, but the passage which immediately follows it is an indication of the sheer hard grind of practising. At the time, Paderewski had just arrived in New York for his first American tour. To his consternation, he discovered that he was expected to play six different concertos in the first week, two of which he scarcely knew. He also had to prepare for six recital programmes to be given on the subsequent fortnight. Small wonder that he was worried.

When I was a student, I had the good fortune to study with Cyril Smith, whose virtuosity in Rachmaninoff and Liszt was breathtaking. It is interesting to read what he has to say about practice, for at the time it seemed that technical difficulty just did not exist for him. As Christopher Robin's nanny, Alice, might have said had she but known,

'The life of a pianist is terrible 'ard . . .'

Rules for practising the piano

1. PRACTISE the passage with the most difficult fingering; when you have mastered that, play it with the easiest.

2. If a passage offers some particular technical difficulty, go through all similar passages you can remember in other places; in this way you will bring system into the kind of playing in question.

3. Always join technical practice with the study of the interpretation; the difficulty often does not lie in the notes, but in the dynamic shading prescribed.

4. Never be carried away by temperament, for that dissipates strength, and where it occurs there will always be a blemish, like a dirty spot which can never be washed out of a material.

5. Don't set your mind on overcoming the difficulties in pieces which have been unsuccessful because you have previously practised them badly; it is generally a useless task. But if, meanwhile, you have quite changed your way of playing, then begin the study of the old piece from the beginning, as if you did not know it.

6. Study everything as if there were nothing more difficult; try to interpret studies for the young from the standpoint of the virtuoso; you will be astonished to find how difficult it is to play a Czerny or Cramer, or even a Clementi.

7. Bach is the foundation of piano playing, Liszt the summit. The two make Beethoven possible.

8. Take it for granted from the beginning that everything is possible on the piano, even when it seems impossible to you, or really is so.

9. Attend to your technical apparatus so that you are prepared and armed for every possible event; then, when you study a new piece, you can turn all your power to the intellectual content; you will not be held up by the technical problems.

10. Never play carelessly, even when there is nobody listening, or the occasion seems unimportant.

11. Never leave a passage which has been unsuccessful without repeating it; if you cannot do it in the presence of others, then do it subsequently.

12. If possible, allow no day to pass without touching your piano.

COMPOSERS ON MUSIC (Busoni): Sam Morgenstern

Chopin's teaching methods

CHOPIN POSSESSED a most highly cultivated technique, and was a thorough master of his instrument. In all kinds of touch, piano or forte, staccato or legato, the smoothness of his scales and runs was unsurpassed, indeed marvellous; under his hands the piano needed to envy neither the violin its bow, nor a wind-instrument its living breath. The tones blended as harmoniously together as in the sweetest chorus. His true pianoforte hand, not so very large, but wonderfully elastic, enabled him to master chords of the most difficult harmonies, and passages requiring the very widest stretches, such things of his own as no one up to his time had dared to introduce into piano literature – in fact, he played anything and everything without the least apparent effort. His playing was characterised by freedom and facility, and the tone which he knew how to charm from the instrument was always, especially in cantabile passages, marvellously full; perhaps Field alone could be compared with him in this respect. A noble, manly energy lent to passages requiring such a quality an overpowering effect, an energy without coarseness; as on the other hand he knew how to charm his hearers by the delicacy of his soul-felt rendering, a delicacy, without over-ornamentation. And yet, in spite of the intense feeling habitual to his performance, it was nevertheless always well-balanced, chaste, even elegant, and sometimes sternly held in check. But, unfortunately, these finely shaded differences, like so much else belonging to the ideal field of art, have, by the tendency of the piano-playing of today, been thrown into the lumber-room of superannuated ideas, as a prejudice detrimental to progress; and we are nowadays told to regard a mere development of power, which takes no account of the capacities of the instrument nor of the beauty of each tone to be produced, as great style and fine expression!

In the matter of keeping time Chopin was blameless, and it will surprise many to learn that the metronome stood always upon his piano; and even in his much calumniated tempo rubato, one hand, the accompanying one, always played in strict time, while the other, as if singing, either with an undecided hesitation, or more rapidly with a certain impatient excitedness as if in passionate speech, kept the musical expression free from all rhythmical fetters.

Although Chopin mostly played his own compositions, yet his wonderfully faithful memory mastered everything that was great and beautiful in piano literature, particularly Bach, and it is difficult to say whether he loved him or Mozart more. In executing the works of these masters he was incomparably great. Together with Messrs Alard and Franchomme he fairly threw the blasé Parisian public into raptures with the G *Major Trio* of Mozart in one of his last concerts. Of course, Beethoven possessed an equally warm place in his heart. He took great pleasure in playing Weber's music, particularly the *Concert-piece*, and the *Sonatas in E Minor* and *A Flat Major*, as well as Hummel's *Fantasy*, *Septette* and Concertos, and Field's *A Flat Major Concerto* and *Nocturnes*, to which he improvised the most charming variations. Neither I myself nor probably any one else has ever seen upon his piano a single specimen of 'virtuoso-music' of any kind, although its growth was fearfully rank in his time: and he only very seldom took advantage of the many opportunities proffered to, ay even urged upon him to hear such music. On the other hand he was a regular and enthusiastic listener at the Habeneck Société de Concerts, and the Alard-Franchomme string quartet concerts.

It may perhaps be of interest to many readers to learn here something about Chopin as a teacher, if only from a very general sketch.

So far from regarding his labour in that capacity (which he could not easily give up, owing to his artistic and social position in Paris) as a heavy burden, Chopin devoted to it all his powers daily for several hours. Naturally, he made great demands upon the talent and industry of the pupil, and there were often *des leçons orageuses*, as the idiom of the school called them, after which many a tearful eye left the high altar of the Cité d'Orléans, Rue St Lazare, but always without the slightest ill-will towards the dearly beloved master. The strictness which was so hard to please, the feverish excitement with which the master endeavoured to raise his pupils to his own standard, the incessant repetition of a passage until it was completely comprehended – are these not proofs that he had the progress of his pupils at heart? A sacred zeal for art glowed in his breast, every word from his lips was encouraging and inspiring. Certain lessons often actually lasted two or three hours consecutively, until exhaustion overpowered both master and student.

Chopin's endeavour at the outset of the instruction was, to emancipate the pupil from all stiffness and cramp-like, convulsive movement of the hand, and to give him the prime quality necessary for a good performance – *souplesse*, suppleness, and, along with that, independence of the individual fingers of each other. He pointed out indefatigably that the exercises used for this purpose were not merely mechanical, but that they depended greatly upon the intelligence and will of the student, and did not therefore require inane repetition for a countless number of times (as unfortunately is taught in so many schools), not to mention the ridiculous advice of Kalkbrenner to busy oneself at the same time with some kind of reading (!). Chopin paid great attention to the different kinds of touch, particularly the melodious legato.

For gymnastic exercises he recommended bending the wrist up and down, repeated wrist-exercises on the piano, stretching the fingers, in a word everything of that kind, but with an earnest warning against fatigue. He made his pupils play the scales with a full tone, the notes connected as much as possible, with the evenness of a metronome, and he had them run into a faster tempo only slowly and very gradually. The putting of the thumb under the fingers and of the fingers over the thumb were to render the necessary holding of the hand inwards easier. The scales needing most black keys (B Flat Major, F Sharp Major, D Flat Major) were the first to be studied, and the last, as the most difficult, C Major. After, or at the same time with the scales, he used Clementi's *Preludes and Exercises*, a work which on account of its utility he valued highly. According to Chopin, the evenness of a scale or an arpeggio depended not so much upon an equal strengthening of all the fingers to be obtained through five-finger exercises, and keeping the thumb quite free in its movements, as upon a regular and flowing sideward movement of the hand over the keyboard, which he tried to make understood by comparing it with the glissando; and the elbow was always to hang perfectly free.

After these exercises he used to give his pupils a number of studies selected from Cramer's *Études* and Clementi's *Gradus ad Parnassum*, which seemed to him good exercises in style, and for higher finish Moscheles, Bach's Suites, and some Fugues from the *Wohltemperiertes Klavier*. In some degree Field's and his own Nocturnes served also as studies, for in these they were to learn, by grasping his explanations and through comparison and imitation (Chopin often played his own things to his pupils), to recognise, appreciate, and put into practice the genuine, beautiful, singing tone, and the true legato. In playing all kinds of chords he required all the fingers to strike at exactly the same instant, and spread chords were only allowed where the composer himself indicated them.

The important point about the trill, which he usually began with the upper auxiliary note, was not rapidity so much as perfect evenness, and the end of a trill was to be played quietly and without hurry. For the *gruppetto* and the *appogiatura* he recommended the great singers as patterns.

Octaves were to be played indeed from the wrist, but by no means at the expense of fullness of tone. Such studies as his own *Études*, Opus 10 and Opus 25, were only given to the most advanced students.

In regard to wrong phrasing he often repeated the well-timed remark that it always seemed to him as if someone were reciting in a language which he did not understand – it was a speech, laboriously impressed upon the memory, in which the speaker not only neglected the natural quantity of the syllables, but even sometimes made a pause in the very middle of a word.

The pseudo-musician who used bad phrasing, he used to say, in like manner proved that music was not his mother-tongue, but something to him foreign and not understood, and such a player, like the reciter just mentioned, would be obliged wholly to give up the idea of moving his hearers in the faintest degree by his performance. In supplying music, especially his own, with fingering, Chopin was not sparing, and in this field art owes to him great innovations, which on account of their manifest utility soon found permanent acceptance, in spite of the fact that, at first, authorities such as Kalkbrenner were scandalised by them.

For instance, Chopin unhesitatingly used the thumb upon the black keys, and even passed it under the little finger (of course holding the wrist well in where this made the passage easier or lent it more quietness and smoothness). He often took two keys in juxtaposition with the same finger (and not only in slipping the finger from a black key on to a white one), without the slightest break in the series of tones. He used also to put the longer fingers over each other without the help of the thumb (*Étude No 2, Opus 10*), and not alone where this was rendered necessary by the first finger holding a tone. His fingering of chromatic thirds founded on this principle (as he has expressed it in the *Étude No 5, Opus 25*), offers in a much higher degree than any previous system the possibility of the most beautiful legato with a hand perfectly free from nervousness, even in the quickest tempo. In shading the tone he insisted upon a really gradual increase and decrease of the tone-power. He gave his pupils invaluable lessons and hints in regard to declamation and rendering in general, and his whole influence was without doubt the more valuable and lasting because in his lessons he repeatedly played not only single passages but whole pieces, and that too with a conscientiousness, an inspiration, such as few ever heard him play within a Concert-hall. Often a whole lesson went by without the student playing more than a few measures, while Chopin, interrupting and correcting him upon a Pleyel upright, offered him for his admiration and emulation the living ideal of the highest beauty. His pupils always played upon an excellent concert-piano, and they were allowed to practise upon none but the best instruments. One may assert without exaggeration that only his pupils knew Chopin the pianist in all his unequalled greatness.

CARL MIKULI, Lemberg, September 1879

Paderewski and the spider

ONE DAY I was practising in my little room in Vienna. Among the pieces I was then studying, and which I had to play every day as a finger exercise, was a certain study by Chopin, a study in thirds. I was just starting to work – I lit the candles and sat down at the piano. The room was very dark, you know, there were so many tall shrubs growing close to the window. Then suddenly in the midst of my playing, there came down from the ceiling right on to the piano desk, something like a tiny silver thread. It attracted my attention and I looked a little closer, and then I saw – a spider attached to it. He hung there motionless and appeared to be listening to my playing, and as long as I played that particular study in thirds, the little spider remained there perfectly still on his line.

And now comes the interesting thing. After finishing the study in thirds, I went on to another study – in sixths this time, and the moment I began it, the spider turned himself quickly about, and hurried up to the ceiling. Well, it struck me at the moment as very funny, and I was interested and deeply intrigued. I said to myself, 'Now, I must see whether that spider is really musical or not – whether he meant to come down to listen on purpose, or by accident.' So I suddenly stopped my study in sixths, and quickly started again the one in thirds. Instantly, down came the little spider! He seemed to slide down his line, and this time to the very end, and sat on the piano desk and listened. He did not seem at all frightened, only deeply interested in the music.

He had aroused my interest greatly and I wondered if he would appear the next morning. I was very curious about him – I felt sure I should see him again. Well, he did appear the moment I began my day's work with the thirds. That little thread still hung from the ceiling, and down he came the moment I touched the piano, and this same thing continued all that day, and the next day and for many weeks he came – he was a faithful companion. Whenever I started the study in thirds, the little spider came quickly to the piano desk and listened. After a time I arrived so far as to be able to see his eyes – so brilliant, like tiny, shining diamonds. He would sit immovable, or hang immovable I should say, during the Chopin *Étude*, perfectly content and perfectly quiet. But the moment I stopped that particular study, back he went quickly to the ceiling and disappeared. Sometimes, I used to think quite angrily.

When the vacation time came I confess I felt strangely anxious about the spider. What would become of him, I wondered. 'Shall I find him when I return?' I asked myself. He had become a part of my daily practice, a kind of companion, and I knew I should miss him. When I returned in September, I looked for him everywhere. I looked for the little line, but it no longer hung from the ceiling. I played my study in thirds, again and again I played it, but I could not find my spider friend. The room seemed empty and lonely without him. What had happened to him? Had some careless housemaid crushed out his little life, or had he, lonely and discouraged with the closed piano and silent room, gone elsewhere? I could only hope so. But the days went on, and I never saw my spider friend again.

THE PADEREWSKI MEMOIRS: *Ignace Jan Paderewski* and *Mary Lawton*

Ten seconds of bliss

IN THE MUSICAL PROFESSION there is no such thing as an overnight leap to fame. Success has to be earned slowly, painfully, by the steady acquisition of much craftsmanship, by the discipline of thousands of hours of practice, by the perfecting of co-operation between mind and hands. A concert pianist has to devote much of his early life to training his little finger to be stronger than other people's little fingers. He needs to learn, not only how to play a piece of music, but also to master ever gradation of its every note. There are a million degrees of quality in the playing of any piano work, and it is quite possible to practise a piece for hours on end without getting a single note wrong, and yet to be playing it appallingly. Every phrase has countless problems, some of which can be solved only with great difficulty, and some never at all – at least by me.

I would estimate that, even with eight hours' practice a day, few pianists are able to achieve more than ten consecutive seconds of absolutely perfect playing a year. In fact, I could count on one hand the number of times in my life when I have played a phrase to my complete satisfaction. Once was when I was a student, living at the Orrey's house in Barnes, I was practising the Chopin *B minor sonata* as I had done every day for some weeks. There was one particularly elusive phrase which I had tried, unsuccessfully, to work out many times . . . and then it happened, for some reason which I cannot explain even to myself, that as I went over the piece yet again, everything clicked into place – the comprehension of the music and the method of playing it – and for the space of about ten seconds I played to what I thought to be perfection. Those ten seconds were so significant that I can still remember in detail my surroundings at the time. The piano was our hired Grotrian-Steinweg, standing against a wall in the dining-room. There were French windows leading on to a verandah and a small garden. It was very peaceful and there was no one else to hear my brief moment of triumph. Even if others had done so, they might well have disagreed about my interpretation of the phrase, but it was perfect to my ears. I tried again many more times that day, and many days afterwards, to recapture those ten seconds of playing, but I have never been able to do so.

DUET FOR THREE HANDS: *Cyril Smith*

Aria

A vocal piece, especially in opera or oratorio, formally more highly organised than a song.

Caruso's sketch of himself as Don José in *Carmen*

Aria

'MUCH IS TO BE LEARNED from singers male and female. But do not believe all they tell you.'

So said Schumann in his *Aphorisms*. The cautionary note he adopts is valuable, for there can be little doubt that the teaching of singing is an area into which the layman probes at his peril. Peter Ustinov tells most entertainingly of a few lessons that he once had in Rome when he was required to sing in the film *Quo Vadis*; he was variously exhorted to sing with the forehead, the eyes, or the stomach; the voice, it seemed, never entered into it. To analyse and describe a physical process that is taking place in someone else's larynx is admittedly a difficult task, and one can sympathise with pupil and teacher alike when the problem of 'placing' the voice is being discussed. 'Put it in the dome, dear,' was Elizabeth Schumann's infallible cure for all technical problems, the instruction being accompanied by an illustrative gesture of the hand not unlike the one with which, as boys at school, we made the shadow-figures of swans' heads appear on the dormitory wall.

I have gathered into this section a number of helpful tips that should assist the reader in acquiring a singing technique. If, like Neville Cardus, he finds self-instruction ineffectual but singing teachers even more disastrous, it may simply be a matter of trying to find a better teacher. Geraldine Farrar sets a high standard, involving as it does 'the sacrifice of gluttony and dissipation'. There is a wealth of good sense in her recommendations.

Not wishing to appear prejudiced, I have presented two opposing views on dress on the concert stage. Neither Anna Case nor Ursula Greville has remembered one very important point, however, and that is that if you are to appear on the stage in oratorio, it is essential if you are a soprano to discover in advance what the alto is going to wear, and *vice versa*. There is only one disaster worse than standing next to a lady whose colour scheme clashes violently with your own, and that is if she should be so tactless as to wear an absolutely identical garment. Having acquired both technique and wardrobe, it is as well to know what to eat, and here Anna Case's words may strike a responsive chord.

The first big opportunity – fame overnight – is this not the dream of every young artist? I thought it would be nice to include at least one example of what one might term the Cinderella syndrome, Lotte Lehmann's description of her first appearance in *Lohengrin* with Klemperer. To those of us who only know him as a partially paralysed ageing giant, it is interesting to read of him attacking the piano like a tiger. Lastly, we have Melba describing a very curious episode in her life; to our ears, the idea of introducing *The Star-spangled Banner* into a performance of *The Barber of Seville* seems stylistically so incongruous as to be totally unacceptable. Concepts of musical propriety have changed much over the years, as this unique incident reveals.

My career as a singer, by Neville Cardus

IT WAS HARFORD, when he sang the *Dichterliebe* cycle of Schumann, who made me decide to try to become a great lieder singer; like Harford I had little tone in my voice, so his example was encouraging. As I couldn't pay yet for singing lessons I consulted the library. At random, for I knew nothing of the subject of voice production, I hit upon a book by Emil Behnke, with illustrations showing the insides of the lungs and throat, all abstract, removed from any personal identity and very vivid. 'Chubes!' as Mr Polly said.

One of Behnke's vocal exercises involved the repetition of 'Koo, koo, koo, koo-oo-oh-ah' on eight repeated notes of the same pitch throughout one's range, the idea being to 'place' the voice forward. A lot was written in those days by experts in voice-production about 'placing'. There were breathing exercises too; I would stand in front of an open window, at break of dawn, and take in a Manchester fog, releasing the air very slowly until I nearly burst myself. Another breathing exercise was performed lying on one's back, looking at the ceiling. I paid a widowed woman in the back-street hovel of Hulme a shilling each time to allow me use of an unfurnished attic one night every week; and I climbed the rickety stairs, carrying a candle in a candlestick, for the attic had no means of illumination and the night was sure to be pitch black and cold as charity. I used a tuning-fork to keep my bearings. Up and down the scale I koo-koo-oh-ah'd for an hour, advancing my studies gradually to Herculean attempts at *crescendi* on sustained chest-notes. Also I practised while walking along the Manchester streets when other pedestrians were not too close to me. The roar of the traffic easily concealed my *coup de glotte*. But now and again a sudden lull would occur in the city's roar; a tram would stop and create a vacuum in which I was exposed – or as the music-hall comedians used to say, 'left' – on a strangled high E flat; I never could really cope with anything higher than D. I was a circumscribed baritone.

My career as a singer came to an end a year or so after I had delivered myself into the care of teachers of voice production. I do not indict them altogether; the odds were against them, no doubt, but before consulting them I at least could produce, even if only ventriloquially, the impression that a singer really was somewhere about or around. After a dozen or so lessons I was reduced to a state of what might be called congestion of the larynx. And, of course, as I tried different professors in turn, each assured me that I had come to him 'just in time'. I was instructed by one master to practise on the vowel A, only to be told by another that my urgent need was the sound OO; another advocated the *coup de glotte*; another threw up his hands in horror at the very mention of it. I was introduced to nasal resonance and made stiff of chin. I was rendered tongue-conscious. I had so far not been aware that the tongue possessed the power to waggle and flop about the mouth by its own volition. From the moment I was told that a singer, while enunciating 'ah', must keep his tongue flat and still, with the tip relaxed next the lower teeth, my tongue clove to the roof of my mouth. I was made to hold a lighted candle and to sing scales at it; if it fluttered in the slightest, something needed doing to 'concentrate' my tone. I suppose there was a grain of sense in all this quackery; and I suppose it is still taught and swallowed. My own experience of the teachers of singing, the voice-builders and so on, is that they have little more wisdom to impart than that, granted a good voice from nature, a student will go ahead if he keeps the muscles of his chin and throat free and not clenched, trains his ear, controls his diaphragm, and has nothing whatever to do with theories of vocal colour, but allows his imagination to do the shading.

SECOND INNINGS: *Neville Cardus*

How to become a prima donna by Geraldine Farrar

THE VERY FIRST requisite is an iron will, to work like a galley slave, and to concentrate every energy of many talents combined. An operatic career should commence early. No singer at fifty can sing as she did at twenty, for although the great artiste may put her spirit, her soul, her experience behind her voice when she is older, she cannot restore to it the intangible bloom of youth. The singer who plans an operatic career must be willing to submit herself to a hard regime of study and sacrifice. She must eat, exercise, live generally with an ever present thought of its effect on her voice and appearance. Of what use is the projection of a beautiful mental picture by means of a fine voice if the physical attributes do not correspond, if the singer's appearance contradicts her voice? Nowadays the public demands the ultimate.

Ceaseless vigilance is the price of operatic mastery. For twenty years I have followed the same regular course of sitting down at the piano at nine o'clock and working until one. There are certain phrases in each opera of the repertory, which are individually difficult to different individual singers. And these phrases must be smooth, must be perfect, must lie ready in the consciousness and voice of the artiste against a call at any time. Keeping them there is a matter of practice, of thinking, of concentration. The singer must always keep in perfect working trim, just like the fencer or football player.

But all too many opera singers are deficient in the very things in which they should excel. Though they should work like galley slaves there is no reason why they should look like them. The public idealises its operatic heroines, and they should try to live up to the ideal portrayed. There is no excuse on their part for frowsiness, for lack of neatness and charm. It means the sacrifice of gluttony and dissipation. Why have a glorious voice, and when you come on the stage look like something which has been delivered by auto truck? Perhaps it is easier to forgive a man in this connection than a woman. I am quite free to say that there are few opera singers who can read at sight, who do not have to have their music pounded into their heads, and who are capable of singing without having their eyes glued agonisingly on the conductor. The world is full of books, of sculpture, of paintings, or interests for mind and soul. Yet they never read, they never have an intellectual reaction: food, drink and sleep seem to sum up their idea of spending the hours when free from the footlights.

The aspirant to operatic honours must always remember that operatic singing is the 'limping sister' of music, even if the most gaudily attired, that seventy-five per cent of the people who go to 'hear' opera, want first to 'hear' it through the medium of the eye. She must bear in mind that the world of opera is one of illusion, of fantasy, of exaggeration – and that it is hard to nurse poetic and fantastic illusions, no matter how fine a voice is trying to convey them, when the eye is oppressed by the sight of some three hundred pounds of human avoirdupois, ill-fitting costumes, wigs, awkward stage deportment or ill-timed mannerisms.

THE ART OF THE PRIMA DONNA (*Geraldine Farrar*): Frederick H Martens

* * *

...by Anna Case

THE CONCERT SINGER should make legitimate most of her personal advantages. An attractive personality, a face and figure which pleases, help to establish the bond of sympathy between audience and singer which should be welded with her entrance. It is the singer's duty to be attractively gowned, as well as she can afford; and it is far better to wear a bright dress, a sparkling, brilliant dress of some kind rather than one dark and sombre in colour. Audiences are very susceptible to colours; a bright dress emphasises the mood of happiness and lightness which the singer wishes to establish; it underlines her smile. A dark dress, on the other hand, is apt to lessen an appreciative attitude.

THE ART OF THE PRIMA DONNA (*Anna Case*): Frederick H Martens

* * *

...by Ursula Greville

BUT ASIDE from the concert singer's voice and personality, she has – if she chooses to make use of it – another factor at hand which may aid greatly in her success – the frock! I mean by this the right frock for the right song or group of songs. The singer's frock is very valuable in helping her make clear the meaning of her songs, in lending them charm of local colour, and giving a touch of appropriate beauty of colour and design to their interpretation. I was told of a man who went to one of my London concerts, a man who knew nothing about music and cared less, and who after I had sung a few songs said:

'Why, that girl is no singer! She's a revue artiste. Hope she'll keep right on for a long time.' It was a sincere compliment, coming from him. And what drew it forth? – the frock.

Music is not as interesting to some people who attend concerts as to others, but if they can be prevented from finding it dull by having something beautiful to look at while they listen, they may in the end be led to like it more and more. It seems so stupid to see a woman who sings away about spring, spring which is so fresh, and green and delicately joyous, in a gown of flaming red brocade. How can she make her audience feel that she is expressing the mood of her song? I think it is just as legitimate for the artiste to support and embellish her song with beauty of dress, in the way of design, colour and historic or regional suggestion, as she does with her piano accompaniment, the natural movement of her hands and body, and facial expression.

'Here,' continued the singer, 'let me show you some of my frocks – I have more than sixty of them – all designed by me.' Miss Greville's maid, undoing their tissue-paper wrappings, reverently brought forth a number of exquisite creations which fully bore out the artiste's contentions anent the charm a lovely frock has for the eye. 'This,' continued Miss Greville, as she held up a lovely thing in gold, Russian greens and blues, with a dull gold buckle heavily studded with uncut rubies, 'this is my frock when I sing *The Hymn to the Sun* from Rimsky's *Coq d'Or*. Is it not beautiful? And the buckle – I should not want to tell you what it cost for it comes from a famous collection of antiques and is as old as the hills,' she added with a little sigh. 'This other' – it was a gossamer thing of soft shades of rich blues and silver – 'is my *Moonlight* frock. I am very fond of it because I used it in England on the stage to try out my theories with regard to frocks as factors in winning success in concert singing, and it justified itself. I use it for songs with a distinct atmospheric quality, a moonlight quality of appeal, soft, clear, cool songs whose charm lies in the silver clarity of their melodies rather than in any sentiment of warmth or passion. This almost early Victorian frock – its design is really older, however – I use for groups of Elizabethan songs. Some little time back I sang a group of songs accompanied by the lute, probably the first time the lute had been used in public for many generations, and for that I wore a little white velvet stomacher and full skirt. I never bother to get the exact period frock for in those days I'm sure there were women who refused to follow fashion, and altered the period frocks, just as they do today. It is the suggestion which counts. To begin with, it would be impossible to sing in many of the garments owing to the restriction. I could spend hours on this subject, which I believe to be a most important factor in getting the man in the street interested visually as well as aurally.

    THE ART OF THE PRIMA DONNA (*Ursula Greville*): *Frederick H Martens*

★   ★   ★

... by Anna Case

BEFORE A CONCERT I eat a light dinner at about five o'clock – preferring chicken or the breast of guinea fowl, rice and vegetables to beefsteak – to gain the strength necessary to sing in the evening. After the performance I sometimes eat some additional food.

 In my opinion, a great deal of the 'colds' trouble singers have with their voices results from colds more or less directly due to improper food. Every singer should understand her own physique perfectly, and learn what food she can or cannot eat. If the body is kept free from poisonous toxins, the voice will be in good condition. I use neither lozenges nor atomiser, but I have one certain gargle, a special prescription, of astringent qualities, which I employ only when my voice is fatigued, as a stimulant. And you may form an idea of how frequently I resort to it when I tell you that I used it two weeks ago for the first time in two years.

 Nearly all the colds which affect the voice result from indigestion, in my opinion. I know that I once, when I was in the best of health, had a bad attack of laryngitis as a result of eating plum pudding. Not until I had taken glass after glass of hot water and thoroughly washed the poison out of my system could I sing again. I never eat sea food or canned goods of any kind while on tour. It is better to do without lobster or oysters than run the chance of ptomaine poisoning and find yourself incapable of filling your engagements.

 I never risk deranging my stomach or nerves with patent medicines.

    THE ART OF THE PRIMA DONNA: *Frederick H Martens*

The Cinderella syndrome

THE NEXT SEASON started off just as usual: one nice part on a Sunday afternoon in Altona – as makeshift for someone else – otherwise pages and apprentices, mere walk-on parts.

 One day Klemperer called me. I still had my old passion for him, and stood before him in some confusion.

 'Do you think you could manage to take on Elsa's part? You'd only have a week. Frau Wagner is on holiday, Fleischer-Edel is away too at the moment, and we're in a fix. I've persuaded Dr Loewenfeld to let you risk it. Well – do you think you can do it?'

 Did I think I could do it?

I had, of course, studied Elsa's part by myself, and came proudly to the rehearsal. But if I thought I knew the part, I realised my mistake after the first five minutes. Klemperer sat at the piano like an evil spirit, thumping on it with long hands like tigers' claws, dragging my terrified voice into the fiery vortex of his fanatical will. Elsa's dreamy serenity became a rapturous ecstasy, her anxious pleading a challenging demand. For the first time I felt my nervous inhibitions fall from me, and I sank into the flame of inner experience. I had always wanted to sing like this – it was like flying in a dream: a bodiless gliding through blissful eternity. . . . But usually one wakens from this lovely kind of dream with the terror of falling. And so I was dragged back from those ecstasies by Klemperer's voice saying:

'No idea of the part. We must work hard if you're to manage it.'

I managed it.

I sang Elsa in spite of the indignant looks of Pennarini, my *Lohengrin*, in spite of the producer's shrugged shoulders, in spite of Klemperer's discouraging interpolations at the orchestral rehearsal. . . .

Theo Drill-Orridge was singing *Ortrud* on a visiting-engagement, and her eyes grew wider as she noticed at the rehearsal how simply everyone was against me – even Klemperer, who grew furious every time I forgot anything, seemed to lose all confidence in me and shouted up:

'What's the matter? Has the big part gone to your head and made you forget everything?'

But now I set my teeth, and plunged into the hazards of this great undertaking.

I didn't see the audience – probably a sceptical one, expecting nothing very special – on the evening. Nor did I see Dr Loewenfeld's dreaded face spying from the box. . . . I was just Elsa! I felt only the blissful pulsation of my voice, I forgot everything that conductor and producer had pumped into me – I was just myself alone. Tears stood in my eyes as I passed down the minster steps through the bowing throng.

'Hail to thee, Elsa of Brabant,' sang the chorus – and 'Hail to thee' my whole heart sang, greeting this day that was the real beginning of my rise to fame.

Of course, that Elsa was far from being a mature artistic achievement. Probably a great deal of it was primitive and gauche, yet that evening is one of the sacred high-points of my life, for whose sake life has been worth living.

It was a great and decisive success both with the audience and the Press. With one stroke I was 'made'.

WINGS OF SONG: *Lotte Lehmann*

The star-spangled manner

WHEN I ARRIVED at San Francisco, it was to find a city in the grip of the fever of war. The crisis which had long brooded between Spain and the United

States was reaching its climax. Great headlines denouncing the Spanish policy flared across the tops of the newspapers, demonstrations were held in the streets, and the question on all men's lips was, 'When will war be declared?'

I could not have chosen any part of the States more inopportune for the commencement of an opera season than San Francisco, because as you are probably aware, this city was the centre of Spanish settlement in days gone by, and even at that time many descendants of Castilian pioneers still lived in the city. However, that was not what troubled me. The most agitating problem before me was the fact that I was due to open in *The Barber of Seville* – to sing the leading rôle of an intensely Spanish opera in a city where the very name of Spain was anathema.

What should I do? Would there be a public demonstration against me? Would there – even worse – be a demonstration of Spaniards in favour of their national ideals? I sat in my hotel, sent wires right and left to try and alter the performance, saw my manager, held conferences with the leading artistes – all to no purpose. It was too late. *The Barber* had been announced, and we must go through with it.

War was declared. In the harbour of the Golden Gate itself we heard something of the echo of the strife. All day and all night there was marching and counter marching in the streets. It seemed incredible that I should ever sing the rôle of Rosina without some untoward event.

However, I shrugged my shoulders and hoped for the best. 'After all,' I said to myself, 'I am not a politician or a diplomat. I am an artiste. Music is international, and this opera shall be one in which no echo of the war shall be heard.'

How little I anticipated what actually happened when I said these words! How little I looked forward to the extraordinary scene in which I was about to play a leading part!

If you are acquainted with *The Barber of Seville*, you will of course remember that in the second act occurs a scene in which Rosina, the heroine, is being given a singing lesson. Rossini, the composer, with his well-known laziness, left this scene a blank, leaving it to the discretion of the prima donna to sing whatever song she chose during the lesson. It was rather a charming innovation in opera, and in the part I had often left the song I was going to sing till the last minute, choosing *Mattinata*, *Still wie die Nacht*, or even the Mad Scene from *Lucia*, as the mood suited me.

I was still undecided as to the song I should sing during the Lesson Scene when I went on the stage. I was too preoccupied with the mentality of the audience. An uncanny silence hung over the vast auditorium, crammed though it was to capacity. All the artists were nervous. I felt – I know not how – that instead of the usual electric chain of sympathy which I had been used to creating between the audience and myself, there was a cloud of sullen hostility, which needed only the most trivial incident to cause it to break.

The first act passed by without any serious trouble, but every minute the atmosphere was becoming more electric. As the curtain rose on the second act,

I stood in the wings, in my gaudy Spanish dress, thinking furiously. Was there any means by which I could stop the demonstration that was looming all too clearly ahead?

The cue for my entrance was played and with a heavy heart I went on to the stage. Mechanically I sang the music that precedes the Lesson Scene, noticing as I did so, that the audience was becoming more and more restive. Suddenly I remembered that I had not yet decided which song I should sing during the lesson. I bit my lip with vexation, and quickly ran through in my mind a selection of songs that might be suitable on this most disastrous of nights.

Suddenly, at the very moment when I had to walk to the piano, an idea flashed through my mind. Whether it was right or wrong, I know not, but I determined to put it into practice. Trembling with emotion, I found my way to the piano, sat down, and instead of the *Aria* which the audience were expecting, I played the opening bars of the *Star-spangled Banner*.

The effect was miraculous. As my voice floated out I could hear the sound of the vast gathering rising to their feet. By the end of the first few lines every man and woman in the audience was shouting their National Anthem, and my own voice was drowned and inaudible.

MELODIES AND MEMORIES: *Nellie Melba*

Sonata

A term designating both a type of composition and a musical form. The Sonata as a type is normally a composition in three or four movements, only the first of which is, with few exceptions, in Sonata form, and often the last, though that is at least as frequently a Rondo. The word is derived from *suonare* or *sonare*='to sound'; a Sonata is originally simply 'a thing sounded', ie played, as distinct from a Cantata (from *cantare*), 'a thing sung', etc etc etc.

Ludwig van Beethoven, 1814

Sonata

FORM is probably the most misunderstood factor in music; it is the academician's delight and the student's despair. How many aspiring youngsters are led to believe that the proper identification of the termination of the bridge passage is the most important step on the road to musical enlightenment? Periodically I am asked to give a lecture on one of the 'set works' for an O or A level examination to an assembly of young people gathered from some thirty different schools. For an hour or more I will treat them to an impassioned discourse revealing, as it seems to me, profound insight and understanding – only to be asked at question-time, 'Will you please tell me whether the second subject begins in bar 121 or 123?' Why do they ask? Does it matter to the child? Does it matter to *anybody*? Certainly, the composer never devoted any great thought to this particular detail; he may have fought a mental battle for days deciding how to solve the problem of the transition involved, but never in his wildest dreams would he have thought of saying to himself, 'Here beginneth the second subject'.

The trouble is that examiners want cut-and-dried answers; it saves endless time if they can put a cross or a tick against a factual reply, rather than having to wade through pages of ill-digested generalisations. Much of the teaching of music seems to me to be hopelessly misguided, in that it is directed towards the wrong goals. Why do harmony teachers persist in passing on rule-of-thumb methods for writing non-music, when they would be infinitely better employed developing a susceptible response to the emotional power of harmony? Where will you even find the emotional characteristics of chords mentioned in harmony textbooks? It is like teaching the grammar and spelling of a language without ever elucidating the meaning of the words. The meaning – 'aye, there's the rub'. The meaning of music is something far too nebulous to be discussed in the examination room. It is a subject that most teachers shy away from, except in terms so obvious that they can be taken for granted. It is unnecessary to indicate that this is a 'sad' piece or a 'happy' one, except to a child so lacking in musical perception that he or she ought not to be learning at all; and since there is little virtue in pointing out the obvious, we may as well avoid the risk of becoming too deeply entangled in the obscure.

Form is not a corset, enclosing the over-ample flesh of a sonata and giving it coherence. It is the very stuff of which the musical drama is made. I call as witness Donald Francis Tovey, for my taste the most consistently illuminating writer on music of all time.

Tovey may be a little too technical for the lay reader at times, and he makes the common mistake of assuming that other minds are as well-stocked as his. To read him is as sharply invigorating to the mind as a plunge into a rough sea is to the body. For this reason I have included an excerpt from his writings, though, needless to say, it is incomplete. It is taken from an essay called *Some aspects of Beethoven artforms*.

This extract is followed by a novelist's view. I am not at all literary in my tastes; I respond to language, I love poetry, I am spell-bound by the paradoxes that Bernard Shaw constructs with such delight in his plays, or deeply moved by drama, whether it be by Shakespeare, O'Neill or James Saunders. But though my shelves are well stocked with the classic novels, they remain largely unread. A normal week leaves little time for anything but the Sunday papers and a couple of motoring magazines; holidays, I regret to say, are an occasion for reading thrillers and detective stories by the dozen. It is not that I do not feel I will enjoy a great novel, but rather that I do not wish to be exercised in that particular way. A writer like Proust then has remained for me literally a closed book. Inevitably, though, in the course of compiling an anthology of this nature, I asked my friends if they had any especial favourites; it was a doctor at the Hammersmith Hospital who suggested that I looked in *Swann's Way*, and there I found a remarkably perceptive passage. It admirably reveals the way in which an uninitiated listener responds to musical form without being really aware of what is happening. When it describes Swann hoping 'with a passionate longing' that a theme might reappear a third time, it pinpoints precisely that psychological need upon which sonata form is based, the need to compare, to re-evaluate, to be aware of change and yet to be reassured by repetition.

I return to earth with the two final entries in this section, a brief but clear-sighted dismissal of conventional analysis by Deryck Cooke that reinforces Tovey's viewpoint, and an essay on the performance of Beethoven by Eric Blom which seems to me a model of what musical criticism ought to be and so seldom is. The advice he gives is so constructively illuminating that it deserves to be read by every musician, amateur or professional.

I make no apology for the relatively serious tone that these four excerpts have in common; although a sonata movement may contain much feeling, its prime purpose is to think – to think out loud without the use of words, for that indeed is what a great deal of music is really concerned with. It is a thought-process in which the emotional reaction is a mere incidental by-product.

The dramatic situation

IMPORTANT THINGS in musical history can be learnt from a bird's-eye view, just as photography from aeroplanes has revealed unexpected and abundant traces of Roman camps, and even Roman towns, which no study on the level of the ground could ever discover; but what matters in the enjoyment of music is, not the history, nor the bird's-eye view, but precisely the ground-level view; and my complaint against most of our text-book knowledge of musical form is just that it is all up in the clouds, and distracts the listener's attention from everything which can help him to listen to the music. Now, the essentially dramatic quality of the music of Haydn, Mozart, and Beethoven is precisely the quality which the listener can find present all the time. Even in such merely symmetrical dance-forms as minuets and scherzos without any codas or digressions, the tunes have a quality which is not anticipated by Bach's lightest gavottes and other *Galanterien*. Of course, when the scale is so small and the form so merely lyric, the dramatic quality of the things in themselves cannot be more than subtleties; but these little minuets and scherzos do not exist in themselves. They are dramatic by position. Nothing, for instance, can be more dramatic in this way than the position of the tiniest of all, the middle movement of the C sharp minor (*Moonlight*) *Sonata, op 27, no 2*, which Liszt finely described as '*une fleur entre deux abîmes*'.

BEETHOVEN: *Donald Francis Tovey*

'A vista of joys unknown'

AFTER THE PIANIST had played, Swann felt and showed more interest in him than in any of the other guests, for the following reason:

The year before, at an evening party, he had heard a piece of music played on the piano and violin. At first he had appreciated only the material quality of the sounds which those instruments secreted. And it had been a source of keen pleasure when, below the narrow ribbon of the violin-part, delicate, unyielding, substantial, and governing the whole, he had suddenly perceived, where it was trying to surge upwards in a flowing tide of sound, the mass of the piano-part, multiform, coherent, level, and breaking everywhere in melody like the deep blue tumult of the sea, silvered and charmed into a minor key by the moonlight. But at a given moment, without being able to distinguish any clear outline, or to give a name to what was pleasing him, suddenly enraptured, he had tried to collect, to treasure in his memory the phrase or harmony – he knew not which – that had just been played, and had opened and expanded his soul, just as the fragrance of certain roses, wafted upon the moist air of evening, has the power of dilating our nostrils. Perhaps it was owing to his own ignorance of music that he had been able to receive so confused an impression, one of those that are, notwithstanding, our only purely musical impressions, limited in their extent, entirely original and irreducible into any other kind. An impression of this order, vanishing in an instant is, so to speak, an impression *sine materia*. Presumably, the notes which we hear at such moments tend to spread out before our eyes, over surfaces greater or smaller according to their pitch and volume; to trace arabesque designs, to give us the sensation of breadth or tenuity, stability or caprice. But the notes themselves have vanished before these sensations have developed sufficiently to escape submersion under those which the following, or even simultaneous, notes have already begun to awaken in us. And this indefinite perception would continue to smother in its molten liquidity the motifs which now and then emerge, barely discernible, to plunge again and disappear and drown; recognised only by the particular kind of pleasure which they instil, impossible to describe, to recollect, to name; ineffable; – if our memory, like a labourer who toils at the laying down of firm foundations beneath the tumult of waves, did not, by fashioning for us facsimiles of those fugitive phrases, enable us to compare and to contrast them with those that follow. And so, hardly had the delicious sensation, which Swann had experienced, died away, before his memory had furnished him with an immediate transcript, summary, it is true, and provisional, but one on which he had kept his eyes fixed while the playing continued, so effectively that, when the same impression suddenly returned, it was no longer uncapturable. He was able to picture to himself its extent, its symmetrical arrangement, its notation, the strength of its expression; he had before him that definite object which was no longer pure music, but rather design, architecture, thought, and which allowed the actual music to be recalled. This time he had distinguished, quite clearly, a phrase which emerged for a few moments from the waves of sound. It had at once held out to him an invitation to partake of intimate pleasures, of whose existence, before hearing it, he had never dreamed, into which he felt that nothing but this phrase could initiate him; and he had been filled with love for it, as with a new and strange desire.

With a slow and rhythmical movement it led him here, there, everywhere, towards a state of happiness noble, unintelligible, yet clearly indicated. And then, suddenly, having reached a certain point from which he was prepared to follow it, after pausing for a moment, abruptly it changed its direction, and in a fresh movement, more rapid, multiform, melancholy, incessant, sweet, it bore him off with it towards a vista of joys unknown. Then it vanished. He hoped, with a passionate longing, that he might find it again, a third time. And re-appear it did, though without speaking to him more clearly, bringing him, indeed, a pleasure less profound. But when he was once more at home he needed it, he was like a man into whose life a woman, whom he has seen for a moment passing by, has brought a new form of beauty, which strengthens and enlarges his own power of perception, without his knowing even whether he is ever to see her again whom he loves already, although he knows nothing of her, not even her name.

SWANN'S WAY:Marcel Proust

The language of programmes

CONSIDER the normally intelligent commentary, so often encountered in musical biographies and concert programmes, on a sonata-movement of an expressive masterpiece. The writer has obviously apprehended the basic emotions of the music through his innate musicality, since he has labelled the themes with emotional adjectives – say, 'the heroic first subject' and 'the sorrowful second theme'; but the moment that he has encountered the 'transition section' with its 'busy passage-work', and the 'development' with its 'fragmentation and re-integration of the main material', he has moved on to another plane altogether. It seems as if he must feel that expression gives way entirely to 'pure form' at these points, for we are suddenly faced with arid technical description such as 'in a short transition section a four-note rhythmic figure deriving from the second bar of the first subject is worked up in imitation, reaching a powerful climax in the key of the submediant'. After which we may well be switched back suddenly to the expressive plane: 'then follows the sorrowful second theme'.

Such writing is quite useless, not only because the layman cannot understand it and the professional does not need it, but for the more fundamental reason that the expressive significance of the 'transition section' (ie, the emotion conveyed by this working-up of a fragment of the first subject) is not stated, and thus the ultimate point of the passage is ignored. Having stated that the composer began with a 'heroic' theme, the writer has neglected to tell us what happened to it, considered as a heroic theme; why should we care, then, whether it is heroic or not, if it suddenly becomes nothing more than a technical gambit? Of course, the actual sound of any such passage is instinctively apprehended as emotion by all genuinely musical listeners – a category which may well include the commentator himself, who is merely defeated by the problem of trying to get it all into words; nevertheless, the fact remains that in all our writing and thinking about music, we do most unfortunately tend to preserve the fallacy that musical form cannot function continuously as expression, whereas, in fact, the two things are only two aspects of another of our indissoluble unities.

THE LANGUAGE OF MUSIC: *Deryck Cooke*

On playing Hamlet and Beethoven

THE GREAT PROBLEM that confronts all performers, indeed the circumstance that accounts more than any other for the rarity of great reproductive artists, is the fact that while countless bad interpretations of a work of art are possible, only a comparatively limited number of good ones are acceptable. Some artists, of course, go to the length of asserting that only one single interpretation of each work is interesting – their own. But that is preposterous and shows deplorable limitations, not in the work, but in the player, who makes up for narrowness of sympathy and imagination by an arrogant conceit that may relieve him of the discomforts of an artistic conscience, but is apt to make him impressive only to the least desirable section of his audience.

Most of us know from experience that there are a hundred ways of performing *Hamlet* badly or perversely; but no one, except possibly an actor whose self-esteem exceeds discretion to an almost fabulous extent, would be so absurd as to pretend that there is only one way of doing the title part of that work – not to mention others – convincingly. And we may say much the same of Beethoven's sonatas, for it is an almost mathematically exact truth that the greater the works of art confronting the interpreter, the wider becomes the range of possible great performances. Still, that range does remain definitely limited, if only we could say exactly where the limitations begin, whereas to the risks of bad performance there is no end.

It follows that it must always be much easier, but also far less useful, to say how Beethoven should not be played than to suggest what can be done to render him justice, and, unfortunately, it cannot be taken for granted that any bad habit which has been condemned will automatically become a valuable artistic precept by being turned into its opposite. If I tell a child that it is a sin to steal a sack of coal from a Tyneside merchant, this does not mean that it is therefore a virtue to carry coals to Newcastle. One may thus say, for instance, that no phrase of Beethoven's should ever be played in a slovenly way; but it is not enough simply to play every phrase carefully. There are various ways of careful playing, and some of them may be nearly as bad as slovenliness at its worst.

Perhaps one may go so far in safety as to say that carefulness should only be technical – the kind of mechanical assurance that can be taught and learnt – and that it should never cramp a spiritual adventurousness. The more certain the pianist is of having every detail of a work technically in hand, the more ready will he be to yield to momentary promptings of his imagination during a performance. These promptings, again, must, however, be subject to a kind of moral control that never lets him violate a code of general conduct he has established for himself beforehand. Within the exigencies of this code he is free, and the more free the greater the care he has taken to think out the laws to which he intends to submit.

Two sonatas that happen to be known by descriptive titles may serve as illustrations of the point. It would be ridiculous to sit down to their study with the intention of seeing how every phrase of the *Pathétique* can be made pathetic and every incident of the *Appassionata* impassioned. That is the way to reduce the *Moonlight Sonata* to mere moonshine. But the player may, so to speak, set the stops marked 'Pathos' or 'Passion' before he settles down to work on either of these two sonatas. It is not a matter of forcing himself to feel certain things. If he is obliged to do that, he is no artist and may as well give up all attempts at interpretation from the beginning. It is a matter of letting a mental process induce an emotional reaction, not with cold deliberation, but certainly with a distinct predominance of mind over feeling. Once the mind is made up definitely, feeling will respond quite spontaneously, but without running away with the player and leaving him helplessly floundering in a morass of uncontrolled emotionalism. Nothing could be worse than that, not even the most mechanical of performances. The pianist who hands Beethoven to his public cut and dried, without daring for a moment to let the music sway him by its own power, is as lifeless as the actor who simply follows the producer's instructions like an automaton; but to sit down to a great sonata trusting to the feelings of the moment is like going on the stage to play Hamlet with no clear notion of what one is going to do at any moment, but with the optimistic amateur's conviction that 'it will be all right on the night'. A performance approached in this frame of mind is never all right on any night.

Thinking before feeling is what it comes to; that is the first principle. Then, during actual performance, emotion may be safely given the lead. Having been controlled by the mind during preparation, it will be in no danger of mocking the composer by letting the interpreter interpose his own personality too obtrusively. But the performance will not be mechanically like any of the artist's trial playings, nor will it be quite the same again when it is repeated in public.

Yet the notes will have been the same each time. One has a right to expect that, though if something must be slightly amiss, one would rather have a wrong note now and again than a wry phrase or a dry phrase. Accurate pianists are as plentiful as word-perfect actors, and among them are as many dull musicians as there are mediocre stage-players among the latter. It is what lies behind the words or the notes we listen for. But what is that? And how does the interpreter bring it out? Formidable questions to which no technical answer is enough, yet which can be answered only technically, if at all. And, since we have discovered that there are infinitely more wrong than right ways of playing Beethoven, it is easier to say what the pianist who tackles the sonata should avoid than what he should do.

The most useful precept, generally speaking, is perhaps to begin by approaching Beethoven's instrument in the right way. They say nowadays that the piano is a percussion instrument. This is as obviously true, in a technical sense, as it is ridiculous to draw the inference that all music must be played as though it had been written for the dulcimer or the xylophone. It all depends on how the composer regards his medium. If Stravinsky chooses to write for the piano as an instrument of percussion, by all means let his music be hammered upon it like nails into a coffin. But Beethoven, in spite of the fact that he affected the German name of Hammerklavier for a time, did not think of it in that way. For him the piano was substitute for the orchestra. This is not by any means to suggest that his writing in the sonatas is unpianistic. On the contrary: keyboard writing is often the better the more orchestral it sounds. Liszt's piano music, always most congenially written for the instrument, is richly orchestral in its effect, and so often is Schumann's – in whose case we see in fact the curious phenomenon of a substitute that sounds a great deal better than the real thing. Schumann's symphonies are very poorly scored for orchestra and very much more satisfying in sound in their arrangement as piano duets.

Beethoven's piano sonatas are often not particularly good piano music as such; they are great music requiring a medium of expression manageable by a single performer, because that expression is meant to be intimate and flexible. But that medium is to some extent makeshift. The music seems to call now for this string or wind instrument, now for that, and the player's business is to suggest these instruments by every device of touch and every power of imaginative mimicry at his disposal. This is no reproach to the piano; no greater tribute could in fact be paid to it than that of demonstrating how far it can surpass itself, how much more than the mere aggressive instrument of percussion it can be.

What other hints could be useful? Phrasing, phrasing and again phrasing: that is perhaps the most important. It is astonishing how few pianists, even professional pianists, know that good phrasing not only heightens the plasticity and significance of the music as it comes, but saves making all kinds of exaggerated points as a composition progresses. Something has to be done to herald the return of a rondo subject, let us say. Well, instead of doing it by means of an obvious rallentando, it can be less blatantly yet just as eloquently done by means of a little extra emphasis on significant delivery. One cannot explain this on paper and it makes a difference if shown on the piano only to players imaginative enough to do similar things for themselves in any case, though perhaps they will do them differently. For it is a matter of musical response that comes from within and cannot be instilled.

BEETHOVEN'S PIANOFORTE SONATAS DISCUSSED: *Eric Blom*

Theme & Variations

...being an enquiry into the nature and meaning of music.

Part of Beethoven's manuscript for *Sonata for piano and violin in G major*

Theme & Variations

How many thousands of words have been written in an endeavour to elucidate the meaning of music! 'I enjoyed your broadcast on the Brahms symphony so much, but you neglected to tell us what it meant,' wrote one correspondent to me, as though Brahms's intention was to describe a picnic by the Wörther-See, a visit to an historical church, a drinking party at the Red Hedgehog and a trip down the Tunnel of Love. What *does* music mean? It is easy enough to divert our imaginative response into the proper channel when the composer gives us a clue by calling the piece *The Sorcerer's Apprentice* or *The Dance of Puck*. But if we are listening to a sonata, a quartet or a symphony, what should our reaction be? Is the music no more than a series of stimuli, creating now a condition of gloom or subsequently a feeling of elation? Certainly, the composer would rate the function of music a good deal higher than this. But composers themselves disagree considerably on the nature of music, and, in particular, on that elusive quality, so beloved by novelists who write about music, Inspiration.

The simplest explanation is that this mysterious visitation is literally Divine. Bach was in the habit of putting the letters SDG at the end of his compositions – *Soli Dei Gloriae*, but to give the glory to God is not quite the same thing as attributing the inspiration directly to Him. Haydn went on his knees daily when he was composing the *Creation*, asking for strength to finish the work, but normally his approach was fairly haphazard.

'I would sit down and begin to improvise,' he told a friend, 'whether my spirits were sad or happy, serious or playful. Once I had captured an idea, I strove with all my might to develop and sustain it in conformity with the rules of art. In this way I tried to help myself, and this is where so many of our newer composers fall short; they string one little piece onto another, and break off when they have scarcely started.'

We all know of the struggle that Beethoven had to mould his ideas to his satisfaction, evidence of conscious craftsmanship if ever there was; but, when on one occasion the violinist Schuppanzigh complained to him that a passage was so awkwardly written as to be virtually unplayable, he is supposed to have replied, 'When I composed that, I was conscious of being inspired by God Almighty. Do you think I can consider your puny little fiddle when He speaks to me?'

Brahms, too, had something to say on the same lines, and quoted Beethoven in his support:

'To realise that we are one with the Creator, as Beethoven did, is a wonderful and awe-inspiring experience.' He went on: 'When I feel the urge to compose, I begin by appealing directly to my maker and I first ask Him the three most important questions pertaining to our life here in this world – Whence, wherefore, whither.' Although in this revealing confession Brahms claimed that he used to go into a trance-like state, and that he had to be careful not to lose consciousness, he also admitted that these inspired moods were rare events. 'Don't make the mistake,' he said, 'of thinking that because I attach such importance to inspiration from above, that that is all there is to it. Structure is just as consequential, for without craftsmanship, inspiration is a mere reed shaken in the wind, a "sounding brass or tinkling cymbal".'

This is all very well, but it pre-supposes that all composers are deeply religious, which is not necessarily so. An even more dangerous supposition would be to equate religious sincerity with musical worth: some of the worst abominations of Victorian church music were written in a condition of irreproachable piety, but it appears that the Almighty was less forthcoming to the composers than He was to (say) Moussorgsky who was not only cynical about religion, but a drunkard to boot. A man believes what he believes, and it may be that the most practical attitude is to make the best of both worlds, as Stravinsky did when he inscribed the title page of his *Symphony of Psalms*: 'This symphony was composed to the glory of God and dedicated to the Boston Symphony Orchestra on the occasion of their fiftieth anniversary.'

Whatever the cause, religious, aesthetic, amorous, descriptive or autobiographical, something prompts a composer to put pen to paper. Once he is committed to the act, it is more than likely that the original incentive will fast disappear from his mind. Beethoven may have started the *Eroica* symphony as a tribute to Napoleon, but the demands of the music superseded all considerations of programme long before the first movement had even taken shape in his mind. What fascinates me most about composition is what I call the two-way process, the way in which the music acts on the composer as much as the composer on the music. Much as the grain of the wood may govern the direction of the wood-carver's chisel, or an accidental fusion of colours may affect a painter's conception of a picture, so does the music react upon its creator. When an idea comes into his mind, and let us leave aside the vexed question of where it comes from, it bears its own emotional aura with it. What he does with it is up to him to decide but in the process of moulding it to his will, it may resist and prove intractable. It is at such moments that the creative artistic struggle can be seen at its most dramatic.

The theme which I have postulated for this section is the meaning of music. The first quotation comes from a book which gave me keen delight, Hindemith's *A Composer's World*, in which a penetrating analysis of the relation between music and feeling is to be found. Hindemith is under a cloud at the moment, but the classical lucidity of his music appeals to me as strongly as ever, and I shall never forget his penetrating gaze on the one occasion I talked to him, his eyes the brightest blue I ever saw. I wonder what he would have made of E M Forster's *Howard's End*, in which there is a famous description of the audience's reaction at a performance of Beethoven's *Fifth Symphony*. The book dates from 1910, and it is interesting to read that applause was apparently quite acceptable after the slow movement of the symphony, a custom which we today would look on as barbarous. Those of us who look back nostalgically to the Queen's Hall might take exception to Forster's condemnation of it as 'the dreariest music-room in London', but otherwise his writing is a fair enough depiction of the lack of contact that exists between most members of an audience and the music they are listening to. How much more matter-of-fact is the letter that Mendelssohn wrote to his friend Marc-André Souchay in October 1842, a model of how to write lucid sense on musical topics without recourse to jargon.

The various books in which Robert Craft has played Boswell to Stravinsky will be marvellous material for scholars to play with in the next century. Stravinsky's mercurial mind is scarcely notable for consistency and while there is a great deal of sense in what he says, he often contradicts himself. I have included an extract from one of the lectures that he gave at Harvard University when occupying the Charles Eliot Norton chair of poetics; their title, *Poetics of Music*, is likely to frighten off the casual reader, but the language in which Stravinsky expresses his ideas is wonderfully clear. His is the only excerpt that touches on the 'chance' element in composition which I have described earlier as a two-way process.

Lastly, and there is a very personal reason for this, I include a brief interview with Michael Tippett, taken from Murray Schafer's *British Composers in Interview*. Tippett was the most important formative influence on my life; I never had an official lesson with him, but conversations with him over a canteen table at Morley College were the greatest revelation of musical truth that I have known. My entire attitude to music was shaped by him, and I shall always be in his debt, not only for introducing me to the music of Purcell, Weelkes, Monteverdi and Gesualdo, but for giving me what insight into music I may possess.

Music and memory-images

THE MOST GENERALLY accepted explanation of the effect music has upon a listener is: it expresses feelings. Whose are the feelings it expresses? Those of the composer, the performer, the individual listener, or the audience? Or does it express feelings of a general character, the specification of which is left to the members of any of these groups?

Music cannot express the composer's feelings. Let us assume a composer is writing an extremely funereal piece, which may require three months of intensive work. Is he, during this three months' period, thinking of nothing but funerals? Or can he, in those hours that are not devoted to his work because of his desire to eat and to sleep, put his grief on ice, so to speak, and be gay until the moment when he resumes his sombre activity? If he really expressed his feelings accurately as they occur during the time of composing and writing, we would be presented with a horrible motley of expressions, among which the grievous part would necessarily occupy but a small place.

Perhaps we are to believe that the composer need have the feeling of grief only once at the beginning of his work, in order to drench the opus with sombreness, notwithstanding his own feelings of hilarity, jocularity, and whatever else he is going to experience during the time of incubation? This idea is even more ridiculous than the preceding one, because there is no reason why in a series of feelings just the first one, due to its position, should be of greater importance. If the feelings of the series occur with equal intensity, it is most likely that the latest one, as the most recent experience, has the greatest significance; and if the intensity is variable, then it will be the points of greatest intensity that are predominant.

If the composer himself thinks he is expressing his own feelings, we have to accuse him of a lack of observation. Here is what he really does: he knows by experience that certain patterns of tone-setting correspond with certain emotional reactions on the listener's part. Writing these patterns frequently and finding his observations confirmed, in anticipating the listener's reactions he believes himself to be in the same mental situation. From here it is a very small step to the further conviction that he himself is not only reproducing the feelings of other individuals, but is actually having these same feelings, being obsessed by them whenever he thinks he needs them, and being urged to express them with each stroke of his ever-ready pen. He believes that he feels what he believes the listener feels; he tries to construct musically the ultimate ring of this strange chain of thought – and consequently he does not express his own feelings in his music.

Can music express the feelings of the performer? Even if performers of any kind – singers, players, conductors – were actually the demi-gods that many of them want us to think they are and some of them believe themselves to be, in reality they are, in respect to the current that flows from the composer's brain to the listener's mind, nothing but an intermediate station, a roadside stop, a transformer house, and their duty is to pass along what they received from the generating mind. Although our system of notation can give them no more than approximations of the composer's intentions, they are supposed to understand his written symbolism and by means of their own interpretational liberties and changes add merely what is the minimum requirement for a realisation of the composition in sound. The ideal performer will never try to express his own feelings – if ever he thinks that feelings are to be expressed – but the composer's, or what he thinks the composer's feelings were. Covering a piece with a thick layer of the performer's so-called feelings means distorting, counterfeiting it. A performer, in doing this, changes his function from that of transformer to a competing generator – and the shocks received from the clashing of two different currents always hit the innocent listener. Whether the performer trusts he is adding a minimum of his own feelings to a piece he performs, or whether he soaks it thoroughly in these feelings like a piece of pot roast in brown gravy, he is in the same state of self-deception as was the above-mentioned composer. What he thinks are his feelings is again the series of conclusions mentioned before: observed correspondence of music and emotional effect on the listener – confirmation by frequent recurrence – identification of himself with those effects – the belief that he himself 'feels' them.

The case is somewhat more involved with the feelings of the individual listener or the collective feeling of an entire audience. All listeners, individually or collectively, are also the victims of the treacherous chain of thought, although their unconscious reasoning enters at another point of its course. The composers' and performers' unconscious starting point was the listeners' emotional reaction, intellectually anticipated. The listeners, having these emotional reactions as the final result of the musical process, do not actually start with the intellectual anticipation of them. Their chain of reasoning is: (1) The composer expresses his feelings in his music – which opinion, although wrong, is excusable, since the listener is unaware of the composer's previous miscalculations. (2) The performer expresses the composer's or his own feelings (equally wrong, as we have seen). (3) The composer's and performer's feelings, expressed in their musical production, prompt me to have the same feelings.

Since the listeners' conclusions are based on the composers' and the performers' false suppositions, they cannot contain any truth, and we can also state that the listeners' individual or collective feelings are not expressed in music.

If music does not express feelings, how then does it affect the listener's emotions? There is no doubt that listeners, performers, and composers alike can be profoundly moved by perceiving, performing, or imagining music, and consequently music must touch on something in their emotional life that brings them into this state of excitation. But if these mental reactions were feelings, they could not change as rapidly as they do, and they would not begin and end precisely with the musical stimulus that aroused them. If we experience a real feeling of grief – that is, grief not caused or released by music – it is not possible to replace it at a moment's notice and without any plausible reason with the feeling of wild gaiety; and gaiety, in turn, cannot be replaced by complacency after a fraction of a second. Real feelings need a certain interval of time to develop, to reach a climax, and to fade out again; but reactions to music may change as fast as musical phrases do, they may spring up in full intensity at any given moment and disappear entirely when the musical pattern that provoked them ends or changes. Thus these reactions may within a few instants skip from the most profound degree of grief to utter hilarity and on to complacency without causing any discomfort to the mind experiencing them, which would be the case with a rapid succession of real feelings. In fact, if it happened with real feelings, we could be sure that it could be only in event of slight insanity. The reactions music evokes are not feelings, but they are the images, memories of feelings. We can compare these memories of feelings to the memories we have of a country in which we have travelled. The original journey may have taken several weeks or months, but in conjuring up in our memory the events of it, we may go through the entire adventure in a few seconds and still have the sensation of a very complete mental reconstruction of its course. It is the same trick dreams play on us. They, too, compress the reproductions of events that in reality would need long intervals of time for their development into fractions of a second, and yet they seem to the dreamer as real as adventures he has when he is wide awake. In some cases these dream-events may even be the 'real' life of the individual, while the facts they reflect, distort, or re-arrange are nothing but an inconsequential and sober succession of trifles.

Dreams, memories, musical reactions – all three are made of the same stuff. We cannot have musical reactions of any considerable intensity if we do not have dreams of some intensity, for musical reactions build up, like dreams, a phantasmagoric structure of feelings that hits us with the full impact of real feeling. Furthermore we cannot have any musical reactions of emotional significance, unless we have once had real feelings the memory of which is revived by the musical impression. Reactions of a grievous nature can be aroused by music only if a former experience of real grief was stored up in our memory and is now again portrayed in a dream-like fashion. 'Musical' gaiety can be felt only if a feeling of real gaiety is already known to us; 'musical' complacency arises in our memory only if complacency felt before without musical prompting was already part of our experience. It is only with the memory of feelings in our mind that we can have any feeling-like reaction caused by music. This can be proved. If, for example, we assume that music is able to arouse a reaction, which in the mind of a mass murderer uncovers the memory of the satisfaction he felt after having slaughtered a row of twenty victims, that feeling cannot be reproduced in our own minds unless we do as he did – murder twenty people and then listen to the adequate music. Certainly, we can imagine what the fellow felt and we can direct our reactions to music so that in their dreamlike way they make us feel as if we had the mass murderer's experience and the memories thereof released by music. But these reactions can never be like the genuine ones of the mass murderer, as we do not have the actual experience that left its imprints in his mind; they can be nothing but reactions of a similar – never identical – nature; reactions based on the feeling of satisfaction we had after other cruelties we committed. These are now substituted by us for the lacking experience of greater cruelty, and are rather artificially brought into contact with a musical impression.

If music did not instigate us to supply memories out of our mental storage rooms, it would remain meaningless, it would merely have a certain tickling effect on our ears. We cannot keep music from uncovering the memory of former feelings and it is not in our power to avoid them, because the only way to 'have' – to possess – music, is to connect it with those images, shadows, dreamy reproductions of actual feelings, no matter how realistic and crude or, on the contrary, how denatured, stylised, and sublimated they may be. If music we hear is of a kind that does not easily lend itself or does not lend itself at all to this connection, we still do our best to find in our memory some feeling that would correspond with the audible impression we have. If we find nothing that serves this purpose, we resort to hilarity – as in the case of oriental music – and have a 'funny feeling', but even this funny feeling is merely the image of some real funny feeling we had with some former non-musical experience, and which is now drawn out of its storage place, to substitute for the memory of a more suitable feeling.

This theory gives us a reasonable explanation for the fact that one given piece of music may cause remarkably diversified reactions with different listeners. As an illustration of this statement I like to mention the second movement of Beethoven's *Seventh Symphony*, which I have found leads some people into a pseudo feeling of profound melancholy, while another group takes it for a kind of scurrilous scherzo, and a third for a subdued pastorale. Each group is justified in judging as it does. The difference in interpretation stems from the difference in memory-images the listeners provide, and the unconscious selection is made on the basis of the sentimental value or the degree of importance each image has: the listener chooses the one which is dearest and closest to his mental disposition, or which represents a most common, most easily accessible feeling.

We may ask: what is the relation of the reaction to music as described here to the form of perceiving or imagining music? The intellectual act of building up in our mind a parallel structure of a piece heard or imagined, simultaneously with its performance or with its imagination, is not to be confused with the emotional reaction to music as described now. Although the presence of both is the indispensable condition for our mental absorption of musical impressions, they are not interdependent. They are independent, and their independence may go so far, that a piece which we relish emotionally may have a very discomforting, even disgusting effect on us while we are producing its parallel form mentally; and a piece which gives us the highest satisfaction intellectually may have only a minor effect on our emotions. Examples for the first category can be found in many of Tchaikovsky's, Dvorak's, Grieg's, and other composers' pieces, in which the audible structure frequently is enchanting and is apt to release easily and pleasantly all the images of feelings as mentioned before, but intellectually sometimes makes us ask: 'Do these fellows really assume that we are so naïve as to take their jesting for serious creation?' For the second category we find examples in many super-contrapuntal or otherwise overconstructed compositions, when our intellectual faculty of understanding may be carried to very high spheres, but emotionally we are left with dissatisfaction, because these structures are so involved or overburdened or unpredictable, that our activity of reconstructing them tellectually absorbs all our attention and prohibits emotional enjoyment.

A COMPOSER'S WORLD, HORIZONS AND LIMITATIONS: *Paul Hindemith*

The goblins of the Fifth

IT WILL BE generally admitted that Beethoven's *Fifth Symphony* is the most sublime noise that has ever penetrated into the ear of man. All sorts and conditions are satisfied by it. Whether you are like Mrs Munt, and tap surreptitiously when the tunes come – of course, not so as to disturb the others – or like Helen, who can see heroes and shipwrecks in the music's flood; or like Margaret, who can only see the music; or like Tibby, who is profoundly versed in counterpoint, and holds the full score open on his knee; or like their cousin, Fräulein Mosebach, who remembers all the time that Beethoven is *echt Deutsch*; or like Fräulein Mosebach's young man, who can remember nothing but Fräulein Mosebach; in any case, the passion of your life becomes more vivid, and you are bound to admit that such a noise is cheap at two shillings. It is cheap, even if you hear it in the Queen's Hall, dreariest music-room in London though not as dreary as the Free Trade Hall, Manchester; and even if you sit on the extreme left of the hall, so that the brass bumps at you before the rest of the orchestra arrives, it is still cheap.

'Who is Margaret talking to?' said Mrs Munt, at the conclusion of the first movement. She was again in London on a visit to Wickham Place.

Helen looked down the long line of their party, and said that she did not know.

'Would it be some young man or other whom she takes an interest in?'

'I expect so,' Helen replied. Music enwrapped her, and she could not enter into the distinction that divides young men whom one takes an interest in from young men whom one knows.

'You girls are so wonderful in always having – Oh dear! one mustn't talk.'

For the Andante had begun – very beautiful, but bearing a family likeness to all the other beautiful Andantes that Beethoven had written, and, to Helen's mind, rather disconnecting the heroes and shipwrecks of the first movement from the heroes and goblins of the third. She heard the tune through once, and then her attention wandered, and she gazed at the audience, or the organ, or the architecture. Much did she censure the attenuated Cupids who encircle the ceiling of the Queen's Hall, inclining each to each with vapid gesture, and clad in sallow pantaloons, on which the October sunlight struck. 'How awful to marry a man like those Cupids!' thought Helen. Here Beethoven started decorating his tune, so she heard him through once more, and then smiled at her cousin, Frieda. But Frieda, listening to Classical Music, could not respond. Herr Liesecke, too, looked as if wild horses could not make him inattentive; there were lines across his forehead, his lips were parted, his pince-nez at right angles to his nose, and he had laid a thick, white hand on either knee. And next to her was Aunt Juley, so British, and wanting to tap. How interesting that row of people was! What diverse influences had gone to the making! Here Beethoven, after humming and hawing with great sweetness, said 'Heigho', and the Andante came to an end. Applause, and a round of '*wunderschöning*' and '*pracht*' volleying from the German contingent. Margaret started talking to her new young man; Helen said to her aunt: 'Now comes the wonderful movement: first of all the goblins, and then a trio of elephants dancing'; and Tibby implored the company generally to look out for the transitional passage on the drum.

'On the what, dear?'

'On the *drum*, Aunt Juley.'

'No; look out for the part where you think you have done with the goblins and they come back,' breathed Helen, as the music started with a goblin walking quietly over the universe, from end to end. Others followed him. They were not aggressive creatures; it was that that made them so terrible to Helen. They merely observed in passing that there was no such thing as splendour or heroism in the world. After the interlude of elephants dancing, they returned and made the observation for the second time. Helen could not contradict them, for, once at all events, she had felt the same, and had seen the reliable walls of youth collapse. Panic and emptiness! Panic and emptiness! The goblins were right.

Her brother raised his finger: it was the transitional passage on the drum.

For, as if things were going too far, Beethoven took hold of the goblins and made them do what he wanted. He appeared in person. He gave them a little push, and they began to walk in a major key instead of in a minor, and then – he blew with his mouth and they were scattered! Gusts of splendour, gods and demi-gods contending with vast swords, colour and fragrance broadcast on the field of battle, magnificent victory, magnificent death! Oh, it all burst before the girl, and she even stretched out her gloved hands as if it was tangible. Any fate was titanic; any contest desirable; conqueror and conquered would alike be applauded by the angels of the utmost stars.

And the goblins – they had not really been there at all? They were only the phantoms of cowardice and unbelief? One healthy human impulse would dispel them? Men like the Wilcoxes, or President Roosevelt, would say yes. Beethoven knew better. The goblins really had been there. They might return – and they did. It was as if the splendour of life might boil over and waste to steam and froth. In its dissolution one heard the terrible, ominous note, and a goblin, with increased malignity, walked quietly over the universe from end to end. Panic and emptiness! Panic and emptiness! Even the flaming ramparts of the world might fall.

Beethoven chose to make all right in the end. He built the ramparts up. He blew with his mouth for the second time, and again the goblins were scattered. He brought back the gusts of splendour, the heroism, the youth, the magnificence of life and of death, and amid vast roarings of a superhuman joy, he led his *Fifth Symphony* to its conclusion. But the goblins were there. They could return. He had said so bravely, and that is why one can trust Beethoven when he says other things.

Helen pushed her way out during the applause. She desired to be alone. The music had summed up to her all that had happened or could happen in her career. She read it as a tangible statement, which could never be superseded. The notes meant this and that to her, and they could have no other meaning. She pushed right out of the building, and walked slowly down the outside staircase, breathing the autumnal air, and then she strolled home.

HOWARD'S END: E M Forster

A letter from Mendelssohn

TO MARC-ANDRÉ SOUCHAY, *who had asked the meaning of some of the Songs Without Words.*

... THERE IS SO MUCH talk about music, and yet so little is said. For my part, I believe that words do not suffice for such a purpose, and if I found they did suffice I would finally have nothing more to do with music. People often complain that music is too ambiguous; that what they should think when they hear it is so unclear, whereas everyone understands words. With me it is exactly the reverse, and not only with regard to an entire speech, but also with individual words. These, too, seem to me so ambiguous, so vague, so easily misunderstood in comparison to genuine music, which fills the soul with a thousand things better than words. The thoughts which are expressed to me by music that I love are not too indefinite to be put into words, but on the contrary, too definite. And so I find in every effort to express such thoughts, that something is right but at the same time, that something is lacking in all of them; and so I feel, too, with yours. This, however, is not your fault, but the fault of the words which are incapable of anything better. If you ask me what I was thinking of when I wrote it, I would say: just the song as it stands. And if I happen to have had certain words in mind for one or another of these songs, I would never want to tell them to anyone because the same words never mean the same things to different people. Only the song can say the same thing, can arouse the same feelings in one person as in another, a feeling which is not expressed, however, by the same words.

Resignation, melancholy, the praise of God, a hunting-song, do not conjure up the same thoughts in everybody. Resignation is to the one what melancholy is to the other; the third can form no lively conception of either. Why, to anyone who is by nature a keen sportsman, a hunting-song and the praise of God would come to pretty much the same thing, and to him the sound of the hunting-horn would actually be the praise of God, while to us it would be nothing but a hunting-song. And however long we might discuss it with him, we should never get any farther. Words have many meanings, but music we could both understand correctly. Will you allow this to serve as an answer to your question? At all events, it is the only one I can give, although these, too, are nothing, after all, but ambiguous words!

MENDELSSOHN LETTERS: G Selden-Goth

Stravinsky as inventor

WE HAVE A DUTY towards music, namely, to invent it. I recall once during the war when I was crossing the French border a gendarme asked me what my profession was. I told him quite naturally that I was an inventor of music. The gendarme, then verifying my passport, asked me why I was listed as a composer. I told him that the expression 'inventor of music' seemed to me to fit my profession more exactly than the term applied to me in the documents authorising me to cross borders.

Invention pre-supposes imagination but should not be confused with it. For the act of invention implies the necessity of a lucky find and of achieving full realisation of this find. What we imagine does not necessarily take on a concrete form and may remain in a state of virtuality, whereas invention is not conceivable apart from its actual being worked out.

Thus, what concerns us here is not imagination in itself, but rather creative imagination: the faculty that helps us to pass from the level of conception to the level of realisation.

In the course of my labours I suddenly stumble upon something unexpected. This unexpected element strikes me. I make a note of it. At the proper time I put it to profitable use. This gift of chance must not be confused with that capriciousness of imagination that is commonly called fancy. Fancy implies a pre-determined will to abandon one's self to caprice. The aforementioned assistance of the unexpected is something quite different. It is a collaboration which is immanently bound up with the inertia of the creative process and is heavy with possibilities which are unsolicited and come most appositely to temper the inevitable over-rigorousness of the naked will. And it is good that this is so.

'In everything that yields gracefully,' G K Chesterton says somewhere, 'there must be resistance. Bows are beautiful when they bend only because they seek to remain rigid. Rigidity that slightly yields, like Justice swayed by Pity, is all the beauty of earth. Everything seeks to grow straight, and happily, nothing succeeds in so growing. Try to grow straight and life will bend you.'

The faculty of creating is never given to us all by itself. It always goes hand in hand with the gift of observation. And the true creator may be recognised by his ability always to find about him, in the commonest and humblest thing, items worthy of note. He does not have to concern himself with a beautiful landscape, he does not need to surround himself with rare and precious objects. He does not have to put forth in search of discoveries: they are always within his reach. He will have only to cast a glance about him. Familiar things, things that are everywhere, attract his attention. The least accident holds his interest and guides his operations. If his finger slips, he will notice it; on occasion, he may draw profit from something unforeseen that a momentary lapse reveals to him.

One does not contrive an accident: one observes it to draw inspiration therefrom. An accident is perhaps the only thing that really inspires us. A composer improvises aimlessly the way an animal grubs about. Both of them go grubbing about because they yield to a compulsion to seek things out. What urge of the composer is satisfied by this investigation? The rules with which, like a penitent, he is burdened? No: he is in quest of his pleasure. He seeks a satisfaction that he fully knows he will not find without first striving for it. One cannot force one's self to love; but love pre-supposes understanding, and in order to understand, one must exert one's self.

It is the same problem that was posed in the Middle Ages by the theologians of pure love. To understand in order to love; to love in order to understand: we are here, not going around in a vicious circle; we are rising spirally, providing we have made an initial effort, have even just gone through a routine exercise.

Pascal has specifically this in mind when he writes that custom 'controls the automaton, which in its turn unthinkingly controls the mind. For there must be no mistake,' continues Pascal, 'we are automatons just as much as we are minds. . . .'

So we grub about in expectation of our pleasure, guided by our scent, and suddenly we stumble against an unknown obstacle. It gives us a jolt, a shock, and this shock fecundates our creative power.

POETICS OF MUSIC: Igor Stravinsky

Tippett's Inception of Creation

TIPPETT: I like to think of composing as a physical business. I compose at the piano and like to feel involved in my work with my hands, but I wouldn't say putting my hands on the keyboard means as much to me as it might to, say, Stravinsky who, being a good pianist, probably feels composing as something of a fingertip operation. What is certainly clear to me is that I need to make actual sounds, even if they are imperfect and never identical with the sounds of the composition in performance. But with this general aura of sound I make with my voice and the piano, I produce what appears to me to be quite clearly a physical atmosphere; and within this physical atmosphere my creative process is at its strongest – I mean the critical part of the creative process is at its strongest. The inception of creation may be quite apart from anything physical whatsoever.

SCHAFER: Is it possible to describe this 'inception of creation'?

TIPPETT: I feel a need to give an image to an ineffable experience of my inner life. I feel the inner life as something that is essentially fluid in consistency. The process, which may be rapid or slow, is one of giving articulation to this fluid experience, and appears in successive stages. I begin by first becoming aware of the overall length of the work, then of how it will divide itself into sections (perhaps movements), and then of the kind of texture of instruments that will perform it. I prefer not to look for the actual notes of the composition until this process has gone as far as possible. Finally, the notes appear and, in general, I find that during the purely mental process of articulating my imagination the precise material has been forming itself subconsciously, so that I never have to struggle to find it.

BRITISH COMPOSERS IN INTERVIEW: Murray Schafer

Interlude I

Mendelssohn goes to Buckingham Palace

GRAHL SAYS that the only friendly English house, the house that is really comfortable and where one feels at ease, is Buckingham Palace. I know several others but on the whole I agree with him. Joking apart, Prince Albert asked me to go to him on Saturday at two o'clock so that I may try his organ. I found him all alone but as we were talking away the Queen came in wearing a house-dress. She said she was obliged to leave for Claremont in an hour. Catching sight of the music pages strewn all over the floor by the wind, 'Goodness,' she said, 'how dreadful,' and began to pick up the music. Prince Albert helped and I was not idle. Then Prince Albert began to explain the organ stops to me and while he was doing it the Queen remarked that she would put everything straight again.

I begged the Prince to play something so that, I said, 'I might boast about it in Germany'. Thereupon, he played me a chorale by heart, with pedals, so charmingly and clearly and correctly that many an organist could have learnt something and the Queen (who had finished her tidying up) sat beside him and listened very pleased. Then I had to play and I began my chorus from *St Paul*: '*How lovely are the messengers*'. Before I got to the end of the first verse they both began to sing the chorus very well and all the time Prince Albert managed the stops for me so expertly – first a flute, then full at the forte,

The Prince Consort playing for Queen Victoria and Mendelssohn

the whole register at D major and then making such an excellent diminuendo (all by heart) that I was heartily pleased. Then the Crown Prince of Gotha came in and there was more conversation, the Queen asking me whether I had composed any new songs. 'You should sing one to him,' said Prince Albert, and after a little begging she said she would try my *Frühlingslied in B flat* if 'it is still here as all my music is packed up for Claremont'. Prince Albert went to look for it but came back saying that it had been packed. 'Perhaps it could be unpacked,' said I. 'We must send for Lady . . .' (I didn't catch the name). The bell was rung and the servants went to look but came back embarrassed. Then the Queen went herself and while she was away Prince Albert said to me: 'She begs you to accept this present as a souvenir,' and gave me a case with a beautiful ring on which was engraved 'VR 1842'.

When the Queen came back she said: 'Lady . . . has left and has taken all my things with her. It is most unseemly.' (I cannot tell you how that amused me.) I then begged that I might not be made to suffer for the accident and expressed the hope that she might sing another song. After consultation with her husband he said: 'She will sing something of Gluck's.' Then we five proceeded through the long corridors to the Queen's sitting-room where, next to the piano, stood an enormous fat rocking-horse with two great birdcages and pictures on the walls; beautifully bound books were on the table and music on the piano. The Duchess of Kent came in too, and while they were all talking I rummaged a little amongst the music and found my first set of songs. So naturally I begged the Queen to choose one of those rather than a song of Gluck's to which she consented. What do you think she chose? '*Schöner und schöner*' and sang it beautifully in tune, in strict time and with very nice expression. Only where, after '*Der Prosa Last und Mühe*' (where it goes down to D and then comes up by semitones) she sang D sharp each time. The first and second time I gave her the D natural, but the last time (when it should be D sharp) she sang D natural. Except for this mistake it was very charming and on the long G at the end I have never heard better or purer tone from any amateur. I felt obliged to confess that the song had really been written by Fanny (I found it difficult; but pride must have a fall) and begged the Queen to sing one of my own. She said she would if I gave her some help and sang *Lass dich nur nichts dauern* without a mistake and with charming feeling and expression. I thought that one must not pay too many compliments on an occasion of this sort so I merely thanked her very much, but she said: 'If only I hadn't been so nervous; I have really a long breath.' Then I praised her heartily and with a clear conscience as she had sung the last part with the long C so well, taking the C and the next three notes in the same breath as is seldom done. . . .

After this Prince Albert sang '*Er ist ein Schnitter*' and then he said I must play (improvise) something before I went and gave me as themes the chorale which he had played on the organ and the song he had just sung. If everything had happened as usual I should have improvised very badly for that is what happens to me when I am specially anxious to do well. But I have rarely improvised as well. I was in the mood for it and played a long time and enjoyed myself. Of course I also brought in the songs the Queen had sung but it worked in so naturally that I would have been glad to go on for ever. They followed me with so much intelligence and attention that I felt more at ease than I ever did in improvising before an audience. Then the Queen said: 'I hope you will come and visit us soon again in England.' I took my leave and down below I saw the beautiful carriages waiting with their scarlet outriders and in a quarter of an hour the flag was lowered and the papers said 'Her Majesty left the Palace at thirty minutes past three'. It was a delightful day! I must add that I asked permission to dedicate my A minor symphony to the Queen, that having really been the reason of my visit to England and because the English name would be doubly suited to the Scottish piece. Just as the Queen was going to sing she said: 'The parrot must be taken out or he will scream louder than I can sing,' upon which Prince Albert rang the bell and the Prince of Gotha said: 'I will carry him out,' but I said 'Allow me' and lifted the cage and carried it out to the astonished servants.

MUSICIANS ON MUSIC (*Felix Mendelssohn*): F Bonavia

Images: I

Arnold Schoenberg

IMAGES in Debussy's sense; impressions: the photographer capturing in a fraction of time some part of the elusive total. Musicians' faces vary, some impassive, others contorted, transfigured. In the following pages we look at some who mean a lot to me—Schoenberg and Stravinsky because they are the two most significant figures in the first half of this century; Britten, Walton and Tippett because of what they have done for English music; Toscanini because he is a legend (alas, I never saw him conduct); Holst because my life seems to have shadowed his through Morley College and Brook Green; Maazel and Monteux to show that conductors can be great in youth or age; Giulini for his humility and musicianship; Boult and Cherkassky because they make such a nice picture; Barbirolli in memory of the first time I heard him, which was one of the most exciting concerts of my life; Richard Lewis for his singing; Seefried for bringing tears to my eyes with the first note I ever heard her sing; Cleo Laine for her vitality; Peter Pears for his creation of so many roles; Fischer-Dieskau for bringing Busoni's Doctor Faustus to life, and Marian Anderson for her dignity.

THE PHOTOGRAPHERS: Zoë Dominic—*Benjamin Britten; Cleo Laine; Peter Pears*

Stephen Fry—*Michael Tippett*

Guy Gravett—*Richard Lewis*

Godfrey Macdomnic—*William Walton; Lorin Maazel; Pierre Monteux; Adrian Boult and Shura Cherkassky; John Barbirolli; Fischer-Dieskau*

Lotte Meitner-Graf—*Igor Stravinsky; Carlo Mario Giulini; Irmgard Seefried; Marian Anderson*

Roger Wood—*Arturo Toscanini*

IGOR STRAVINSKY

BENJAMIN BRITTEN

WILLIAM WALTON

MICHAEL TIPPETT

ARTURO TOSCANINI

GUSTAV HOLST

PIERRE MONTEUX

LORIN MAAZEL

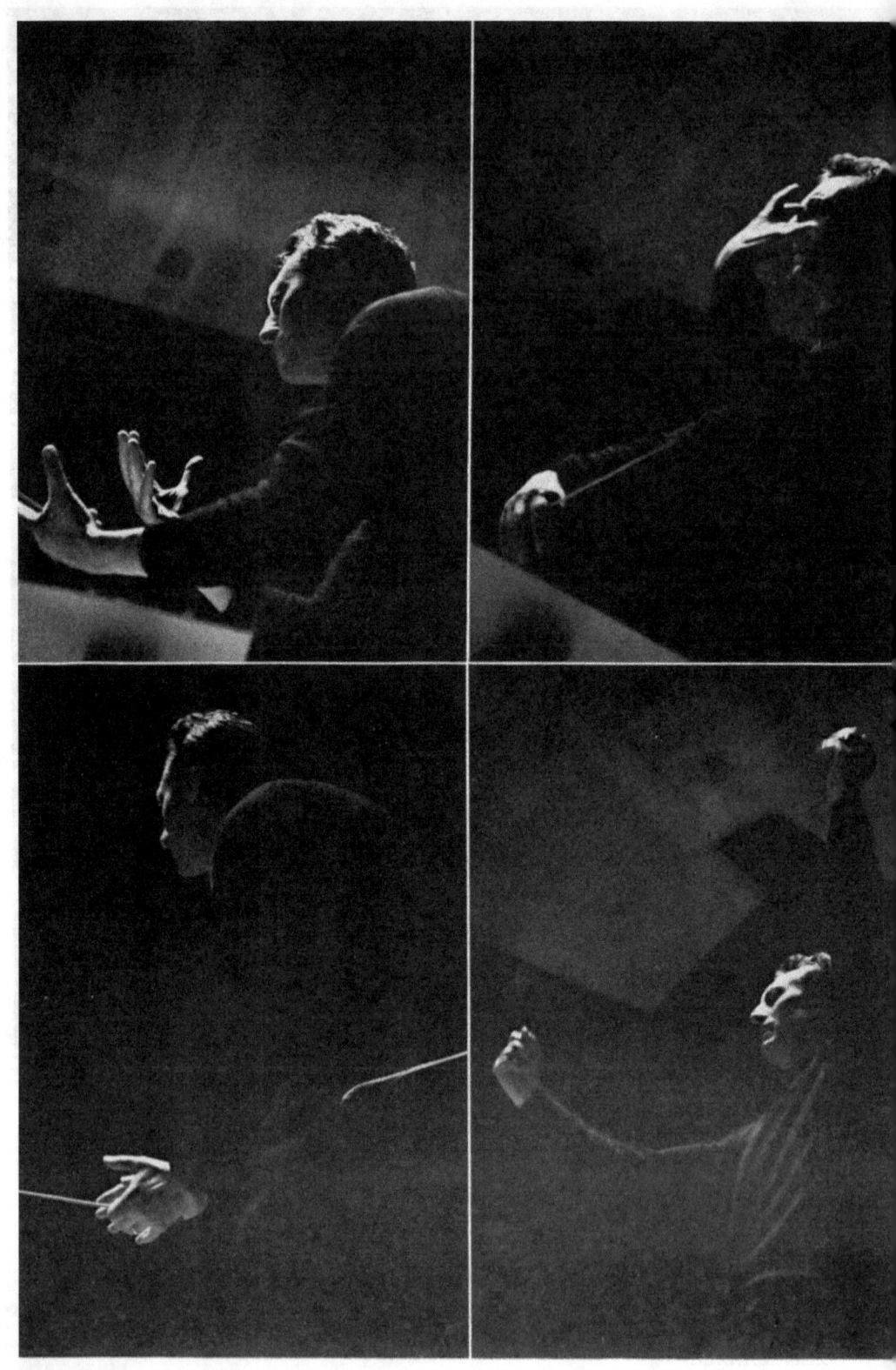

CARLO MARIA GIULINI

SIR ADRIAN BOULT and *SHURA CHERKASSKY*   *SIR JOHN BARBIROLLI*

RICHARD LEWIS as Florestan

IRMGARD SEEFRIED

CLEO LAINE

DIETRICH FISCHER-DIESKAU

PETER PEARS as Peter Grimes

MARIAN ANDERSON

Scherzo

(*From Italian = a joke.*) One of two middle movements, more usually the third, of a four-movement symphony, sonata, or other sonata-form work where it displaced the minuet.

'Lullaby' from *Hoffnung's Companion to Music*

Scherzo

HUMOUR IN MUSIC is looked on with suspicion by the more austere critics. It is accepted that Beethoven's music contains jokes of a sort, at which presumably we are allowed to smile; as for the sudden loud chord that constitutes the surprise in Haydn's *Surprise* symphony, it is acknowledged, but only in such a way as to convey the unspoken wish that the composer had refrained from such a schoolboy prank. Parody of the type that we find in Walton's *Façade* is acceptable since it is witty and sophisticated, but the unmistakable 'raspberry' that Bartok directs towards Shostakovich in his *Concerto for Orchestra* is regarded as in rather poor taste. For myself, I would defend humour more than I would excuse an over-intellectual seriousness. I cannot abide the mentality that believes that all music should purge and purify; one only has to read the letters of Mozart to realise that schoolboy smut and sublime beauty can co-exist in one and the same mind. Psychologists have doubtless explained Mozart's preoccupation with lavatorial jokes in terms of anal fetishism and the like. But he also adored to play with words in a way that suggests a liaison (I would not dignify it with the name of marriage) between Dylan Thomas and Lewis Carroll. What else are we to make of a letter like this one, to his cousin Maria Anna Thekla Mozart, dated 5th November 1777:

> Dearest Coz Fuzz!
> I have received reprieved your dear letter, telling selling me that my uncle carbuncle, my aunt can't and you too are very well hell. Thank God, we, too, are in excellent health wealth. Today the letter setter from my Papa Ha! Ha! dropped safely into my claws paws. I hope that you too have got shot the note dote which I wrote to you from Mannheim. If so, so much the better, better the much so. Now for some sense. I am very sorry to hear that the Abbot rabbit has had another stroke so soon moon. But I trust that with God's cod's help it will have no serious consequences excrescences.

And so on, full of bubbling nonsense rhymes that Emily Anderson has coped with quite brilliantly in her translation. The letter ends with a typical example of his other sort of humour:

As I was doing my best to write this letter I heard something on the street. I stopped writing – I got up – went to the window . . . and . . . the sound ceased. I sat down again, started off again to write – but I had hardly written ten words when again I heard something. I got up again – As I did, I again heard a sound, this time quite faint – but I seemed to smell something slightly burnt – and wherever I went, it smelt. When I looked out of the window, the smell disappeared. When I looked back into the room, I again noticed it. In the end Mamma said to me: 'I bet that you have let off one.' 'I don't think so, Mamma,' I replied. 'Well, I am certain that you have,' she insisted. Well, I thought, 'Let's see,' put my finger to my arse and then to my nose and – *Ecce, provatum est!* Mamma was right after all. Well, farewell. I kiss you 1000 times and remain, as always, your little old piggy wiggy
      Wolfgang Amadé Rosy Posy

 A thousand compliments from us two travellers to my aunt and uncle. My greetings bleatings to all my good friends sends. Addio, booby looby.'

In his childhood travels, Mozart picked up more than a smattering of several European languages, and he loved to show off his prowess by breaking into patches of Italian, Latin or French. One letter to his sister consists in its entirety of this single sentence (12th August 1773):

Hodie nous avons begegnet per strada Dominum Edelbach, welcher uns di voi compliments ausgerichtet hat, et quic sich tibi et ta mère empfehlen lasst. Addio. W M

Soon after his marriage to Constanze, who was then nineteen, he added a postscript to a letter to his parents in which he said: 'My wife is almost ninety-one.'

He frequently broke into doggerel verse, of which perhaps the most charming example is the poem that he sent his sister when she was about to be married.

> Wedlock will show you many things
> Which still a mystery remain;
> Experience soon will teach to you
> What Eve herself once had to do
> Before she could give birth to Cain.
> But all these duties are so light
> You will perform them with delight.
> Yet no state is an unmixed joy
> And marriage has its own alloy,
> Lest us its bliss perchance should cloy.
> So when your husband shows reserve
> Or wrath which you do not deserve
> And perhaps a nasty temper too,
> Think, sister, 'tis a man's queer way.
> Say: 'Lord, Thy will be done by day,
> But mine at night you'll do.'

He loved to play with words and comical nicknames, even in his maturity. The happiest letter he ever wrote (no 544 in Vol III of the collected letters) describes the huge success of *Figaro* in Prague. One portion reads:

> Now farewell, dearest friend, dearest Hikkiti Horky! That is your name, as you must know. We all invented names for ourselves on the journey. Here they are. I am Punkititi. My wife is Schabla Pumfa. Hofer is Rozka Pumpa. Stadler is Notschibikitschibi. My servant Joseph is Sagadarata. My dog Goukerl is Schomanntzky. Madame Quellenberg is Runzifunzi. Mlle Crux is Ramlo Schurimuri. Friestadler is Gaulimauli. Be so kind as to tell him his name.

Schubert appears to have had something of the same delight in fantasy; an early manuscript of his, the fragmentary octet for wind instruments of 1813, is inscribed:

> Finished wi' th' *Quartet*, the which has been composed by Franzo Schubert, Chapel Master to the Imp. Chinese Court. Chappppelll at Nanking, the world-famous residence of his Chinese Majesty. Written in Vienna, on a date I can't tell, in a year which has a 3 at the

end, and a oner at the beginning, and then an eight, and another oner: that is to say – 1813.

Even Brahms, staid as he appeared, enjoyed nonsense. It was his custom to decry those works which obviously pleased him most, as when he wrote to Simrock about his second symphony, that most radiant and sunny work, 'You must put a black edge round the score to give an outward show of grief.' To Elizabeth von Herzogenberg he wrote (of the same piece): 'The musicians play my new work here with crepe round their arms, because it sounds so mournful. It will be printed on black edged paper.'

When I decided to call a portion of this anthology Scherzo, I was faced with the difficult task of deciding which sort of humour I could justifiably include. Musicians as a race certainly enjoy humour in all its forms, and it is sheer folly to attempt to tell a story to an orchestral player – they know them all. Of course, there are innumerable musical legends worth preserving, some of which are dependent on illustration at the piano. I am fond of the story about Ansermet in his early days, when his command of English was not too secure, saying to the orchestra: 'Just play the notes as they are rotten.' Beecham's quips seem to multiply with the years, and to re-tell them here would savour too much of a joke-book.

I have chosen to start with a typical Erik Satie *jeu d'esprit* in which he bemoans the inadequacy of the education that we give to animals. The scene involving Wagner and Dumas strikes me as hilarious, and leads us nicely into the world of opera in which the presumably embroidered fiction of Mark Twain, which I laughed at as a boy, is coupled with the true incident from Tetrazzini's life which amuses me more now.

Berlioz again takes the palm with his Disney-like tale of the piano at the Conservatoire which still delights me after a hundred readings at least. Other excerpts from Spohr, Paderewski, Neville Cardus, John Cage, and sundry anons need no explanation, nor, I trust, justification. Scattered throughout the section are occasional bloomers selected from Fritz Spiegl's truly wonderful collection of howlers, *What the papers didn't mean to say*. I suppose that their correct musical nomenclature would be 'accidentals'!

Musical intelligence among the animals

THE INTELLIGENCE of animals cannot be questioned. But what does man do to improve the mental level of these long-suffering co-citizens? He offers them a mediocre education, full of holes, incomplete, such as no human child would wish on himself, and he would be right, the little dear. This education aims, above all, at developing the instincts of cruelty and vice atavistically resident in the individual. In this curriculum questions of art, literature, natural and moral sciences or other matters do not appear. Carrier pigeons are in no way prepared for their mission by the study of geography; fishes are kept innocent of the study of oceanography; cattle, sheep and lambs are kept totally unaware of the scientific arrangements of a modern slaughter house, know nothing of the nutritive rôle they play in man-made society.

Few animals benefit from human instruction. The dog, the mule, the horse, the donkey, the parrot and a few others are the only animals to receive a semblance of education. And yet, can you call it education? Compare this instruction if you please, to that given the young human undergraduate by the universities, and you will see it is worthless, it can neither broaden the knowledge nor faciliate the learning which the animal might have acquired through his own labours, by his own devotion. But musically? Horses have learned to dance; spiders have remained under a piano throughout an entire concert – a long concert organised for them by a respected master. So what? So nothing. Now and then we are told about the musicality of the starling, the melodic memory of the crow, the harmonic ingenuity of the owl who accompanies himself by tapping his stomach – a purely artificial contrivance and polyphonically meagre.

As for the perennially cited nightingale, his musical knowledge makes his most ignorant auditors shrug. Not only is his voice not placed, but he has absolutely no knowledge of clefs, tonality, modality or measure. Perhaps he is gifted? Possibly, almost certainly. But it can be stated flatly that his artistic culture does not equal his natural gifts, and that the voice of which he is so inordinately proud, is nothing but an inferior useless instrument.

COMPOSERS ON MUSIC (*Satie*): *Sam Morgenstern*

One upmanship

HE CERTAINLY REQUIRED money to keep him going, for he had the most expensive tastes. In a letter to Praeger he said: 'By nature I am luxurious, prodigal, and extravagant, much more than Sardanapalus and all the other old emperors put together.' Here he spoke the sober truth. His voluptuous tastes went far beyond a fondness for rich colours, for harmonious decorations, for out-of-the-way furniture, for well-bound books, and so on. He wore silken underwear at all times, and he employed a high-priced Viennese dressmaker to make the rich garments which he felt indispensable for composition. There is a story about him wanting some flamingo feathers before he could obtain sufficient inspiration to finish the flower-maiden scene in *Parsifal*. Any caller who had not seen him before was likely to suffer a mild shock; for on entering the room where his visitor was seated, Wagner would throw the door wide open before him, as if it were fit that his approach should be heralded like that of a king, and he would stand for a moment on the threshold, a curious mediæval figure in a frame. The mystified visitor, rising from his seat, would behold a man richly-clad in a costume of velvet and satin, like those of the early Tudor period, and wearing a bonnet such as is seen in portraits of Henry VI – his composing costume. He made 'a veritable rainbow of himself, and even wore many-coloured trousers', says one.

Alexandre Dumas, calling upon him, made some good-humoured remark about his own ignorance of music; but his pleasantries were listened to with such a smileless stolidity that he went home in a huff, and wrote his contemptuous protest against 'Wagnerian din – inspired by the riot of cats scampering in the dark about an ironmonger's shop'. On the day before this protest was printed Wagner returned Dumas's visit, and was kept waiting half an hour in an ante-room. Then the author of the *Three Guardsmen* marched in, superbly attired in a plumed helmet, a cork life-belt, and a flowered dressing-gown. 'Excuse me for appearing in my working dress,' he said majestically. 'Half my ideas are lodged in this helmet, and the other half in a pair of jackboots which I put on to compose love scenes.'

MASTER MUSICIANS: *J Cuthbert Hadden*

Tetrazzini awash

THE OPERA HOUSE – I have sung in some strange edifices, all boldly arrogating to themselves the name of opera house – was a sorry structure. The memory of it haunts me still. Sometimes I dream that I am singing in it, and wake up with a gasp of horror. There had been something very much the matter with the roof just before we arrived, for when the time came to raise the curtain we found to our disgust, which was vigorously expressed by every member of the company, that that stage was awash! At first we felt like abandoning the performance, but the manager besought us to appear. There was a full house, which, he said, was badly needed. The other members of my company wavered, and then they, too, not relishing the loss of a night's pay, took the manager's side. So I consented.

The water was baled off the stage as quickly as possible, but the roof still dripped so badly, that the boards were very wet in places when, a little later, the curtain went up. The opera was my old favourite *Lucia*, and not wishing to ruin the expensive long-train gown which I wore in this work, I held it up as I sang, at the same time trying to find one or two dry islands in the stage sea. Perhaps it would have been better to have taken the public into our confidence – although, being natives, they ought to have known the state of their theatre – before we started playing, for some of the aristocratic ladies of Puebla, when they saw me holding my skirts aloft, made motions which revealed how deeply I had shocked them.

One lady, in particular, seated in a box slightly lower than the stage where she was unable to observe the reason for my behaviour, looked frightfully indignant. She frowned, and then ostentatiously turned herself away from me and faced the audience, saying in effect, 'Just fancy! A prima donna attempting to emulate a high-kicking ballet-girl!'

That action of hers and what it implied was too much for me. I decided to help her to clear away a few cobwebs. With my feet fairly soaking and the consciousness that, despite my great efforts, my dress was practically spoiled, I did not feel in the happiest mood, so when a suitable opportunity came I interpolated a few phrases of my own into the libretto of the unfortunate *Lucia*. Advancing gingerly, island by island, across the watery stage, I reached the nearest point to where sat the lady with her back to me. Then I sang, 'Madam, you are shocked, very shocked, I know it, yes I do. But do you know, the stage is soaking wet, and our dresses all are spoiling, yet just to please you I am ready, perfectly ready, to let my dress drag through the wet and be completely ruined if you, dear madam, will promise to buy me a lovely new one.'

My little impromptu serenade did not have the happy result that should have followed. Some of those near by heard what I sang, and laughed; their laughter further offended the dignity of the great local dame in the box. She still sat with her back to me during the rest of the act, and when that was over she gathered up her wraps and haughtily stalked out – to the quiet amusement of others near by and to myself, who happened to be in a position of observation behind the curtain.

MY LIFE OF SONG: *Madame Tetrazzini*

*   *   *

SONOTA IN C MIOR OP 13 BEEHOVEN
(Little-known work apparently played by Denis Matthews according to a programme printed in Afghanistan.)

*   *   *

The piano that played itself

THE CONSERVATOIRE competitions began last week. On the first day Monsieur Auber determined, as the saying goes, to take the bull by the horns, and began with the piano classes. The intrepid jury summoned to hear the candidates learns without apparent agitation that they number thirty-one – eighteen women and thirteen men. The piece chosen for the competition is Mendelssohn's *Concerto in G minor*; so that, barring an apoplectic fit striking down one of the candidates during the seance, the concerto is going to be played thirty-one times running; you can see that for yourself. But what you perhaps cannot see as yet, and what I myself did not know until a few hours ago, not having had the temerity to attend one of these affairs, is what I was told this morning by one of the Conservatoire attendants when I was crossing the courtyard of the institution, still worrying about the epithet of old bestowed on me by the Amaryllis of Montmorency.

'That poor M Érard!' he said. 'What a misfortune!'

'Érard, what has happened to him?'

'What, weren't you at the piano competition?'

'No indeed, so tell me what took place.'

'Well, M Érard had been so obliging as to lend us for that day a magnificent piano he had just finished, which he intended to send to London for the Universal Exhibition of 1851. That is as good as to say that he was satisfied with his work. It had a tremendous tone, a bass never heard heretofore; in a word, an extraordinary instrument. Its only fault was that the keyboard was a little hard, but that is why he had sent it to us. M Érard is no fool, and he had said to himself: "The thirty-one pupils, by pounding their concerto, will liven up the keys of my piano, and that can only improve it." True, but the poor man did not foresee that his keyboard would be livened up in so terrible a fashion. When you think of it, a concerto played thirty-one times in succession on the same day! Who could imagine the result of so much repetition?

'Well, the first pupil comes forward, and finding the piano somewhat hard, does not spare himself to get the tone out of it. The second ditto. For the third the piano does not resist as much; the fifth it resists still less. I do not know how the sixth found it; just as he came on, I had to go out for a bottle of ether for one of the gentlemen of the jury who had fainted. When I returned, the seventh had finished, and I heard him say, as he was returning into the wings: "This piano isn't as hard as they pretend; on the contrary, I find it excellent." The next ten or twelve competitors were of the same opinion; the last-comers even declared that, far from being too hard to the touch, it was too soft.

'Towards a quarter to three we had come to No 26 (we had begun at ten o'clock); it was the turn of Mademoiselle Hermance Lévy, who detests hard pianos. Conditions could not have been more favourable for her, since by that time everybody was complaining that the keyboard hardly needed touching to make it sound; and so she played the concerto so lightly that she won the first prize outright. When I say outright, I am not quite accurate; she shared it with Mademoiselle Vidal and Mademoiselle Roux. These two young ladies also profited by the advantage offered them by the softness of the keyboard; a softness such that the keyboard moved if one merely breathed on it. Whoever saw a piano like that? Just as they were about to hear No 29 I once more had to go in search of a doctor; another of our gentlemen of the jury had become very red in the face, and it was absolutely necessary to bleed him. A piano competition is no joke; when the doctor turned up, it was only just in time. As I was returning to the foyer of the theatre, I saw No 29, young Planté, returning from the platform, very pale and trembling from head to foot; he said: "I don't know what's wrong with the piano, but the keys move of their own accord; you would think there was someone inside it moving the hammers. I'm scared." – "Come now, youngster, you're daft," replied young Cohen, who is three years older than he. "Let me pass. I'm not afraid!" Cohen (No 30) comes on, sits down to the piano without glancing at the keyboard, plays his concerto very well, and after the final chord, just as he is leaving his seat, the piano begins the concerto again by itself! The poor youth had screwed up his courage; but after remaining petrified an instant he bolted as fast as his legs would carry him. From that time on, the piano, getting louder and louder every minute, goes its own gait, turning out scales, trills, arpeggios. The public, not seeing anyone at the instrument and hearing it make ten times the noise it did before, gets very excited; some laugh, others begin to be frightened; all are astounded as you can imagine. One member of the jury alone, who could not see the platform from the back of his box, thought that Mr Cohen had begun the concerto over again, and shouted at the top of his voice: "Enough, enough, enough, be quiet! Send for No 31, the last one." We had to shout to him from the stage: "No one is playing, sir; it's the piano, which has acquired the habit of Mendelssohn's concerto and is playing it on its own, according to an idea of its own. You can see for yourself." – "But this is preposterous; send for M Érard. Hurry up; perhaps he can master this awful instrument!" We go in quest of M Érard. Meanwhile, that brigand of a piano, having finished its concerto, began it all over again without losing a minute, and ever and ever with more row; you would have thought it was four dozen pianos going at once, throwing out rockets, tremolos, runs of sixths and thirds in octaves, chords of ten notes, triple trills, a cascade of sound, the loud pedal, the devil and all his tricks.

'M Érard arrives; do what he will, the piano, which no longer knows its own self, recognises him no more. He sends for holy water and sprinkles the keyboard with it, but in vain; a proof that it wasn't witchcraft, but the natural effect of the thirty performances of the same concerto. They take the instrument down, detach the keyboard, which is still moving, and throw it into the middle of the courtyard of the Garde-meuble, and there the furious M Érard has it chopped up with an axe. All very fine! What made matters worse than ever; each fragment danced, jumped, frisked about on its own, on the paving stones, between our legs, against the wall, in all directions, so much so that the locksmith of the Garde-meuble picked up an armful of this lunatic mechanism and flung it into the fire of his forge to make an end of it. Poor M Érard! Such a fine instrument! We were heartbroken! But what could we do? It was the only way to deliver us from it. Besides, how can a piano, after hearing a concerto played thirty times in succession in the same hall on the same day, help acquiring the habit of it? M Mendelssohn won't be able to complain that his music isn't played! But look at the results!'

I will not add a word to the story we have just heard read, a story that has all the appearance of a fantastic tale. No doubt you won't believe a word of it; you will go so far as to say that it is absurd. Now, it is precisely because it is absurd that I believe it, for no Conservatoire attendant could have invented anything so extravagant.

EVENINGS IN THE ORCHESTRA: Hector Berlioz

* * *

JOHN PRITCHARD conducts the London Philharmonic Orchestra's second concert of the winter season at the White Rock Pavilion, Hastings, on Tuesday. (7.30) Soloist will be Ronald Smith, who will play *Tchaikovsky's Piano Concerto No 1*.

There will be another wrestling tournament at the Pavilion on Wednesday. (7.45 pm)

* * *

An orange at the opera

THE MOST CURIOUS scene of this sort that I remember took place one evening when Sacchini's *Œdipe* was being played. I had dragged one of my friends, who cared for no art but that of billiards, but of whom I was nevertheless determined to make a musical proselyte, to the Opera. To my disgust, my friend was but moderately affected by the sufferings of Antigone and her father, so after the first act I gave him up as hopeless and went to a seat in front, where I should not be disturbed by his insensibility. As though to throw his impassibility into further relief, however, chance had placed on his right hand a spectator who was as impressionable as he was the reverse. I soon became aware of this. Absorbed though I was by the beauty and truly antique character of the scene, I could not help overhearing the dialogue which was going on behind, between my man, quietly peeling an orange, and his unknown neighbour, who was evidently suffering from the most intense emotion.

'Good God, sir, be calm.'
'No, it is too much; it is overwhelming! – it is terrible!'
'But, sir, you are wrong to give way like this. You will be ill.'
'No; let me be . . . Oh!'
'Sir, come sir, cheer up! After all it is only a play. Will you have a piece of this orange?'

'Ah! how sublime!'
'It is Maltese!'
'What heavenly music!'
'Do not refuse.'
'What music!'
'Yes; it is very pretty.'

During this discordant discourse we had got to the fine trio, *O doux moments*, which follows the scene of reconciliation; I was deeply affected by the penetrating sweetness of the simple melody, and, hiding my face in my hands, was weeping silently. Scarcely was the trio ended when I felt myself raised from my seat by two powerful arms which clasped me like a vice; they belonged to the unknown enthusiast, who, perceiving that I alone of all his neighbours shared his feelings, and unable any longer to control his emotion, was embracing me with wild enthusiasm, exclaiming convulsively, '*Sac-r-r-re Dieu*, monsieur, how beautiful it is!' Without expressing any surprise, and turning my face all blurred with tears towards him, I said, 'Sir, are you a musician?' . . . 'No! but I could not love music more if I were.' 'What matter? Shake hands; you are a right good fellow.'

And, thereupon, regardless of the jeers of the spectators who had formed a circle round us, and of the flabbergasted look of my orange-eating friend, we whispered to each other our names and professions. He was an engineer! a mathematician! In what strange soils can keen susceptibility thrive!

MEMOIRS OF HECTOR BERLIOZ: *Edited by Ernest Newman*

* * *

3.00 Greenwich Time Signal
Conducted by
Lt Col S Rhodes, MBE
Edith Lewin (mezzo-soprano)

Radio Times

* * *

Friedman interrogated

NOBODY HAS PLAYED the smaller pieces of Chopin with quite Friedman's touch and absorption. His interpretation of the *Mazurkas* were legend and history rendered into tone. He would play the postlude to a mazurka as though reluctant to take leave of the music; his fingers seemed to contain throbs of fancy, love and relish, straight from his mind. He was the best I have known at telling a story. His face became histrionic, with a Grimaldi droop of the mouth. His masterpiece was his account of his appearance at a Sydney police station when it was necessary for him to register, in wartime, as an alien. He appeared before a policeman who sat at a small table upon which his helmet reposed, for the morning was hot.

'Name?'

'Friedman.'

'Howjer spell it?'

Friedman asked for a pencil. 'I will write it down for you.' The constable inspected the signature.

'Fried-man? Huh. And what's your first, your Christian name?'

'Ignaz – also I spell it for you – so.'

The constable again pored over the signature, then spoke again.

'What are yer?'

Friedman was here naturally a little at a loss.

'What am I? – pleas' explain.'

'I mean what are yer, whadjer do for a livin'?'

'Oh,' collaborated Friedman, 'I am a pianist.'

'Pianist?'

'Yes.'

'Yer meanter say yer play the pianner?'

Friedman murmured a modest affirmative. The constable pondered again, then said:

'And where jer play?'

Friedman didn't wish to bring in the suspect names of Berlin, Vienna and Rome at such a moment, so he replied:

'Brisbane, Sydney –'

'What? You've played in public in Sydney and Brisbane?'

'Yes.'

'Anywhere else?'

'Yes, Melbourne, Adela-ide' (pronounced as the Germans pronounce the name of Beethoven's song), 'Tasmania –'

'So you plyed the pianner in all these plices?' He went into a deeper than ever session of silent thought, before abruptly and rather officiously asking: 'Who's yer boss?'

SECOND INNINGS: *Neville Cardus*

* * *

Our strings are used by a cross section of the Hallé orchestra. – *Advertisement in 'The Strad'*.

* * *

Cadenza

HE CONCLUDED his second concert with a long cadenza in which he put all the tricks he knew. At the rehearsal he asked the orchestra to enter after the cadenza with a chord of startling resonance for which he was to give the signal by stamping his foot. At the concert Boucher began the cadenza which seemed to last so long that the players quietly began at first to put away their instruments and, finally, to depart. Boucher, absorbed in his performance, noticed nothing; he played a long final trill, satisfied that with the vigorous entry of the orchestra the enraptured audience would break into enthusiastic applause. He raised his foot at last and let it fall with a loud thump. When nothing happened he stared round and saw nothing but empty desks. The audience, who had anticipated this moment, burst into uproarious laughter in which Boucher had to join with as much grace as he could muster.

MUSICIANS ON MUSIC (Louis Spohr): F Bonavia

Paderewski's awful moment

EVERY ARTIST has lived through trying and agonising experiences. I have had my full share of them and there was one audience in my early career, when I was still quite young, that I furnished unwittingly with a rare bit of comedy. I remember this concert very distinctly, and that I was late in arriving and in a great hurry, which did not often happen. At any rate, I came very late to dress and had to hurry. I jumped into a cab and drove to the concert hall, quite unconscious of the appearance I presented. But as I stepped on to the platform I realised that something was quite wrong, for even before I reached the piano, the people sitting near the stage entrance burst into laughter, hearty laughter I may say. I took a few more steps towards the piano, but as the laughter increased, I turned to look at the offenders and found to my horror on turning, that my braces, or as you call them, suspenders, were hanging and dangling far down below my coat! It was an awful moment. There was only one thing to be done.

I ran away, of course, literally made a dash for the exit, which I accomplished successfully but with more laughter. In a minute or two I got myself in order and returned to the stage. I must say that my second entrance was a difficult one to make, but the audience was splendid – there was no more laughter, only very encouraging applause, and the recital went on without further disaster.

THE PADEREWSKI MEMOIRS: Ignace Jan Paderewski and Mary Lawton

★   ★   ★

The Liverpool Philharmonic Society

resents the

ROYAL
LIVERPOOL
PHILHARMONIC
ORCHESTRA

★   ★   ★

Too good for J Walter Thompson

ONE DAY while I was composing, the telephone rang. A lady's voice said, 'Is this John Cage, the percussion composer?' I said, 'Yes.' She said, 'This is the J Walter Thompson Company.' I didn't know what that was, but she explained that their business was advertising. She said, 'Hold on. One of our directors wants to speak to you.' During a pause my mind went back to my composition. Then suddenly a man's voice said, 'Mr Cage, are you willing to prostitute your art?' I said, 'Yes.' He said, 'Well, bring us some samples Friday at two.' I did. After hearing a few recordings, one of the directors said to me, 'Wait a minute.' Then seven directors formed what looked like a football huddle. From this one of them finally emerged, came over to me, and said, 'You're too good for us. We're going to save you for *Robinson Crusoe*.'
SILENCE: Lectures and Writings by John Cage

* * *

The clergy witnessed the rehearsal and broadcast of this and of the daily service at home. The actual broadcast of both was a revelation, and a wonderful example of recollected concentration, preparation, and what must be called teamwork at its best. Nor will anyone forget the delicious touch when George Thalben Ball walked in and promptly pushed his organ round till he got it in the right place. Then he accompanied the service superbly. – *The Church Times.*

* * *

Schoenberg asks a girl to play . . .

ON ONE OCCASION, Schoenberg asked a girl in his class to go to the piano and play the first movement of a Beethoven sonata, which was afterwards to be analysed. She said, 'It is too difficult. I can't play it.' Schoenberg said, 'You're a pianist, aren't you?' She said, 'Yes.' He said, 'Then go to the piano.' She did. She had no sooner begun playing than he stopped her to say that she was not playing at the proper tempo. She said that if she played at the proper tempo, she would make mistakes. He said, 'Play at the proper tempo and do not make mistakes.' She began again, and he stopped her immediately to say that she was making mistakes. She then burst into tears and between sobs explained that she had gone to the dentist earlier that day and that she'd had a tooth pulled out. He said, 'Do you have to have a tooth pulled out in order to make mistakes?'
SILENCE: Lectures and Writings by John Cage

Blues

An American dance stemming from the foxtrot, the speed of which it reduced, and into which it brought a deliberately continued dismal atmosphere. When Blues are sung, their words seem to aim at attaining to the utmost depths of gloom and inanity.

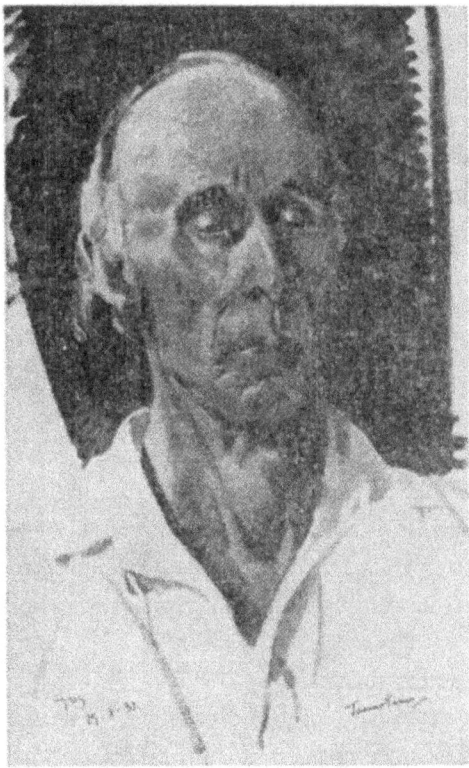

Delius, from a sketch in oils by James Gunn

Blues

ERIC BLOM's definition of the Blues betrays a certain lack of sympathy with a form of self-expression which the jazz enthusiast regards as the deepest manifestation of grief. I toyed with the idea of calling this section Lament, but while the occasional piece may be called Lament, it is scarcely a generic form, which the Blues certainly can be said to be. Within the next few pages there are a number of cries of sorrow, evidence of the pain and despair that musicians have so frequently felt. In the nature of things, a musician is a sensitive soul, likely to assume emotional attitudes that may seem a little hysterical to a more balanced mind. One of the paradoxes of music though is the apparent lack of any relationship between what a composer feels and what he writes. Tchaikovsky, who was quite a one for the blues, wrote one of his gayest works, the *Rococo Variations for Cello and Orchestra*, when he was at a very low ebb. As is made clear in another section of this book, you can scarcely expect a composer to feel sad when he writes the slow movements and happy when he gets to work on the scherzo. The music is greater than he, and while a romantic composer like Berlioz may well use music as a means of self-projection, to do so is far less common than most people realise.

I suppose that the classic expression of personal anguish, the *De Profundis* of music, is the so-called *Heiligenstadt Testament* of Beethoven, in which he resigns himself to the bitterness of his fate:

> ... for six years past I have fallen into an incurable condition, aggravated by senseless physicians, year after year deceived in the hope of recovery, and in the end compelled to contemplate a *lasting malady*, the cure of which may take years or even prove impossible. ... O how should I then bring myself to admit the weakness of *a sense* which I once possessed in the greatest perfection.

... O I cannot do it! ... Recreation in human society, the more delicate passages of conversation, confidential outpourings, none of these are for me; I must live like an exile. ...

This famous document has been reprinted so often that I felt that I might be excused from including it, so long as I admitted its unquestioned position as the supreme testimony of anguish amongst composers. Instead I have concentrated on the more personal and intimate expressions of despair – Mozart's abject plea for recognition from the city fathers of Vienna, or his cries for financial assistance to Michael Puchberg. (The letters BO after his name stand for Brother of the Order of Freemasons.) Health as much as money troubled poor Mozart at this time, his wife's as well as his own; despite these ever-present miseries, music poured from his pen. The piano sonata in D, K576, was written in July 1789, the clarinet quintet not long after.

Schubert's last letter deserves a place for the interesting light that it sheds on his literary tastes. Less well-known is the *cri-de-cœur* of 1824 to his friend Kupelwieser, the painter. The quotation, 'My peace is gone, my heart is sore' is an allusion to one of Schubert's best-known songs, *Gretchen am Spinnrade*.

The harrowing description of Beethoven's corpse given in Van Hartmann's diary, and quoted in Deutsch's monumental book on Schubert, does not quite fit into the same category, but I felt that it belonged to this section of the anthology; but to escape from this somewhat morbid pre-occupation with death, I have followed it by Schumann's letter to Clara describing the painful interview he had just endured with her obdurate father. From Schumann to Chopin seemed a logical enough step, since Schumann was partly responsible for the early recognition of Chopin's genius (*see p* 249). The story of Chopin's final years is too well-known to need any comment here, but the letter I have chosen is particularly revealing. That this man, whose music is so full of pride and fire, should have had to be carried up and down stairs seems extraordinarily pathetic. His vague speculations about marriage, the evidence of boredom, the intimations of death, all add up to a chronicle of despair.

Brahms's visits to Schumann in the asylum must have been a torment in more ways than one. Not only did he have the pain of seeing the disintegration of a man who had been a profound influence on his development as a composer, but he must also have felt an intense guilt that he was in love with Clara. His description of Schumann's last days is all the more moving to us in consequence.

The Puccini extract is included for the interesting information that it gives us about his early days, and the relationship his own experiences had to his most famous opera. But this was a sad story with a happy ending for, unlike Mozart or Schubert, Puccini was to become successful and prosperous. By the time this interview was given he could afford to look back almost romantically at his early poverty.

I was determined to include at some point an excerpt from one of the most remarkable books on music that I have ever read, remarkable not so much for its historical significance as for the unique character of the story it tells. Delius as a composer may not be to everyone's liking, but no one could question the extraordinary courage of a man who could go on trying to compose against the virtually insuperable obstacle of paralysis. Eric Fenby, a young Englishman, went to France to act as Delius's amanuensis; in the long run, the relationship was to be quite a fruitful one, but the passage I have quoted describes Fenby's despair when, on his arrival at the Delius home, he realised quite how difficult a task he had taken on. As a testament to human courage this must rank pretty high on both their parts.

The path of genius is a singularly lonely one at times, and those to whom the music of Schoenberg is unsympathetic should never forget the derision and mockery this man had to face for virtually his whole life. Like it or not, Schoenberg is the most significant father-figure in twentieth-century music, and his influence now extends to a very large proportion of composers. In May 1947, when he was in his early seventies, recognition had at last come in that he was awarded a prize of one thousand dollars by the American Academy of Arts and Letters for his outstanding achievements. The letter that he wrote thanking them for this honour is a revelation of the struggle that he had fought for so long.

In such a life, when the feeling of isolation must at times seem overwhelming, friendship is invaluable. Schoenberg gathered around him a devoted group of disciples, inspired by his fanatical belief in the New Music, their own thinking coloured by the intensity of his convictions. Of these, perhaps the greatest musician was Alban Berg. Like Schoenberg, he endured more than his fair share of ostracism. His master outlived him by sixteen years, for Berg died in 1935 of blood-poisoning, exacerbated by a bee-sting. The two brief letters I quote reveal the wretched health which was a cross he had to bear; they come from Hans Redlich's biography of Berg, which I wholeheartedly recommend to anyone wanting to understand his music.

Lastly, we have something about which I experience a stupid and irrational sense of identification. I live in Brook Green, Hammersmith, in an old house close to St Paul's girls' school. For a significant part of his life, Gustav Holst was the director of music there, and I feel his presence time and again. I never pass the school gates without imagining this quiet unassuming man for whose music I have such a deep affection. His daughter Imogen has written two books about him, one about his life, the other about his works; her analysis of his compositions is clear, unbiased and dispassionate. But in spite of her determination to present the story of his life in equally lucid terms, I found much of it painfully moving. As a tribute to the courage of an under-estimated man, I end this sad chapter with an extract from her biography of her father.

Mozart's letter to the Municipal Council of Vienna

MOST HONOURABLE AND MOST LEARNED MUNICIPAL COUNCILLORS OF VIENNA! MOST WORTHY GENTLEMEN!

When Kappellmeister Hofmann was ill, I thought of venturing to apply for his post, seeing that my musical talents, my works and my skill in composition are well known in foreign countries, my name is treated everywhere with some respect, and I myself was appointed several years ago composer to the distinguished court of Vienna. I trusted therefore that I was not unworthy of this post and that I deserved the favourable consideration of our enlightened municipal council.

Kapellmeister Hofmann, however, has recovered his health and in the circumstances – for I wish him from my heart a long life – it has occurred to me that it might perhaps be of service to the Cathedral and, most worthy gentlemen, to your advantage, if I were to be attached for the time being as unpaid assistant to this aging Kapellmeister and were to have the opportunity of helping this worthy man in his office, thus gaining the approbation of our learned municipal council by the actual performance of services which I may justly consider myself peculiarly fitted to render on account of my thorough knowledge of both the secular and ecclesiastical styles of music.

Your most humble servant,

WOLFGANG AMADÉ MOZART
Royal and Imperial Court Composer

Mozart to Michael Puchberg

DEAREST, MOST BELOVED FRIEND AND MOST HONOURABLE BO

Great God! I would not wish my worst enemy to be in my present position. And if you, most beloved friend and brother, forsake me, we are altogether lost, *both my unfortunate and blameless self* and my poor sick wife and child. Only the other day when I was with you I was longing to open my heart to you, but I had not the courage to do so – and indeed I should still not have the courage – for, as it is, I only dare to write and tremble as I do so –

and I should not even dare to write, were I not certain that you know me, that you are aware of my circumstances, and that you are wholly convinced of my *innocence* so far as my unfortunate and most distressing situation is concerned. Good God! I am coming to you not with thanks but with fresh entreaties! Instead of paying my debts I am asking for more money! If you really know me, you must sympathise with my anguish in having to do so. I need not tell you once more that owing to my unfortunate illness I have been prevented from earning anything. But I must mention that in spite of my wretched condition I decided to give subscription concerts at home in order to be able to meet at least my present great and frequent expenses, for I was absolutely convinced of your friendly assistance. But even this has failed. Unfortunately, Fate is so much against me, *though only in Vienna*, that even when I want to, I cannot make any money. A fortnight ago I sent round a list for subscribers and so far the only name on it is that of Baron van Swieten! Now that (the 13th) my dear little wife seems to be improving every day, I should be able to set to work again, if this blow, this heavy blow, had not come. At any rate, people are consoling me by telling me that she is better – although the night before last she was suffering so much – and I on her account – that I was stunned and despairing. But last night (the 14th), she slept so well and has felt so much easier all the morning that I am very hopeful; and at last I am beginning to feel inclined for work. I am now faced, however, with misfortunes of another kind, though, it is true, only for the moment. Dearest, most beloved friend and brother – you know *my present circumstances*, but you also know *my prospects*. So let things remain as we arranged; that is, *thus or thus*, you understand what I mean. Meanwhile, I am composing six easy clavier sonatas for Princess Friederike and six quartets for the King, all of which Kozeluch is engraving at my expense. At the same time, the two dedications will bring me in something. In a month or two my fate must be decided *in every detail*. Therefore, most beloved friend, you will not be risking anything so far as I am concerned. So it all depends, my only friend, upon whether you will or can lend me another five hundred gulden. Until my affairs are settled, I undertake to pay back ten gulden a month; and then, as this is bound to happen in a few months, I shall pay back the whole sum with whatever interest you may demand, and at the same time acknowledge myself to be your debtor for life. That, alas, I shall have to remain, for I shall never be able to thank you sufficiently for your friendship and affection. Thank God, that is over. Now you know all. Do not be offended by my confiding in you and remember that unless you help me, the honour, the peace of mind, and perhaps the very life of your friend and brother Mason will be ruined.

    Ever your most grateful servant, true
        friend and brother
            W A MOZART.

Mozart to Michael Puchberg

DEAREST FRIEND AND BROTHER,

Whereas I felt tolerably well yesterday, I am absolutely wretched to-day. I could not sleep all night for pain. I must have got overheated yesterday from walking so much and then without knowing it have caught a chill. Picture to yourself my condition – ill and consumed with worries and anxieties. Such a state quite definitely prevents me from recovering. In a week or a fortnight I shall be better off – certainly – but at present I am in want! Can you not help me out with a trifle? The *smallest* sum would be very welcome just now. You would, for the moment at least, bring peace of mind to your true friend, servant and brother.

W A MOZART
THE LETTERS OF MOZART & HIS FAMILY: *Emily Anderson*

Schubert: 'My peace is gone'

DEAR KUPELWIESER,

For a long time I have felt the urge to write to you, but I never knew where to turn. Now, however, Smirsch offers me an opportunity, and at last I can once again wholly pour out my soul to someone. For you are so good and honest, you will be sure to forgive many things which others might take in very bad part from me. – In a word, I feel myself to be the most unhappy and wretched creature in the world. Imagine a man whose health will never be right again, and who in sheer despair over this ever makes things worse and worse, instead of better; imagine a man, I say, whose most brilliant hopes have perished, to whom the felicity of love and friendship have nothing to offer but pain, at best, whom enthusiasm (at least of the stimulating kind) for all things beautiful threatens to forsake, and I ask you, is he not a miserable, unhappy being? – 'My peace is gone, my heart is sore, I shall find it never and nevermore,' I may well sing every day now, for each night, on retiring to bed, I hope I may not wake again, and each morning but recalls yesterday's grief. Thus, joyless and friendless, I should pass my days, did not Schwind visit me now and again and turn on me a ray of those sweet days of the past. – Our society (reading circle), as you probably know already, has done itself to death owing to a reinforcement of that rough chorus of beer-drinkers and sausage-eaters, for its dissolution is due in a couple of days, though I had hardly visited it myself since your departure. Leidesdorf, with whom I have become quite well-acquainted, is, in fact, a truly thoughtful and good fellow, but so hugely melancholy that I am almost afraid I owe him more than enough in that respect; besides, my affairs and his do badly, so that we never have any money. The opera by your brother (who did not do any too well in leaving the theatre) has been declared unusable, and thus no claim has been made on my music. Castelli's opera, *The*

Conspirators (*Die Verschworenen*), has been set in Berlin by a local composer and received with acclamation. In this way I seem once again to have composed two operas for nothing. Of songs I have not written many new ones, but I have tried my hand at several instrumental works, for I wrote two Quartets for violins, viola and violoncello and an Octet, and I want to write another quartet, in fact I intend to pave my way towards grand symphony in that manner. – The latest in Vienna is that Beethoven is to give a concert at which he is to produce his new Symphony, three movements from the new Mass and a new Overture. – God willing, I, too, am thinking of giving a similar concert next year. I will close now, so as not to use too much paper, and kiss you a thousand times. If you were to write to me about your present enthusiastic mood and about your life in general, nothing could more greatly please

Your
faithful Friend
FRZ SCHUBERT
Fare well!
Very well!!

Schubert's last letter

DEAR SCHOBER

I am ill. I have eaten nothing for eleven days and drunk nothing, and I totter feebly and shakily from my chair to bed and back again. Rinna is treating me. If ever I take anything, I bring it up again at once.

Be so kind, then, as to assist me in this desperate situation by means of literature. Of Cooper's I have read *The Last of the Mohicans*, *The Spy*, *The Pilot*, and *The Pioneers*. If by any chance you have anything else of his, I implore you to deposit it with Frau von Bogner at the coffee-house for me. My brother, who is conscientiousness itself, will most faithfully pass it on to me. Or anything else.

Your friend
SCHUBERT

Beethoven in death

28TH MARCH 1827: Out to the Schwarzspanierhaus, where I contemplated the body of the divine Beethoven, who died the day before yesterday, at six in the evening. Already on entering his room, which is large and somewhat neglected, I was moved by its desolate look. It is scantily furnished, and only the pianoforte, of which the English made him a present, as well as a very fine coffin, struck a note of beauty in it. In some places lay music and several books. No catafalque had as yet been erected, but he still lay on the mattress of his bed. A cover was spread over him, and a venerable old man, whom I would regard rather as a servant than as a watcher, uncovered him for me. There I saw his splendid face, which unhappily I had never been able to see in life. Such a heavenly dignity lay spread over him, in spite of the disfigurement he is said to have suffered, that I could scarcely look my fill. I departed full of emotion; and only when I was downstairs could I have wept for not having begged the good old man to cut me off a few of his hairs. Ferdinand Sauter, whom I had arranged to meet, but whom I missed, ran across me, and I turned back with him, telling him of my plan. The old man showed him to us once more and also uncovered the chest for us, which, like the greatly swollen abdomen, was already quite blue. The smell of corruption was very strong already. We pressed a gratuity into the old man's hand and asked him for hair from Beethoven's head. He shook his head and motioned us to be silent. So we sadly trundled down the stairs, when suddenly the old man softly called us from the banisters upstairs, asking us to wait at the gate until the three fops had departed who were viewing the dead hero, tapping their swagger-canes on their pantaloons. We then re-ascended the stairs and, issuing from the door and putting his fingertips to his lips, he gave us the hair in a piece of paper and vanished. We left, sorrowfully happy about it. Fritz met us, and I told him of our errand, whereupon he did the same. – In the Kohlmarkt we looked at the latest portrait that has appeared of him and found that his corpse still resembled it very much.

SCHUBERT, A DOCUMENTARY BIOGRAPHY: Otto Erich Deutsch

A letter to Clara, from Schumann

MY INTERVIEW with your father was terrible. He was frigid, hostile, confused and contradictory at once. Truly his method of stabbing is original, for he drives in the hilt as well as the blade....

Well, and what now, my dear Clara? I am at a loss – absolutely – to know what to do. My reasoning power is quite exhausted, and any display of feeling is worse than useless in dealing with your father. What in the world can we do? You must be particularly on your guard against any attempt he may make to *sell you*.... I believe in you – God knows – with all my heart. This is, indeed, my chief support. But you will have more need of strength than you suspect. Did not your father give me the grim assurance to my face that he was 'not to be shaken'? You must be prepared for anything, for if he cannot succeed by force he will employ cunning. Be prepared for anything, I repeat.

I feel so lifeless, so *humiliated*, today that I am incapable of a single fine thought. Even your picture is so blurred that I almost forget what your eyes are like. I am not so reduced in spirit as to think of giving you up, but so embittered by this outrage to my most sacred feelings, by being treated like one of the common herd. If I could only have a word from you! Tell me what

I must do. If I do not hear from you, the mockery of the whole thing will drive me to flight. To think that I am not allowed to see you! He will only allow it in some public place, where we should be a laughing-stock for everybody. What a cold sting there is in all this! He further permits us to correspond when you are travelling, and that is the sum total of his concessions. . . . I always considered your father a good and humane person, but I look in vain for anything that might excuse him, in vain for any nobler reason underlying his refusal, such as a fear that your artistic career might suffer through an early engagement, the plea that you are too young, or any similar objection. No sign of anything of the sort! Believe me, he will fling you at the first suitor who comes, provided he has money and titles enough. It is as if he could conceive of nothing higher than touring and concert-giving. To this end he would sacrifice your heart's blood and cripple my strength at the moment when I am striving to do great things in the world, over and above which he mocks at all your tears.

Your ring is looking at me in such a charming way, as if it would chide me for reproaching my Clara's father. The word 'steadfast' which you uttered three times the other day, seemed to come from the very depths of your soul. That day did so much for me, Clara; don't be angry if I am weak today and have hurt your father's feelings. I have right on my side.

Remember what is at stake. Exert yourself to the utmost, and if your gentleness fails, use your strength. Silence seems to be my only refuge, for every new attempt to persuade your father would provoke fresh insult. Do all you can to find a way out; I will follow like a child. . . . How my poor head swims! I could laugh for very anguish. This cannot go on much longer – my health will not stand it. . . . God preserve me from despair. My life is torn up by the roots.

THE COMPOSER IN LOVE (*Schumann*): *Cyril Clarke*

Chopin's chronicle of despair

To Wojciech Grzymala

MY DEAREST FRIEND,

Have you forgotten what I am like, that you go and deduce from my letters, in which I have told you that I am every day weaker, more bored, without a shadow of hope, without a home of my own, that I am going to be married? On the day I received your good kind letter I wrote a sort of list of instructions for the disposal of my stuff in case I should happen to expire somewhere.

I have been wandering about all over Scotland but it's already too cold for that, and tomorrow I am returning to London, for Lord Dudley Stuart has written to ask me to play on the 16th at a benefit concert for the Poles, to be given before the ball begins. Coming back from Hamilton Palace (sixty miles from here), where I spent a few days with the Duke and Duchess of Hamilton, I caught cold and I haven't been out for five days. I am staying with Dr Lyszczynski who is giving me homoeopathic treatment. I decline all invitations to stay with people, for the cholera is on our doorstep. Besides, if I collapse anywhere, it will be for the whole winter, the way I am now. I have promised that if the weather improves I shall return to Hamilton Palace and go from there to the Isle of Arran (the whole of which belongs to them) to stay with the Baden princess who has married their son, the Marquis of Douglas. But I already know that nothing will come of all this. During my stay at Hamilton they had not only many local aristocrats and members of the family but also the Prince and Princess of Parma and the Prince of Lucca. The Princess is the sister of the Duc de Bordeaux: she and her husband are a very gay young couple, and they have invited me to their house at Kingston on my return to London. Since they have been forced to leave Italy they will now be living in England.

All these things are very fine but they are now beyond me, and if I hastened to get away from Hamilton it was once again because I could not remain at table from eight till ten-thirty without suffering pains, as I did at Gutmann's – do you remember? Although I breakfasted in the morning in my own room and came down late, and was carried up and down the stairs, I was ill at ease with it all. Before I received your letter, I wrote to you while I was at Wishaw, at Lady Belhaven's, but my letter was so despairing, so awful, that it was just as well I did not send it.

After the sixteenth November, if the situation in Paris improves somewhat, or if the London fogs drive me away, I shall return to Paris, provided it is not too late in the season for me to travel.

My good Scots ladies, whom I have not seen for a week or two, will be coming here today. They would like me to stay longer and go trotting from one Scottish palace to another, here, there and everywhere that I am invited. They are kindhearted but so tiresome!! – may God be with them! I get letters from them every day but I never answer a single one; and as soon as I go anywhere they come running after me if they possibly can. Perhaps that is what has given somebody the idea that I am going to be married. But there must be some sort of physical attraction; and the unmarried one is far too much like me. How can one kiss oneself? . . . Friendship is friendship, I have said so distinctly, but it gives no claim to anything else.

Supposing that I could fall in love with someone who loved me in return, and as I would wish to be loved, even then I would not marry, for we should have nothing to eat and nowhere to live. But a rich woman looks for a rich husband – and if she does choose a poor man he must not be a feeble creature, but young and vigorous. A man on his own can struggle along, but when there are two, poverty is the greatest misfortune. I may give up the ghost in an institution, but I won't leave a wife to starve.

Anyhow it's a waste of time to write all this – you know how I feel. [*Sentences blacked out.*] And so I am not thinking at all of a wife, but of those at home, my mother and sisters. God fill their hearts always with happy thoughts! But in the meantime what has become of my art? and where have I squandered my heart? [*Crossings-out.*] I can scarcely remember what songs they sing at home. This world seems to slip from me, I forget things, I have no strength. I no sooner recover a little than I sink back lower still.

I am not *complaining* to you; but you wanted an explanation, so I am merely making it clear that I am nearer to a coffin than a bridal bed. I am fairly calm in my mind. [*Words blacked out, the only legible phrase being:* 'I am resigned.']

Send me a few lines. Address to Szulczewski Esq, 10 Duke Street, St James's. Lord Dudley Stuart has his Polish Literary Society there. I wrote a fourth letter but I am not sending it – only one page of another letter which I wrote in a moment of impatience. I send it to show you how black my mood sometimes is.

Yours till death,
Ch

SELECTED CORRESPONDENCE OF FRÉDÉRIC CHOPIN: *Bronislaw Edward Sydow*

Brahms visits Schumann in the asylum

To Clara Schumann

MY MOST BELOVED FRIEND!

I feel that I have so many beautiful things to tell you this evening that I really don't know where to begin. From two o'clock till six I was with your beloved husband, and if you could see my blissful expression you would know more than any letter could tell you. He received me as warmly and cheerfully as he did the first time, but did not show the same subsequent excitement. Then he handed me your last letter and told me what a delightful surprise it had been to him. We spoke about your travels. I told him that I had seen you in Hamburg, Hanover, Lübeck, and even in Rotterdam. He then asked particularly whether you had occupied the same room in Holland as you had the previous winter. I told him your chief reason for avoiding it, which he quite understood. He was very much pleased with the Bach, Beethoven, Schumann programme.

Then I showed him your portrait. Oh, if only you could have seen how deeply moved he was, how the tears almost stood in his eyes as he looked ever more closely at it. 'Oh, how long have I wished for this!' he said at last, and as he laid it down his hands trembled. He continued to look at it and often stood up to get a closer view of it. He was delighted with the inkstand and also with the cigars. He said he had not had any since Joachim's. This is probably true and he may have left some of those lying about. But he told me that he does not like to ask the doctors for anything (he also said to me most emphatically, 'Clara must certainly have sent me some often, but I do not get them').

He then invited me to go into the garden with him, but as to what we talked about, I cannot possibly remember it all, but I don't think you could mention anything we did not discuss. I asked him quite calmly whether he was composing anything. He then told me that he had written some fugues, but that I was not to hear them because they were not properly arranged yet. He spoke much and often about you – how wonderfully, how magnificently you play, for instance the canons, particularly those in A flat and B, the Sketches. 'It would be impossible to hear *Abend* and *Traümeswirren* played more beautifully than by her!' He inquired after all the children and laughed heartily over Felix's first tooth. He also asked after Frl Bertha, Frl Leser, Frl Junge, and Frl Schönerstedt, Joachim (and how earnestly!), Hasenclever, etc, etc. Later on he asked after Bürgermeister Hammers, Nielo, Massenbach, etc inquiring whether they were still in Düsseldorf. He told me a lot about your travels, the Siebengebirge, Switzerland and Heidelberg, and also spoke of Gräfin Abegg. He looked through my *C major Sonata* with me and pointed out many things. I begged him to send you a greeting (in writing) and asked him whether he did not wish to write to you more often. 'I should love to,' he replied, 'always and always, if only I had paper.' And he really hadn't any. For he does not like to ask the doctors for anything and they think of nothing unless he asks for it.

Whereupon I had paper brought. He disliked its large size very much, nor was he at all pleased with my way of reducing its dimensions. Again and again he sat down and with a most friendly expression on his face seemed as if he wished to write. But he declared that he was much too excited and would write the next day. I can only hope that the next day will not keep us waiting as long as usual. He wrote in my notebook with a pencil the things I was to get for him – a scarf; his everyday one is worn out and the one he was wearing was too 'grand' for his taste! As for the copies of the *Signal*, I will look through this year's numbers and send them to him (when I have made my selection), then I will write to Senff to tell him that Herr Sch wishes to read this paper. We also spoke about the new *Zeitschrift für Musik* and what a lot of nonsense and gossip it contained. . . . He spoke very enthusiastically of Joachim, as enthusiastically as he usually speaks only of you. He talked a good deal about the musical festival, and of how beautifully J had already played at the rehearsal. Surely such sounds had never been heard on the violin before! We then played a duet. He asked me to play the *César Overture* with him, but he would not take the lead. 'I am the bass,' he said. We did not keep strictly together but how long it must be since he played a duet! He said that with you he used to play it much faster or else that you used to play it so. He thought highly of the arrangement. . . . The piano was badly out of tune; I have arranged for it to be tuned.

When I wished him goodbye, he insisted on accompanying me to the station. On the plea of going to fetch my coat I went downstairs and asked the doctor whether this could be allowed, and to my great joy he said it could. (I did not say any more to the doctor and had not even seen him before this.) An attendant followed us or walked beside us all the time (a few steps away).

It was very fine to see the heavy doors, which are usually bolted, opened for us to go out.... He was very pleased with my Hungarian hat just as he used to be in the old days with the cap etc. You can imagine my joy when I found myself walking cheerfully along with my friend for quite a long time. I never once looked at my watch and in reply to his questions always said that there was no hurry. So we went to the cathedral, and to the Beethoven monument, after which I brought him back to the road.

He often made use of my glasses because he had forgotten his own and incidentally found no difficulty in keeping up with the well-known Brahms pace which is often too much for you. On the way he asked me whether his Clara also took a walk every day. I told him (though not quite truthfully) that whenever you were in Düsseldorf or any other place with me I took you for a walk every day, as you did not like going out alone. 'That I readily believe,' said your Robert, very sadly, 'in the old days we always went out for walks together.' We talked a good deal about his books and his music and he was as happy as a king when he saw how well I knew them all and their proper places. We chaffed each other a good deal over this, for in the case of some of the books he had to stop to think and I had to do the same in the case of others.

I left him on the Endenich Road. He hugged and kissed me tenderly, and on parting sent greeting to you alone.... On the way there were moments when I felt intoxicated with happiness, and you can well imagine how much I longed for you to be in Düsseldorf. Your letter was a real joy. It made me feel as if I were holding your hand.

I cannot write you anything sad about him except that occasionally he expressed an emphatic wish to be out of the place. At such moments he always spoke in low and indistinct tones, because he is frightened of the doctors; but he said nothing that was not lucid or showed any signs of confusion. He mentioned the fact that in March he would have been in Endenich a year, and it seemed to him as if he had first known the place when everything was beautifully green, the weather perfect and skies blue overhead. But alas! I can only tell you in simple and dry language all that we had to say to each other. The beautiful side of it all I cannot describe – his fine, calm demeanour, his warmth in speaking of you and his joy over the portrait. Just picture all this as perfectly as you can.

Surely you will have no questions to ask after such an exhaustive letter? But how I wish I could write more briefly and more beautifully.... And so with heartiest greetings from your Robert and myself; and be content at least with my good intentions, for you know how gladly I would give you more joy if I could, with heart-felt love and respect,

Your JOHANNES
Heartiest greetings to dear Joachim.

MUSICIANS ON MUSIC (*Johannes Brahms*): *F Bonavia*

Puccini on poverty

WHEN I CHOSE Henri Murger's novel, *La Vie de Bohème*, as a subject on which a libretto could be based, I instructed Illica, my librettist, to construct the first setting in accordance with my description of that miserable room in which I lived when I was a student at the Milan Conservatory. Every time I hear *Bohème*, I see in my mind's eye that bleak vista – those sordid chimney tops and all the squalor that was the bane of my youth. My diet was bread, beans and herrings, and I was sometimes so cold that I actually burned the manuscripts of my early attempts at composition to keep warm, just as Rudolfo does in *La Bohème*.

TALKS WITH GREAT COMPOSERS: *Arthur M Abell*

Delius: a simple little tune

AND SO THE DAYS passed by uneventfully, and I found myself watching him as anxiously as the others. During those periods when Delius was suffering more than usual he could bear pain, but he could not endure the sound of conversation, and we ate and exchanged the usual politenesses of the table in silence. The slightest rattle of a cup or clatter of a spoon was sufficient to lash him into a fury, and if one forgot oneself and found oneself saying, 'Mrs Delius, may I pass you so-and-so?' it was certain to meet with his, 'Will you please be quiet!' The nervous tension one felt in his presence was almost unbearable, and, after sitting beside him for an hour, one left the room feeling as if one had been drained of one's life-blood. The house at such times resembled a tomb from which the living in it could have no hope of escape.

Then came a brighter day, when the sufferer was left in peace.

That evening, after supper, Delius surprised me by saying that he had an idea in his mind – a simple little tune – and that he wanted me to take it down.

I took paper and pen and waited eagerly. I had no idea what he would do – whether he would sing, or call out the names of the notes and their varying time-values. What he did was to stagger and confound me so utterly that I did not recover for the rest of that night.

Throwing his head back, he began to drawl in a loud monotone that was little more than the crudest extension of speech, and which, when there was anything of a ring about it, wavered round a tenor middle B. This is something like what I heard:

'Ter-te-ter – ter-te-ter – ter-te-te-ter' – and here he interjected 'Hold it!' and then went on – 'ter-te-te-ter – ter-ter-ter – te-ter – hold it! – ter-te-te-ter – ter–ter–te–te–ter – hold it! – ter-te-ter-ter-ter-ter-te-ter – hold it! – ter-te-ter-ter-te-ter-ter-te-ter. . . .'

Instantly, my mind went back to those days in the Great War when, as a small boy, I had been accompanist in a concert party and had gone off almost every night to entertain the soldiers. Two or three items were always reserved for such 'Tommies' as cared to sing, and I had learnt something of the good-natured fellow who would come beaming up to the platform and whisper in one's ear, 'I haven't any music, but it goes like this: High-tee-tigh-tee-tigh-tee-tigh!'

When he had finished this amazing recital, he turned to me and asked, 'Have you got that? Now sing it!' I was dumbfounded.

'But – Delius,' I stammered, 'what key is it in?'

'A minor,' came the answer.

In a flash I saw that he evidently heard the tune imaginatively, but was unable to sing it.

'Well, we will try again,' he went on, and there was more suggestion of disgust and impatience in his tone than I cared to admit. It was obvious that he failed to understand how I could be so stupid.

I had observed that he disliked anything in the form of repetition – whether it were musical or verbal – and that if one had the misfortune to repeat oneself, one was never allowed to proceed very far. Unnecessary repetition annoyed him, and he sat there, tossing his head from side to side, and champing and frowning in his anger. This he always did when things went wrong. When I suggested that it would help me if he would call out the names of the notes, he gave a great sigh and added, 'Well, all right then!'

The drawling began again, but now on another note!

'A – BC – BD – E,' etc.

I quickly sketched the shape of this melody, but had no idea of the stresses, nor even the time signature. I was too flurried, too nervous, too upset to go about it in the proper way. I had not thought that it would be like this, and the sting of my emotion pierced me to the heart. My pen flopped about in my fingers, and in my confusion I found myself holding it upside down. My fingers were inky, and the tears that I had been fighting to keep back now blurred my spectacles, and I could not see. The more I looked at this relic of a man, and heard his hopeless attempts to make himself understood in but the rudiments of the glorious art in which he so greatly excelled, the more distressed I became, until in the end the sight and sound of it were too much for me, and I broke down. I had to give it up!

Just then Mrs Delius entered the room, and I pulled myself together as best I could and said, 'I am sorry, I cannot go on! Please excuse me.'

I got up and went out into the porch, and as I groped my way in the pitch darkness round to the door which led up from the garden to the music-room, I overheard Delius say, 'Jelka, that boy is no good! He is too slow. He cannot even take down a simple melody!'

DELIUS AS I KNEW HIM: *Eric Fenby*

An acknowledgement from Schoenberg

THAT YOU SHOULD regard all I have tried to do in the last fifty years as an achievement strikes me as in some respects an overestimate. My own feeling was that I had fallen into an ocean of boiling water; and, as I couldn't swim and knew no other way out, I struggled with my arms and legs as best I could. I don't know what saved me, or why I wasn't drowned or boiled alive – perhaps my own merit was that I never gave in. Whether my movements were very economical or completely senseless, whether they helped or hindered my survival, there was no one willing to help me, and there were plenty who would gladly have seen me go under. I don't think it was envy – what was there to envy? – and I doubt whether it was lack of goodwill, or worse, positive ill-will on their part. Perhaps they just wanted to get rid of the nightmare, the agonising disharmony, the unintelligible thinking, the systematic lunacy that I represented, and I must admit that those who thought in that way were not bad men – though, of course, I could never understand what I had done to them to make them so malicious, so violent and so aggressive. I am still certain that I never took anything from them which was theirs. I never interfered with their rights and privileges, and never trespassed on their preserves. I didn't even know where these lay, or what was the line of demarcation that marked off their estate, or who gave them the right to ownership of the property. I am proud to accept this distinction, awarded on the assumption that I achieved something. Please don't call it false modesty if I say that perhaps something was achieved, but that it is not I who deserves the credit. The credit must go to my opponents. It was they who really helped me.

ARNOLD SCHOENBERG: H H Stuckenschmidt

Letters from Alban Berg

... APART FROM THE FACT that I am quite generally a bad traveller, I would run the risk of ruining the whole day following a night in which I had slept badly. At the same time, if I tried to stimulate myself artificially (a thing I could do very well with tea), I'd risk completely spoiling the next few days. I just have to take my rotten health always into account. I am, too, far from well at present. I am suffering from styes, four on one eyelid. The word 'suffering' is no exaggeration, for this ridiculous and idiotic complaint causes a very painful inflammation of the eye and the whole left part of my face....

I am very ill. It's not only the asthma, to which I have become almost accustomed. Now I've got jaundice again. At least I suppose so, as some of the symptoms fit into the picture. It is like a poisoning of the whole system. I have hardly the strength to lift my arm. I've got racking pains in my glands and muscles, and – worst of all – a constant splitting headache. I have tried to overcome this enigmatic illness by staying up, but high temperature and shivering have compelled me to remain in bed, whence I am writing to you now. . . .

ALBAN BERG: THE MAN AND HIS MUSIC: *H F Redlich*

Gustav Holst: the last days

THE LEISURELY existence was certainly not an entire success. For he had never learnt to be lazy. Life had always consisted of long periods of overwork followed by brief periods of complete rest. And this business of trying to combine the two was a failure. His nerves got worse instead of better. Although it was nearly a year since his accident, he began to have violent pains in the back of his head. Even when the pains ceased, he could hardly bear anything touching his head, whether it was a hat or a pillow or the back of an armchair. Noise was a torture to him. Especially the noise of a crowd of people talking, or of applause at a concert, or the sound of a train coming into an underground station. He dreaded having to cross the road in the middle of the London traffic, and he would stand for a long time at the edge of the pavement, silently holding a most rational argument with himself, before he could gather enough courage to cross over to the other side.

Sleeplessness was an old enemy. But worse than the sleepless nights were the nights when he dreamed such outrageous dreams. He was familiar with all the nightmares that overwork can bring: he knew what it felt like to hear the music he had rehearsed during the day being played over and over in the night, with always the same mistakes in the same places, and the sopranos getting sharp in one bar and the 'cellos hurrying in the next. And he knew the agony of struggling in his sleep to get to the Queen's Hall for a rehearsal that had already begun, or arriving at Morley for a concert and finding that none of the orchestral parts had been brought. But these new nightmares were far worse, and he was haunted by dreams that sent him shuddering into a cold sweat. Not even their utter improbability helped to alleviate the aftermath of horror.

He spent his free days sitting huddled over the fire, sinking lower and lower into a grey region where thought and feeling had ceased to exist, and the spirit itself was numb.

GUSTAV HOLST: *Imogen Holst*

Romance

A piece or song of a 'romantic' nature, usually moderate in tempo and emotional, sometimes sentimental in style. There is no prescribed form, but it is, as a rule, fairly short and in the character of a song, generally contemplative and sometimes narrative in tone.

Clara Schumann

Romance

'IF MUSIC BE THE FOOD OF LOVE . . .' Maybe it is, although I can think of a great deal of music that has less than aphrodisiac qualities. Soft lights and sweet music are the traditional setting for seduction, however, and I suppose it is fair to admit that the right type of music can at any rate be conducive to relaxation or (occasionally) stimulate passion. I recall the glorious scene in *The Seven-Year Itch* when Tom Ewell put on a record of the *Second Rachmaninoff Piano Concerto*, hoping to seduce Marilyn Monroe the while. She listened earnestly for a moment or two and then, with a minute frown, asked, 'When do we get to the vocal?'

In this section I am concerned not with the power of music to stimulate love but with the way in which musicians have expressed love in words. Surprisingly enough, there is a marked lack of really worthwhile love-letters; expressions of affection were normally couched in somewhat formal terms in the eighteenth and nineteenth centuries; twentieth-century lovers use the telephone. Mozart wrote a number of enchanting letters to his wife, and I have included one for the particularly touching way in which he describes the little rituals he observed with her picture. Even so, he ends the letter formally, W A Mozart, which seems surprising to our eyes.

The wild, wild letter from Berlioz to Ferdinand Hiller describes the total frenzy of his love for Harriet Smithson, the actress whom he was to marry, against all the odds. It was, as anyone could have prophesied, an unfortunate match, but Berlioz was the type of person for whom love could never be cosy or undemanding; this letter admirably conveys the burning intensity of his passion.

If the so-called *Heiligenstadt Testament* of Beethoven is the supreme manifestation of despair in a composer, the three short letters 'To the immortal beloved' have become equally famous for a different reason. The fascinating enigma here is that nobody knows who he was writing to, for they were discovered in a secret drawer in his wardrobe, never having been despatched. Much scholarship has been devoted to deciding the identity of the mysterious lady; it is generally thought to have been the Countess Theresa Von Brunswick, but other possibilities are the Countess Giulietta Guicciardi or Amalie Sebald. Beethoven was susceptible, quick to yield to infatuation, but easily hurt. His love-life was far from happy.

The romance of Robert and Clara Schumann was in a quite different category. Despite ferocious opposition from Clara's father, Schumann finally achieved his longed-for goal and married her. Her ambitions for him may not have been entirely beneficial, for she encouraged him to venture into fields which were not his ideal métier. Of their mutual love there can be no doubt, however, and the two letters I have chosen show the same lyrical tenderness that Schumann was to express so magically in the songs that flowed from his pen during this period.

My last excerpt is a curiosity, a letter from Caruso to his wife, Dorothy, in which he wrestles nobly with the English language which he was trying to master for her benefit. (She was an American girl whom he married when she was twenty-five years old and he was in his mid-forties.) For three years they were blissfully happy, and then he contracted pleurisy and died. Under the circumstances, can there be a more touching letter than this one?

Mozart to his wife

DEAREST, MOST BELOVED LITTLE WIFE!

We expected to reach Dresden after dinner on Saturday, but we did not arrive until yesterday, Sunday, at two o'clock in the afternoon, as the roads were so bad. All the same I went yesterday to the Neumanns, where Madame Duschek is staying, in order to deliver her husband's letter. Her room is on the third floor beside the corridor and from it you can see anyone who is coming to the house. When I arrived at the door, Herr Neumann was already there and asked me to whom he had the honour to speak. 'That I shall tell you in a moment,' I replied, 'but please be so kind as to call Madame Duschek, so that my joke may not be spoilt.' But at the same moment Madame Duschek stood before me, for she had recognised me from the window and had said at once: 'Why, here comes someone who is very like Mozart.' Well, we were all delighted. There was a large party, consisting entirely of ugly women, who by their charm, however, made up for their lack of beauty. The Prince and I are going to breakfast there today; we shall then see Neumann and then the chapel. Tomorrow or the day after we shall leave for Leipzig. After receiving this letter you must write to Berlin, Poste Restante. I trust that you got my letter from Prague. All the Neumanns and the Duscheks send their greetings to you and also to my brother-in-law, Lange, and his wife.

Dearest little wife, if only I had a letter from you! If I were to tell you all the things I do with your dear portrait, I think that you would often laugh. For instance, when I take it out of its case, I say, 'Good-day, Stanzerl! – Good-day, little rascal, pussy-pussy, little turned-up nose, little bagatelle, Schluck and Druck', and when I put it away again, I let it slip in very slowly, saying all the time, 'Nu-Nu-Nu-Nu!' with the peculiar *emphasis* which this word so full of meaning demands, and then just at the last, quickly, 'Good night, little mouse, sleep well'. Well, I suppose I have been writing something very foolish (to the world at all events); but to us who love each other so dearly, it is not foolish at all. Today is the sixth day since I left you and by Heaven! it seems a year. I expect you will have some difficulty here and there in reading my letter, because I am writing in a hurry and therefore rather badly. Adieu, my only love! The carriage is waiting. This time I do not say: 'Hurrah – the carriage has come at last', but '*male*'. Farewell, and love me for ever as I love you. I kiss you a million times most lovingly and am ever your husband who loves you tenderly.

W A MOZART
THE LETTERS OF MOZART & HIS FAMILY: *Emily Anderson*

Berlioz to Ferdinand Hiller

My dear Ferdinand!
I must write to you again this evening —— this letter will perhaps be no happier than the others. . . . . . . But no matter ——
Can you tell me what is this overwhelming might of emotion, this *capacity for suffering* that is killing me? . . . . . .
—— . . . .
Let us not groan! . . .
my fire is going out, wait a moment ——
O my friend, do you know? . . . . to relight it I have burnt the manuscript of my *prose elegy*! . . . . . , always tears, sympathetic tears, I see Ophelia shedding them, I hear her tragic voice, the rays from her sublime eyes consume me.
O my friend, I am so unhappy! inexpressibly unhappy!
I have spent some time drying the floods that have fallen from my eyes . . . . . . while I saw Beethoven looking at me severely, Spontini, healed of his woes, regarding me with pity and indulgence —— and Weber, who seems to whisper in my ear like a familiar spirit, inhabiting a happy sphere where he awaits me to console me.
All this is mad —— completely mad, for a domino player in the Café de la Régence, or a Member of the Institut.
No, I still want to live ——
music is a heavenly art, nothing surpasses it but true love —— the one will perhaps make me as unhappy as the other, but at least I shall have lived
        suffering, it is true ——
        with madness, cries, and tears
        but I should have ———————————
        NOTHING
My dear Ferdinand! . . . . I have found in you all the signs of true friendship, my own for you is also true, but I fear it will never bring you the calm happiness that one finds far from the volcanoes ——
absolutely beside myself,
incapable of saying anything
RATIONAL
today it is a year since I saw HER for the last time ——— oh! unhappy woman! how I loved you . . . . trembling I write, HOW I LOVE YOU!
If there is another world shall we find each other again? . . .

Shall I ever see Shakespeare?

Will she know me?.... Will she understand the poetry of my love?.....
oh! *Juliet, Ophelia, Belvidera, Jane Shore,* names that hell repeats unceasingly........

truly;

I am a most unhappy man, a being almost alone in the world... an animal crushed under an imagination it cannot support, devoured by an illimitable love that is rewarded only with indifference and scorn; yes! but I have known certain musical geniuses, I have laughed in the gleam of their lightnings and I gnash my teeth at the mere remembrance.

Oh! sublime ones! sublime ones! annihilate me! summon me to your golden clouds! deliver me!........

Reason says to me

'Be tranquil, fool, in a few years there will be no more question of your agonies than of what you call the genius of Beethoven, the passionate sensibility of Spontini, the dreamy imagination of Weber, the colossal power of Shakespeare!

'Go, go Henriette Smithson
    and   Hector Berlioz
will be reunited in the oblivion of the tomb, which will not prevent other unhappy ones from SUFFERING AND DYING.....'

MEMOIRS OF HECTOR BERLIOZ: *Edited by Ernest Newman*

Beethoven to his beloved

July, 1812.
On the 6th July in the morning.

MY ANGEL, MY ALL, MY VERY SELF,

Just a few words today, and indeed in pencil – (with thine) only till tomorrow is my room definitely engaged. What an unworthy waste of time in such matters – why this deep sorrow where necessity speaks. Can our love endure otherwise than through sacrifices, through restraint in longing? Canst thou help not being wholly mine, can I, not being wholly thine? Oh! gaze at nature in all its beauty, and calmly accept the inevitable – love demands everything, and rightly so. *Thus is it for me with thee, for thee with me,* only thou so easily forgettest, that I must live for myself and for thee – were we wholly united thou wouldst feel this painful fact as little as I should – my journey was terrible. I arrived here only yesterday morning at four o'clock, and as they were short of horses, the mail-coach selected another route, but what an awful road; at the last stage but one I was warned against travelling by night; they frightened me with a wood, but that only spurred me on – and I was wrong, the coach must needs break down, the road being dreadful, a swamp, a mere country road; without the postillions I had with me, I should have stuck on the way. Esterhazi, by the ordinary road, met with the same fate with eight horses, as I with four – yet it gave me some pleasure, as successfully overcoming any difficulty always does. Now for a quick change from without to within; we shall probably soon see each other, besides, today I cannot tell thee what has been passing through my mind during the past few days concerning my life – were our hearts closely united, I should not do things of this kind. My heart is full of the many things I have to say to thee – ah! – there are moments in which I feel that speech is powerless – cheer up – remain my true, my only treasure, my all!!! As I to thee. The gods must send the rest, what for us must be and ought to be.

Thy faithfull,
LUDWIG

Monday evening, July 6.

THOU sufferest, thou my dearest love. I have just found out that the letters must be posted very early Mondays, Thursdays – the only days when the post goes from here to K. Thou sufferest – Ah! Where I am, art thou also with me; I will arrange for myself and Thee. I will manage so that I can live with thee; and what a life!!! But as it is!!! without thee. Persecuted here and there by the kindness of men, which I little deserve, and as little care to deserve. Humility of man towards man – it pains me – and when I think of myself in connection with the universe, what am I and what is He who is named the Greatest; and still this again shows the divine in man. I weep when I think that probably thou wilt only get the first news from me on Saturday evening. However much thou lovest me, my love for thee is stronger, but never conceal thy thoughts from me. Goodnight. As I am taking the baths I must go to bed. O God – so near! so far! Our love, is it not a true heavenly edifice, firm as heavens vault.

Good morning on July 7.

WHILE still in bed, my thoughts press to thee, my Beloved One, at moments with joy, and then again with sorrow, waiting to see whether fate will take pity on us. Either I must live wholly with thee or not at all. Yes, I have resolved to wander in distant lands, until I can fly to thy arms, and feel that with thee I have a real home; with thee encircling me about, I can send my soul into the kingdom of spirits. Yes, unfortunately, it must be so. Calm thyself, and all the more since thou knowest my faithfulness towards thee, never can another possess my heart, never – never – O God, why must one part from what one so loves, and yet my life in V. at present is a wretched life. Thy love has made me one of the happiest and, at the same time, one of the unhappiest of men – at my age I need a quiet, steady life – is that possible in our

situation? My Angel, I have just heard that the post goes every day, and I must therefore stop so that you may receive the letter without delay. Be calm, only by calm consideration of our existence can we attain our aim to live together – be calm – love me – today – yesterday – what tearful longing after thee – thee – thee – my life – my all – farewell – Oh, continue to love me – never misjudge the faithful heart
Of thy beloved
L
Ever thine
Ever mine
Ever each other's

THE COMPOSER IN LOVE (*Beethoven*): *Cyril Clarke*

Robert Schumann to Clara

I HAVE been sitting here a whole hour. Indeed, I meant to spend the whole evening writing to you, but no words would come. Sit down beside me now, slip your arm round me, and let us gaze peacefully, blissfully, into each other's eyes.

This world holds two lovers.
It is just striking the third quarter.
They are singing a chorale in the distance.
Tell me, do you know those two lovers? How happy we are, Clara! Let us kneel together, Clara, my Clara, so close that I can touch you, in this solemn hour.

On the morning of the 1st, 1838.

What a heavenly morning! All the bells are ringing; the sky is so golden and blue and clear – and before me lies your letter. I send you my first kiss, beloved.

THE COMPOSER IN LOVE (*Schumann*): *Cyril Clarke*

Enrico Caruso to Dorothy

MY DORO SWEETHEART:

It is very hot here, but everything is very cold around me. Why? I will tell you. I was accostumated with somebody who was near me all the time, and make the atmosphere full of sweetness and gladness. There was the moment when I steel a kiss with afraid of somebody who don't exist! There was a door which open slowly and a beautiful face came through and say, 'I am here'.

Now all these things are far away from me, and my life is like a piece of meat in the ice-box.

I have very hard time with all the people around me and I don't see how I can get over. They are so stupid and at same time noughty. More I do, more they serve me bad. Punzo is the limit! He try to put Mario in bad light with me and there is fight every moment between everybody, included myself.

It seams that God give me lots of patience to support everyone of this people. The only moment which I am quite is when I am here to write to you, or when I am enclosed in the bath.

Nevermaind! We born for working and for suffrence, and we must took the life as God send to us.

I think is the weather which is so bad, storm, and raining with lots lightning and tunner. Mario have pain in the hand. Zirato in diet, and Fucito also with his head. Punzo live in his ignorency, and so this is the life which we go on and you can imagine how I feel!

My people, perhaps on the bottom of the heart, are not bad, but they don't want any remark. For exemple, last night I made some mistake in the duet with Dulcamara; mistake that was easy to put me at the place if Fucito were attentif. I make the remark and he answer in a way not convenient. At the end of the opera I realise the matter and said something against him. He was not in the dressing-room but Mario and Punzo was there. I dont think that Mario reported what I said but must be Punzo and the consequence was that this morning I had a discussion with Fucito and this thing nearly everyday happens.

But the season of Havana must finish and then everybody his own way.

Oh, my only! If you immagine how I miss you, you will forget everything in the world, even our sweet Gloria! I try to find how I can stop to sing and go near my adorable ones. I hope then, something will happen because I cannot support any more such a life.

Your
RICO

I hope the coming of Mimmi don't truble you – tell him to be a gentleman and not a boy.

ENRICO CARUSO: *Dorothy Caruso*

Images: II

Medieval organ

MORE IMAGES now, starting with the aristocrat of pianists, Artur Rubinstein. I heard him play the Tchaikovsky and the Brahms B^b concertos in the same concert, both flawlessly, and he as unruffled at the end as if he'd strolled across the park. John Ogdon I include for a recital I heard him give in Adelaide in which he conjured sounds from the piano that I'd never heard before; Barenboim for the fun we've shared; Boulanger for her tireless devotion to music; Menuhin because of what he brought us during the war; Milstein and Oistrakh for elegance and mastery; Julian

Bream for being such a lad; the Amadeus because we were all friends when they started; Rostropovich because he is probably the most fully equipped musician of our time; Jacqueline du Pré for her phrasing; Dennis Brain for reading *Autosport* during rehearsals; Gervase de Peyer for playing my favourite woodwind instrument so perfectly; and Albert Schweitzer because he was a great human being.

As for the two photographs of young musicians, they are included for a more personal reason. In 1967 I wrote a mammoth work for the Norwich Triennial Festival; it was performed by over 500 schoolchildren in a most memorable manner. I include some of them in this book to stand in for all the aspiring instrumentalists who give part of their lives to music.

THE PHOTOGRAPHERS: Zoë Dominic—*John Ogdon; David Oistrakh; Nathan Milstein*

Godfrey Macdomnic—*Daniel Barenboim and Antony Hopkins; Gervase de Peyer*

Lotte Meitner-Graf—*Artur Rubinstein; Yehudi Menuhin; Mstislav Rostropovich; Jacqueline du Pré; Julian Bream; Albert Schweitzer*

Axel Poignant—*Nadia Boulanger*

'Eastern Daily Press'—*Young Norwich musicians*

Permission to reproduce the photograph of Dennis Brain has been kindly given by EMI Records; we are also grateful to them for allowing us to use several photographs taken for them by Godfrey Macdomnic

ARTUR RUBINSTEIN

JOHN OGDON

DANIEL BARENBOIM and ANTONY HOPKINS

NADIA BOULANGER

YEHUDI MENUHIN

NATHAN MILSTEIN

DAVID OISTRAKH

JULIAN BREAM

AMADEUS QUARTET

MSTISLAV ROSTROPOVICH

JACQUELINE DU PRÉ

DENNIS BRAIN

GERVASE DE PEYER

YOUNG NORWICH MUSICIANS REHEARSE 'A TIME FOR GROWING'

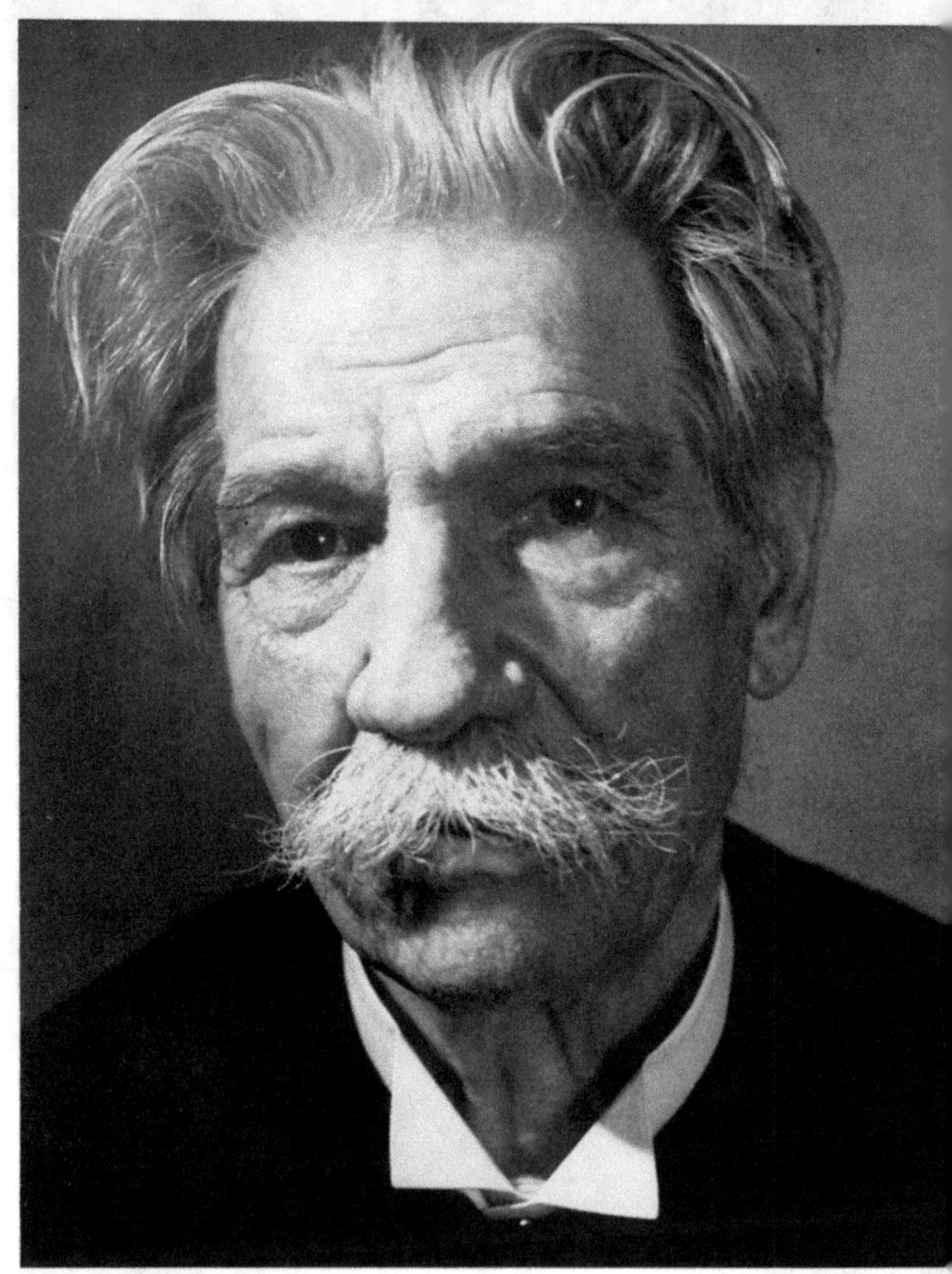

ALBERT SCHWEITZER

Danse Macabre

Not strictly a musical form, and consequently not mentioned as such in *Everyman's Dictionary*, it has been used by several composers as the title of atmospheric pieces, of a supposedly macabre kind.

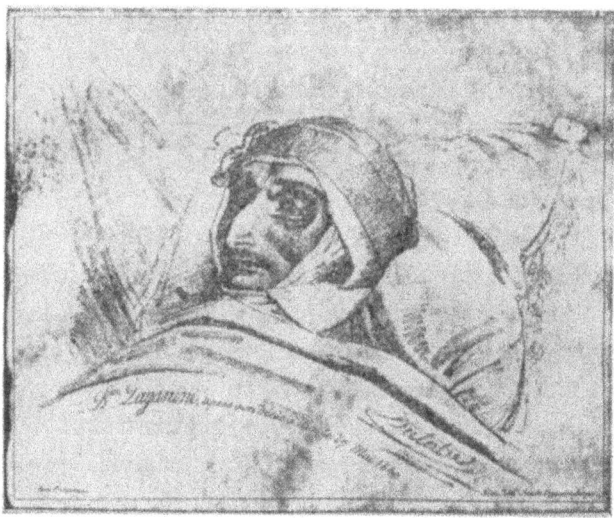

Paganini on his death-bed

Danse Macabre

DEATH HELD a morbid fascination for the nineteenth-century Romantic writer, a fascination which affected the musicians as well. Liszt's *Todtentanz* is only one of many pieces he wrote that were concerned with death. Berlioz tells us a strange story of how he watched the funeral of a young Italian bride, and subsequently bribed the verger to let him go into the chapel where she lay. Moved by her beauty, he impulsively knelt beside her and kissed her hand. Perhaps the extraordinary power and intensity of his music for the scene in Juliet's tomb, where Romeo seems to go out of his mind with despair, reflects something of his own feelings at the time. It was Paganini most of all whose presence seemed to suggest sinister powers; a legend circulated that he had served twenty years as a galley slave for murdering his mistress, when, in fact, he had merely been a slave to his violin. The somewhat exotic section which now follows is designed to reflect something of this preoccupation with death.

First, we have an eyewitness account of Paganini's appearance at a concert, leading to the extraordinary tale of his death and the subsequent journeyings of his corpse. Berlioz in the dissecting-room has always been a favourite passage of mine; his parents intended him to take up medicine, and like a good son, he tried to come to terms with a career which, understandably, lacked appeal. Lastly, and again I draw on Berlioz, we have the splendid story of the decision to avenge himself on his fiancée for her treachery in becoming engaged to another. When Berlioz left Paris for Italy, having at last gained the coveted Prix de Rome, he was in love with a girl called Camille Moke, who taught the piano at the same school at which he taught the guitar. Her mother had publicly referred to him as her son-in-law; protestations of undying love had been exchanged. Once in Rome, Berlioz settled down to enjoy a new existence among sympathetic companions; but as the weeks passed he received no word from his beloved. Finally her mother wrote to say that Camille was going to marry Pleyel, the piano maker. Berlioz's reaction is described in one of the most entertaining episodes in his book.

Paganini takes the stage

AND NOW it was indeed Paganini who approached us. He wore a dark grey overcoat, reaching down to his feet, and making him appear very tall. His long, black hair fell upon his shoulders in wild locks, and, like a frame, encompassed his pale, corpse-like face. . . . A short, self-complacent person in plain attire tripped along at his side. His face, although florid, was full of wrinkles. He wore a light grey coat, with steel buttons, and bowed in every direction with most excruciating politeness, while he, now and then, cast half-fearful, half-insipid glances at the sombre figure walking at his side, serious and wrapt in meditation. It reminded one of Faust and Wagner, walking before the gates of Leipzig. Lyser made me take particular notice of Paganini's long and measured step. 'Does it not,' he asked, 'seem as if he still had the iron bar of the galley slave between his legs? He will never get rid of that prison gait. Do you observe with what contemptuous irony he looks down upon his companion, whenever the latter annoys him with his dull and prosy questions? He cannot get rid of him. A bloody compact binds him to this servant, who is none other than Satan himself. The ignorant imagine his companion to be the dramatist and anecdotist Harrys of Hanover, and believe that Paganini carries him along in his travels that he may attend to the financial management of his concerts. They do not know that Satan has merely borrowed the form of Mr George Harrys, and that, along with other trash, the soul of that poor creature will remain locked up in a chest in Hanover, until the devil returns its carnal envelope, when, in the nobler guise of a black poodle, he will accompany his master Paganini through the world. . . .'

At last a sombre figure, which seemed to have risen from the dark regions, appeared on the stage. It was Paganini in full evening dress. His black coat and vest were of some such horrible cut as infernal etiquette prescribes at the court of Proserpine. The black pantaloons flapped about his legs most wildly. His long arms seemed still longer when he made his strange obeisance to the audience, and bent so far forward that the bow in one hand and the violin in the other almost touched the floor. There was something so terribly wooden and so foolishly animal in the angular bendings of his body, that his bowing produced a great desire to laugh outright. But his pale face, rendered still more deathlike by the glaring lights of the orchestra, seemed so supplicating and so full of shy timidity that shuddering compassion suppressed the desire.

LISZT: *Sacheverell Sitwell*

Paganini: the long, last journey

HIS ENCOUNTER with Berlioz on the concert platform was the last public act of Paganini. His disease developed so rapidly that it was evident he was dying, and the doctors advised his removal to the warmer climate of the south if he was to live through the winter. He spent some months on his way south living in the house of an Englishman with the curiously modern name of Douglas Loveday. I have been unable to discover anything whatever about this individual, except the fact that his hospitality involved him in a lawsuit. He charged Paganini, who must have been part of the time a paying guest, with not contributing his full share of the expenses, and Paganini countercharged with an account for alleged violin lessons given by himself to Loveday's daughter. He also charged Loveday with introducing a doctor to him in order to run up a bill for his own benefit.

From this curious household Paganini removed to Marseilles, whence he was driven by his frayed nerves to Genoa, his birthplace; and from Genoa he fled, as before death, to Nice, where he spent his last few weeks on earth. Here, his love of economy, even in his ultimate moments, made him take up his lodging in two rooms in a mean street. He ate nothing, drank nothing, and had no need of luxuries.

His condition of debility became worse and worse. He was wracked by a terrible cough and suffered from fearful spasms of pain. He died, at last, on May 27, 1840, and, considering the strange rumours with which all his living acts were surrounded, it is no surprise to be told that, on the night before he died, Paganini stretched out his hand for his violin and played for a whole hour, or more. It is no surprise, too, to be told that a friend, the Comte de Cessole, who knew him well, declared that this improvisation during the last hours was the most remarkable feat of his whole life.

But death did not lay his soul to rest. His body led what can only be described as a tormented life, from the very moment that he died. It lay in state on a platform, with aquiline features and glassy eyes, pallid and horrible to behold. A white cotton nightcap, held in place by a blue riband across his forehead, decorated his head; while a white cravat failed to conceal the bandage which kept his jaws closed. There are lithographs to be seen which show the features of Paganini in this ghastly travesty.

A few days later, when it had been embalmed, his body, dressed in the black coat and trousers in which he had appeared on the concert platform, was put into a coffin which had a glass pane above his face. And a dealer in second-hand objects offered the Comte de Cessole, who had been appointed trustee for Achillino, the sum of thirty thousand francs in order to exhibit the corpse in England.

Meanwhile, the clergy had protested against Christian burial for the body. It was alleged that he had not died as a Christian, and that he had committed offences which put him outside the pale of the Church. The coffin was, therefore, taken directly from the house where he died and placed in the waiting-room of the Lazaretto of Villefranche. This was the leper-house where travellers who arrived by sea were forced to spend many weary weeks before they were allowed to enter France. The body remained here for a month, and so many complaints were received because of its state of putrefaction that another move was decided upon, and it was buried in the ground nearby. Once more there were complaints and, this time, Comte de Cessole set out to bury the body, himself. It was interred, by night, at the foot of a Saracen round tower, by the Cap St Hospice, on the property of a friend of the Count. Hastily, so hastily that the burial was incomplete, the coffin was pushed into the ground by the side of a foetid rivulet formed by the refuse from a neighbouring olive-oil factory. A year or so later, the Baron Achillino decided to take his father's body back to Genoa, but there was an outbreak of cholera at Marseilles, whence it had to be shipped, and so his project could not be realised, and the vessel had to put back to Marseilles. It was, therefore, buried once more on the Ile St Ferréol, one of the little Iles dés Lerins, of Hyères, and to this day the ditch in which the coffin was laid is known as Paganini's ditch.

At length, in 1844, the Duchess of Parma, Marie Louise, the widow of Napoleon, gave permission for the body of Paganini to be brought into her dominions, and, Christian burial being still refused to it, the coffin was taken first to the Villa Polevra, a Paganini property, and afterwards, to the Villa Gajona, the estate that the Baron Achillino had inherited from his father. There it remained till 1853, when it was exhumed and subjected to a fresh process of embalming.

Many years later, in 1876, the Baron Achillino prevailed upon the religious authorities to allow a service to be held for his father in the Madonna della Steccata, a church which belonged to the Knights of St George. They were an Order of Chivalry belonging to the Duchy of Parma, and Paganini had been a Knight of the Order. The ceremony was presided over by a nephew, the Baron Attila, yet another member of this sinister family of Barons.

Even now, the troubles of that poor shrivelled body were not over. In 1893, a Czech violinist, Ondriczek, who died as lately as 1922, persuaded the Baron Achillino, then an old man of seventy, to open the coffin in order that he might see the body. And finally, in 1896, what is described as 'urgent necessity' made the authorities open the coffin once more. It is said that fearful as was its state of decay and putrefaction the features of Paganini were still recognisable, but his black coat was in tatters, and the lower part of his body was no more than a heap of bones.

When the Baron Achillino died, and whether he has left any descendants, I have been unable to discover, but, at least, the body of his father has been left undisturbed since then. Fifty-six years had elapsed, by 1896, from the time he died and, as his age at death was fifty-six, it can be said that this kind of ghastly shadow life, these fearful and sinister adventures of his corpse, continued for just the same span of time as his life upon earth.

LISZT: *Sacheverell Sitwell*

Berlioz in the charnel-house

WHEN I ARRIVED in Paris in 1822 with my fellow-student, Alphonse Robert, I gave myself up entirely to preparation for the career which had been forced upon me, and faithfully kept the promise given to my father at parting. But I was sorely tried when Robert announced one morning that he had bought a *subject* (a corpse), and asked me to accompany him to the dissecting-room at the Hospital *de la Pitié*. When I entered that fearful human charnel-house, littered with fragments of limbs, and saw the ghastly faces and cloven heads, the bloody cesspool in which we stood, with its reeking atmosphere, the swarms of sparrows fighting for scraps, and the rats in the corners gnawing bleeding vertebrae, such a feeling of horror possessed me that I leapt out of the window, and fled home as though Death and all his hideous crew were at my heels. It was twenty-four hours before I recovered from the shock of this first impression, utterly refusing to hear the words anatomy, dissection, or medicine, and firmly resolved to die rather than enter the career which had been forced upon me.

Robert wasted much eloquence in combating my disgust and demonstrating the absurdity of my plans. But he finally induced me to make another effort, and I consented to return to the hospital and face the dread scene once more. How strange! I now merely felt cold disgust at the sight of the same things which had before filled me with such horror. I had become as callous to the revolting scene as a veteran soldier. It was all over. I even found some pleasure in rummaging in the gaping breast of an unfortunate corpse for the lungs, with which to feed the winged inhabitants of that charming place.

'Well done!' cried Robert, laughing; 'you are growing quite humane! *Aux petits des oiseaux tu donnes la pâture.*'

'*Et ma bonté s'étend sur toute la nature,*' I retorted, casting a shoulder-blade to a great rat who was staring at me with famished eyes. And so I went on with my course of anatomy, stoically, if not enthusiastically. I was strongly attracted by Professor Amussat, who seemed possessed by the same passion for medicine that I felt for music, and was an artist in anatomy. The fame of this bold scientific explorer has spread all over Europe, and his discoveries have aroused the wonder and opposition of the learned world. Day and night are not long enough for his researches, and, although exhausted by his labours, he pursues his dangerous way with dogged determination. All his traits are those of a man of genius: I often see him, and I love him.

Berlioz's mission of vengeance

IT TOOK ME a long time to get used to this novel kind of existence, and I had something on my mind which prevented me from taking any interest either in surrounding objects or in the society into which I was thus suddenly thrown.

I expected to find letters from Paris waiting for me, and for the next three weeks I watched for them with ever-increasing anxiety.

Unable any longer to control my desire to fathom the reason of this mysterious silence, I determined to return to Paris at once, despite M Horace Vernet's friendly remonstrances, and his warning that he would be obliged to strike my name off the Academy lists if I persisted in my rash resolve. On my way back I was detained for a week in Florence by an attack of quinsy, which confined me to my bed. While there I made the acquaintance of the Danish architect, Schlick, a capital fellow, who is thought very highly of by connoisseurs. During my illness I re-scored the *Scène du Bal,* in my *Symphonie fantastique,* and added the present coda. It was almost finished when I was allowed out for the first time, and I at once proceeded to the post-office for my letters. The packet which was handed to me contained a letter the tenor of which was inconceivably painful to a man of my years and temperament. I was beside myself with passion, and shed tears from sheer rage; but I made up my mind on the spot what to do. My duty was clear. I must at once proceed to Paris, and kill two guilty women and an innocent man. After that, it would, of course, be incumbent on me to commit suicide. I arranged all the details on the spot. Knowing me as they did, my reappearance in Paris would be looked for.... A complete disguise and the greatest precautions were therefore necessary; and I rushed off to Schlick to whom I had already confided my story.

'Good God! what is the matter?' he cried, when he saw my white face.

'Look and see,' I said, handing him the letter.

'This is horrible!' he replied, when he had read it; 'what are you going to do?'

I knew that, if I told him my plan, he would try to dissuade me from carrying it out.

'What am I going to do? Why, return to France, of course; but to my father's house instead of to Paris.'

'That is right, my dear fellow; go home, and in time you will recover from the awful condition into which this unexpected blow has thrown you. Come, cheer up.'

'I will, but I must be off at once. I could not answer for myself tomorrow.'

'We can easily get you off tonight, for I have friends among the police and the postal officials. I will have your passport ready in two hours, and will get you a seat in the diligence which starts five hours hence. Go to your hotel and get ready, and I will meet you there.'

Instead of following his advice, I betake myself to one of the quays of the Arno, where I knew there was a French modiste. I enter the shop, look at my watch, and say: 'It is now twelve o'clock, madame; I leave by the mail this evening, and I want to know if you can let me have, before five o'clock, a costume such as would be worn by a lady's-maid – robe, hat, green veil, and so on? I will pay you whatever you choose to ask.'

After a moment's consideration, it is arranged that I am to have what I want. I deposit part of the price, and return to the Hotel des Quatre Nations, on the opposite bank of the Arno.

I call the head porter.

'I am going to Paris at six o'clock this evening, Antoine, and I cannot take my trunk, so kindly look after it, and send it after me to my father's house as soon as you can. I have written down the address.'

I then took the score of the *Scène du Bal*, and, as the instrumentation of the coda was not quite completed, I wrote across it: 'I have not time to finish this; but, if the Paris Concert Society should take it into its head to perform this work during the ABSENCE of the author, I request Habeneck to double the passage for flutes in the bass octave, with the clarinets and horns, the last time the theme is introduced, and to write the chords which follow for full orchestra; that will do for the ending.'

I then seal it up, address it to Habeneck, and pack it in a bag with some clothes. I have a pair of double-barrelled pistols, which I load carefully, and two little bottles of laudanum and strychnine, which I examine and put in my pocket. Then, my mind being at rest with regard to my arsenal, I spend the remainder of my time in wandering about the streets of Florence, with the restless, disturbing demeanour of a mad dog.

At five I adjourn to my dressmaker's and try on my costume, which fits to perfection. In paying for it I put down twenty francs more than the price agreed; the girl at the desk tries to point out my mistake, but is deterred by her mistress, who hastily sweeps the gold into a drawer, saying: 'Leave the gentleman alone, you little stupid; don't you see that he is too busy to listen to your chatter? A thousand thanks, sir; I wish you success. You will look your part to perfection.' I smiled ironically, and she bowed me gracefully out of the shop.

At last it strikes six, and I bid farewell to my honest friend Schlick, who looks upon me as a lost sheep returning to the fold. I stow away my feminine apparel in one of the side pockets of the coach, give a parting glance at Cellini's Perseus, with the famous inscription, *Se quis te laeserit, ego tuus ultor ero* ('If any offend thee, I will avenge thee') and we are off.

We leave mile after mile behind us, but not a word passes between me and the courier. I had a great lump in my throat, and sat with my teeth tightly clenched, unable either to sleep or eat. About midnight, however, he said something to me about my pistols, which he prudently uncapped and hid under the cushions. He was afraid we might be attacked, and in that case, said he, it is much better to remain passive, unless you wish to be murdered.

'Just as you please,' I replied. 'I don't want to raise any difficulties, and I bear the brigands no grudge.'

My companion did not know what to make of me, and, as I had taken nothing but a little orange juice since we started, he began to regard me as scarcely human. When we arrived at Genoa I discovered that a fresh misfortune had befallen me, and that I had lost my female outfit. We had changed carriages at a village called Pietra Santa, and I had left my disguise behind.

'Fire and thunder!' I said, 'it looks as if some damned good angel were bent on hindering my purpose. But we shall see!'

I sent for a courier who could speak both French and Genoese, and asked him to take me to a dressmaker. It was nearly midday, and the next coach started at six. I demand a costume: impossible to finish one in so short a time. We go to another dressmaker, then to a third, and a fourth, without success. At last we find a woman who is willing to try; she accomplishes the task, and my disaster is repaired. Unluckily, however, upon examining my passport, the police take it into their heads that I am a carbonaro, a conspirator, a patriot, or Heaven knows what, refuse to visa my passport for Turin, and advise me to travel via Nice instead.

'Well, then, visa it for Nice, in Heaven's name! What do I care whether I pass through hell, so long as I pass?' ...

I don't know which of us was the greater fool, the police, who saw a revolutionist in every Frenchman, or I, who feared to set foot in Paris except disguised as a woman, lest my purpose should reveal itself in my face; forgetting, like an idiot, that I could have remained quietly in an hotel in Paris for a few hours and sent for any number of disguises at my leisure.

When people are possessed with any single idea they always fancy, in the drollest way, that everyone else is full of it too, and act upon the supposition.

Still in a rage, I set out on my way to Nice, rehearsing on the way every point of the little comedy I intended to play in Paris. I would go to my friends' house, about nine o'clock in the evening, when the family would be assembled for tea, and send in to say that the Countess M's maid is waiting with an urgent message; I am shown into the drawing-room; I hand over a letter, and while it is being read, produce my pistol and blow out the brains, first of number one, and then of number two; and, seizing number three by the hair, throw off my disguise, and finish her off in the same manner, regardless of her shrieks. Then, before this concert of voices and instruments attracts attention, I hasten to deposit the contents of the remaining barrel in my own right temple; and if the pistol misses fire (which has happened before now), I shall at once resort to my small bottles. A charming comedy! It is really a great pity it was never put on the stage.

And yet there were moments when, in spite of my wrath, I could not help feeling sorry that my plans, excellent as they otherwise were, involved my own suicide. It seemed hard to bid farewell to life and art, to go down to posterity merely as a brute who could not get on in the world; to leave my unfinished symphony, and all the other greater works which were seething in my brain. ... Ah! ... it is ... And then suddenly my fell purpose gained the upper hand once more. ... No, no, no, no, no, they must all die, they must, and they shall! ... And the horses trotted on, bearing me nearer and nearer to France. It was night, and we were travelling along the Corniche road, which is cut out of the steep precipice of rocks overhanging the sea. For more than an hour I had been indulging in bright dreams of what the future might have had in store for me when the postilion stopped the horses to put on the drag, and suddenly, through the stillness, the sound of roaring breakers dashing against the foot of the precipice broke on my ear. The raging fury of the waves raised a corresponding tempest in my breast, fiercer and deadlier than any I had yet experienced. I sat like a raving lunatic, clutching the seat with both hands, ready to spring out and dash myself over the cliff, and uttered such a wild, fierce yell that the unfortunate conductor started away in horror, evidently regarding me as a devil doomed to wander on the earth with a piece of the true cross in his possession.

It must be admitted that, although I was not yet out of danger, the fever was intermittent. When I became aware of this, I reasoned thus with myself – not altogether foolishly, considering the place and the hour: Supposing, in one of these lucid intervals (that is to say, the moments in which life smiled to me; you see I was virtually vanquished), supposing, in one of these lucid intervals, I said, I were to prepare myself for the next attack by tying myself up in some way and having something to cling to . . . I might arrive at some . . . definite . . . conclusion. Let me see.

We were passing through a little village on the seashore (the sea was much calmer), and when we stopped to change horses I told the conductor to wait while I wrote a letter; I go into a little café and write a letter on a scrap of paper to the director of the Académie de Rome, asking M Horace Vernet to be so good as not to strike my name off the Academy lists, if he had not already done so, as I had not yet broken through the rules; and I gave him MY WORD OF HONOUR that I would not cross the Italian frontier until I had received his answer, which I would await at Nice.

Now that I had bound myself by a promise I went on my way most peacefully, feeling that if I were expelled from the Academy and launched penniless on the world, I could still fall back upon my murderous plan; and then . . . I suddenly found out that . . . I was hungry, having eaten nothing since I left Florence. Oh, beneficent nature! I was evidently cured!

                MEMOIRS OF HECTOR BERLIOZ: *Edited by Ernest Newman*

Interlude II

Title page of *Parthenia*

Poets' corner

AGAINST ALL EXPECTATION, there is a notable lack of good poetry about music. Many a promising opening line such as –

'Music, when soft voices die . . .'

turns out to have little relevance to music in the long run. Other poems may describe the poet's mistress playing the lute, but here the music is more of an excuse than the substance of the poem. In the event, my choice has not always been governed by wholly musical factors.

I begin with a poem that occurs in a volume called *Parthenia*, the first music for the virginals that was ever printed in this country. The title-page shows a demure lady, presumably a virgin, playing upon the keyboard with a notable economy of fingers. On the inside page is a poem that cleverly incorporates the names of several of the leading composers of the day – BYRD, BULL and ORLANDO GIBBONS, not to be confused with Orlando di Lasso.

Two examples of madrigal verse follow, the one by Thomas Bateson, the other by Samuel Danyel. Shakespeare must needs be included, and I have chosen what to my mind is the most beautiful of all his musical lyrics, though how much this is governed in my mind by its association with Vaughan Williams's perfect setting it would be hard to say. A rather different poem about Orpheus by Thomas Lisle is an astringent corrective towards any over-romantic tendencies.

On lute-strings Catt-eaten is a curiosity of great charm by an Oxford scholar and divine called Thomas Master or Masters – there is some doubt even about his name. It appears that he came down one morning to find that his cat had eaten the strings of his lute; the poem that he wrote in consequence shows a genuine affection for his pet.

Charles Lamb's diatribe against the whole family of musicians was written to William Ayrton, and must have been as much fun to write as it is to read.

I finish with an Ode written for a concert in aid of the Musicians' Benevolent Fund, St Cecilia's Day, 1949. No poet of our times has been a greater master of the 'occasional' piece than Christopher Hassall; we worked together on an opera for the choristers of Canterbury Cathedral, and I shall never forget the shock of hearing of his death when I chanced to switch on the car radio as I was driving round the Coventry by-pass. To lose a friend of such great charm was a heavy blow. I include his Prologue as a tribute to his memory.

Parthenia

  List to that sweet Recorder;
How daintily this Byrd his notes doth vary,
As if he were the Nightingall's own brother!
  Loe, where doth pace in order
A braver Bull, than did Europa cary:
Nay let all Europe showe me such an other,
  Orlando though was counted Musick's father;
Yet this Orlando parallels di Lasso:
Whose triple praise would tire a very Tasso.
  Then heere in one these three men heare ye rather
And praise thaire songes: and sing his praise who maried
These notes so well which they so sweetely varied.
     from PARTHENIA or the MAYDENHEAD of the first
     musicke that ever was printed for the VIRGINALLS. 1612

  Hark! hear you not a heavenly harmony?
    Is't Jove, think you, that plays upon the spheres?
  Heavens! is not this a heavenly melody,
    Where Jove himself a part in music bears?

  Now comes in a choir of nightingales.
  Mark how the nymphs and shepherds of the dales,
  How all do join together in the praise
  Of Oriana's life and happy days.

  Then sing ye shepherds and nymphs of Diana
  In Heaven lives Oriana.
          THOMAS BATESON

  Like as the lute delights, or else dislikes,
    As is his art that plays upon the same,
  So sounds my Muse according as she strikes
    On my heart strings, high tuned unto her fame.
  Her touch doth cause the warble of the sound,
    Which here I yield in lamentable wise,
  A wailing descant on the sweetest ground,
    Whose due reports give honour to her eyes.
  If any pleasing relish here I use,
    Then judge the world her beauty gives the same;
  Else harsh my style, untunable my Muse.
    Hoarse sounds the voice that praiseth not her name,

For no ground else could make the music such,
No other hand could give so sweet a touch.
                                    SAMUEL DANYEL

    Orpheus with his lute made trees,
    And the mountain tops that freeze,
        Bow themselves when he did sing:
    To his music plants and flowers
    Ever sprung; as sun and showers
        There had made a lasting spring.

    Every thing that heard him play
    Even the billows of the sea,
        Hung their heads, and then lay by.
    In sweet music is such art,
    Killing care and grief of heart,
        Fall asleep, or hearing die.
    KING HENRY THE EIGHTH, Act. III, Scene I: *Shakespeare*

On Orpheus going to hell for a wife

    When Orpheus went down to the regions below,
        Which men are forbidden to see,
    He tuned up his lyre, as our histories show,
        To set his Eurydice free.

    All hell was alarmed that a person so wise
        Should so rashly endanger his life,
    To venture so far: but how great the surprise
        When they found that he came for his wife!

    To find out a punishment due to the fault
        Old Pluto had puzzled his brain;
    But hell had no torments sufficient, he thought,
        So he gave him his wife back again.

    But pity succeeding engaged his heart,
        And, pleased with his playing so well,
    He took her again in regard of his art;
        Such merit has music in hell!
        THE CHAMPION (*Feb. 19, 1740*): *Thomas Lisle*

On lute-strings Catt-eaten

Are these the strings that poets feigne
Have clear'd the Ayre, and calm'd the mayne?
Charm'd wolves, and from the mountaine creasts
Made forests dance with all their beasts?
Could these neglected shreads you see
Inspire a Lute of Ivorie
And make it speake? Oh! think then what
Hath beene committed by my catt,
Who, in the silence of this night
Hath gnawne these cords, and marr'd them quite;
Leaving such reliques as may be
For fretts, not for my lute, but me.
Pusse, I will curse thee; may'st thou dwell
With some dry Hermit in a cell
Where Ratt neere peep'd, where mouse neere fedd,
And flyes goe supperlesse to bedd;
Or with some close-par'd Brother, where
Thoul't fast each Saboath in the yeare;
Or else, prophane, be hang'd on Munday,
For butchering a mouse on Sunday;
Or may'st thou tumble from some tower,
And misse to light upon all fower,
Taking a fall that may untie
Eight of nine lives, and let them flye;
Or may the midnight embers sindge
Thy daintie coate, or Jane beswinge
Thy hide, when she shall take thee biting
Her cheese clouts, or her house beshiting.
What, was there neere a ratt nor mouse,
Nor Buttery ope? nought in the house
But harmlesse Lutestrings could suffice
Thy paunch, and draw thy glaring eyes?
Did not thy conscious stomach finde
Nature prophan'd, that kind with kind
Should stanch his hunger? thinke on that,
Thou caniball, and Cyclops catt.
For know, thou wretch, that every string
Is a catt-gutt, which art doth spinne
Into a thread; and how suppose
Dunstan, that snuff'd the divell's nose,
Should bid these strings revive, as once
He did the calfe, from naked bones;

Or I, to plague thee for they sinne,
Should draw a circle, and beginne
To conjure, for I am, look to't,
An Oxford scholler, and can doo't.
Then with three setts of mapps and mowes,
Seaven of odd words, and motley showes,
A thousand tricks, that may be taken
From Faustus, Lambe, or Fryar Bacon:
I should beginne to call my strings
My catlings, and my mynikins;
And they recalled, straight should fall
To mew, to purr, to catterwaule
From puss's belly. Sure as death,
Pusse should be an Engastranith;
Pusse should be sent for to the king
For a strange bird, or some rare thing.
Pusse should be sought to farre and neere,
As she some cunning woman were.
Pusse should be carried up and downe,
From shire to shire, from Towne to Towne,
Like to the camell, Leane as Hagg,
The Elephant, or Apish negg,
For a strange sight; pusse should be sung
In Lousy Ballads, midst the Throng
At markets, with as good a grace
As Agincourt, or Chevy-chase.
The Troy-sprung Brittan would forgoe
His pedigree he chaunteth soe,
And singe that Merlin – long deceast –
Returned is in a nyne-liv'd beast.
   Thus, pusse, thou seest what might betyde thee;
But I forbeare to hurt or chide thee;
For may be pusse was melancholy
And so to make her blythe and jolly,
Finding these strings, shee'ld have a fitt
Of mirth; nay, pusse, if that were it,
Thus I revenge mee, that as thou
Hast played on them, I've plaid on you;
And as they touch was nothing fine,
Soe I've but scratch'd these notes of mine.

                    THOMAS MASTER (1603–1643)

Some cry up Haydn, some Mozart,
Just as the whim bites. For my part,
I do not care a farthing candle
For either of them nor for Handel.
Cannot a man live free and easy,
Without admiring Pergolesi?
Or thro' the world with comfort go,
That never heard of Doctor Blow?
So help me God, I hardly have;
And yet I eat, and drink, and shave,
Like other people if you watch it,
And know no more of Stave or Crotchet,
Than did the primitive Peruvians,
Or those old ante-queer-Diluvians
That lived in the unwash'd world with Tubal,
Before that dirty Blacksmith Jubal,
By stroke on anvil, or by summ'at,
Found out, to his great surprise, the gamut.
I care no more for Cimarosa,
Than he did for Salvator Rosa,
Being no painter; and bad luck
Be mine, if I can bear that Gluck.
Old Tycho Brahe, and modern Herschel,
Had something in 'em: but who's Purcel?[1]
The devil, with his foot so cloven,
For aught I care, may take Beethoven;
And, if the bargain does not suit,
I'll throw him Weber in to boot.
There's not the splitting of a splinter
To chuse 'twixt *him last named,* and Winter.
Of Doctor Pepusch old Queen Dido
Knew just as much, God knows, as I do,
I would not go four miles to visit
Sebastian Bach – or Batch – which is it?
No more I would for Bononcini.
As for Novello, and Rossini,
I shall not say a word to grieve 'em,
Because they're living. So I leave 'em!
            CHARLES LAMB – THE MUSIC LOVER'S MISCELLANY: *Eric Blom*

[1] *Lamb's incorrect spelling. The name is, of course, Purcell.*—AH

Ode written for a concert

The four winds blow unfettered round the earth.
From shore to shore impartially they send
Such flying news as all may comprehend,
Inklings of cold or budded Spring's rebirth.
Fresh from the rousing of some alien rose
    The South wind blows,
Waking a kindred summer in our trees.
    They, when their branches stir,
    Need no interpreter,
    To expound the breeze,
But all impelled by universal love
    In whispering concord move.
Bending one way, they incline their marshall'd rows
    Like well-strung bows
        On loud orchestral strings aslant
    That simultaneously glide
        Concerted in one chant,
Or only to confirm their unity divide.

Song, like the singing winds, through every land
    Utters what all may understand;
        They to the sluggish root
        Bidding the dust bear fruit,
    She to the mind within
    Where all mankind is kin
        Secretly breathing her profound
    Revivifying strain.
    Oh hark and hark again!
        Cecilia is a Sound.

    A vast unmeaning silence broke
    When first Cecilia spoke.
It was as though immortal hands,
Outstretched along the vague anonymous lands,
    Brought forth the splendours of a feast
    Low in a havock'd East,
And far away on glimmering down and lawn
Laid bare the first experiment of dawn.
    Again the stirring Word!
    And unaccustomed Stillness heard
        Minutely grow
        Infinite grass,

　　　　While over plain and mountain pass
　　　　　　The luminous grooving waters flow,
　　　　Earliest pilgrims of the Sea,
　　　　Shouting aloud in their felicity;
　　And April, quickening in the barren ground, replied
　　　　With flowers full-blown as for a Bride.

Ocean began, but grateful men prolong
　　　　The praise of Song,
Telling of one who to redeem his wife
　　　　Went singing all the way
　　　　Beyond the bounds of day
And all but sang her shadow into life.
　　Of David next they tell,
　　　Stripling of Israel.
He, summoned to the dangerous tent
Alone, put by all argument,
　　Trusting in Beauty to obey his call.
　　　　Invisibly she came,
　　　　　A Phantom and a Flame,
　　　　Lifting the lay till he
　　　　With valiant harmony
　　Shored up the giant shell that once was Saul.

Bright honours these! But we make bold to set
　　Our Saint a task, which to achieve would crown
Her victories with one more glorious yet,
　　And burst the trumpet of Renown.
To us, fair Spirit, who obscurely grope
　　For rescuing strand of rope
Or spar adrift on Time's distracted sea,
　　Restore, like lov'd Eurydice,
　　Radiant Delight long lost as she,
Or like her tears, the slaking dews of Hope.

　　Saint, Echo, Angel, Oh come soon,
With haunted lilies marvellously crowned
　　And bower'd in silence like the moon.
　　At once by sudden glimpse reveal
　　What else these fogs of battle must conceal –
The stern primeval purpose in our strife.
　　Flash on the fragmentary soul
　　One moment's image of the Whole;
　　And so consenting to take part

With us in thy celestial art,
Pour on the troubled heart
Effectual balm, and ease the ache of life.

The world on its jarred axis gyres and groans.
　　Faint hearts can only feel and quake,
　　Succumb at last, and break;
The stronger, still defiant, turn to stones.
　　Who but Cecilia can allay
　　The sickness of our day,
Or heal our planet of its hideous wound?
　　Music, the present help of them that pray,
Shall muster her solemnities of sound
　　And waft the rolling *Benedicite* away.

　　When all sane words are said,
　　Spurn'd, misinterpreted,
　　Love, even logic, dead,
No mortal wit availing,
　　Still shall there be one bond
　　Whereto all hearts respond;
Music shall come on wings of wonder sailing.
　　Wide as the winds that blow
　　Alike on friend and foe,
Serene above the world's continual brawl,
　　Thy voice shall still remain,
　　Dear Saint, when words are vain,
　　Chaos to quell again,
Silence our clash of tongues and conquer all.

　　　　WORDS BY REQUEST – *Christopher Hassall: Spoken in the Albert Hall by Sir Steuart Wilson at a concert in aid of the Musicians' Benevolent Fund, St Cecilia's Day, 1949*

Oratorio & Anthem

A vocal work, usually for solo voices and chorus with some kind of instrumental accompaniment and generally set to sacred words, often direct from the Bible or paraphrased from it, and at any rate nearly always treating a subject of a sacred character.

A composition for a church choir, with or without solo voices and accompaniment.

The anniversary festival of charity children at St Paul's

Oratorio & Anthem

FOR MANY OF US, church music constitutes one of our earliest musical memories. I well remember as a small child at a preparatory school spontaneously singing a descant in one of my favourite hymns. My boyish treble soared up to a high A on the words *Holy, holy, holy Lord* and followed my neighbours down to the end of the verse a third higher. The headmaster stopped the hymn in mid-flight, and angrily forbade me to indulge in such exhibitionism; nobody would believe that it was completely unpremeditated; the higher notes just burst out of me and I could not contain them. Later I was bitterly disappointed when a mastoid operation deprived me of the chance of singing the boy's solo in *Elijah*; I had it off to perfection, and was sure that the substitute who took my place would be inadequate. There was another keenly musical boy at school called Peter Lubbock, and the pair of us would sit together at Glee Club rehearsals; our greatest delight was when the music-master would say: 'Now let's hear it without Hopkins and Lubbock'; thirty faltering voices around us would grope uncertainly for the notes, producing a mewling and puking sound that worked wonders for our morale while shattering theirs. Thereafter, whether it was singing in a village choir in Hertfordshire, exploring madrigals under Michael Tippett's inspired direction at Morley College, or playing for the Bach Choir rehearsals, I have always had a soft spot for choral music.

I have chosen *Psalm 150* because when we sang it at school I used to wonder what sort of a noise the somewhat improbable orchestral combination that it specifies would make. There follows an extract of considerable historical importance, the long account of Mendelssohn's preparation of Bach's *St Matthew Passion*. It should be remembered that Mendelssohn was only twenty at the time, and that to have pushed through this great project against very considerable scepticism, not to say downright opposition, was a notable achievement. Devrient, the writer, was a close friend of Mendelssohn's, and his personal involvement gives his description a marvellous authenticity.

As for the Berlioz excerpt (that name again!), it gives me pleasure not only for its description of a rare ceremony, but also because I like to imagine him in London. I never cease to try to forge personal links between the composers I most love and myself, and I find I can do this more readily if I can stand in a building that they have once visited, or see some of their belongings. I treasure in my home letters by Berlioz, Brahms and Elgar, and on one occasion, a kindly soul pressed into my hand an envelope addressed by Mendelssohn to Sterndale Bennett.

My last two examples of choral singing are at the opposite end of the pole; one is an extract from Thomas Hardy's *Two in a Tower*, in which he describes with delightful wit and observation a choir practice in a small village church. It is of particular interest in that it coincides with the first introduction of the sol-fa method, and reflects the scepticism with which it was greeted by the choristers. The other also concerns itself with sol-fa, as taught to a reluctant schoolboy named Neville Cardus.

PSALM 150

Praise ye the LORD. Praise God in His sanctuary: praise Him in the firmament of His power.

2 Praise Him for His mighty acts: praise Him according to His excellent greatness.

3 Praise Him with the sound of the trumpet: praise Him with the psaltery and harp.

4 Praise Him with the timbrel and dance: praise Him with stringed instruments and organs.

5 Praise Him upon the loud cymbals: praise Him upon the high sounding cymbals.

6 Let every thing that hath breath praise the LORD. Praise ye the LORD.

On Mendelssohn's preparation of the 'St Matthew Passion'

I LONGED more and more ardently to sing the part of Christ in public, and with ever-increasing eagerness we expressed to each other the wish that it might be possible to perform the wonderful work. But all were dismayed, on the other hand, at the insurmountable difficulties, not only in the work itself, with its double orchestra and double chorus, but also in the punctiliousness of the Academy and the reserved, unco-operative attitude of Zelter. Moreover, it was seriously questioned whether the public would take to a work so utterly foreign to this world. In sacred concerts, a short movement by Bach might be accepted now and then as a curiosity enjoyed by only a few connoisseurs, but how would it be to have for an entire evening nothing but Sebastian Bach, whom the public conceived as unmelodious, mathematical, dry, and unintelligible? It seemed a rash undertaking.

Even the parents of Felix, who were nothing loath to see the problem of a revival of the Passion solved by their son, felt doubtful as to the result. Marx hesitated, and the old ladies of the Academy shook their heads. Felix so utterly disbelieved that it could be done that he replied to my entreaties, and those of the more courageous among our friends, Baur, Schubring, and Kugler, only with jest and irony. He offered to contribute to public performance by playing on a rattle and toy trumpet, painted the different phases through which the undertaking would have to pass in the most ludicrous colours, and especially pictured the temerity it would be for him, without any credentials and insignia of office, to attempt to move Berlin out of its time-honoured groove. So hopeless seemed the chance of reviving the *Passion* which had lain buried for a century, even amongst its truest worshippers.

I could not let the matter rest. One evening in January, 1829, after we had gone through the entire first part, Baur singing the Evangelist and Kugler the principal bass parts, and we had all gone home profoundly impressed, a restless night brought me counsel as to how a performance might be brought about. I waited impatiently for the late winter dawn to break; Therese encouraged me, and so I set forth to see Felix.

He was still asleep. I was going away when his brother Paul suggested that it was quite time to wake him; so he commenced the operation. I found on this occasion that Felix had not exaggerated what he told me about his deathlike sleep. Paul took hold of him under the arms and raised him, calling out: 'Wake, Felix, it is eight o'clock.' He shook him, but it was some time before Felix said, dreamily: 'Oh! leave off – I always said so – it is all nonsense!': but his brother continued to shake him and call out to him until he knew that Felix was roused, when he let him fall back on the pillow. Now Felix opened his eyes wide and, perceiving me, said in his usual pleasant way: 'Why, *Eduard*, where do you come from?' I now told him that I had something to discuss with him. Paul took me to Felix's low-ceilinged workroom, where, on the large white writing table, his breakfast was waiting, while his coffee stood on the stove.

When he came in, I told him to make a hearty good breakfast and not to interrupt me too often. With good humour and even better appetite he went at it, and I now roundly told him that during the night I had determined to have the *Passion* publicly given, at the *Singakademie*, and that in the course of the next few months, before his intended journey to England.

He laughed. 'And who is going to conduct?'

'You.'

'The d—— I am! My contribution is going to be –'

'Leave me alone with your toy trumpets! I am not jesting any more, and have seriously thought the matter through.'

'Good heavens, you're really serious. Well, let us hear.'

My argument was that, all of us having the conviction that the *St Matthew Passion* was the greatest and most important of German musical works, it was our duty not to rest until we had brought it to life again so that once more it might edify men's spirits. As Felix could make no rejoinder to this, I was free to draw the conclusion: 'No living man but you can undertake the performance with convincing success, and on this account you are bound to do it.'

'If I were sure I could carry it through, I would.'

I now explained that in case he felt he really could not himself succeed in organising the enterprise, I had hit upon the following solution. He knew that both Zelter and the *Singakademie* felt obliged to me for my co-operation at all their concerts over a period of almost ten years. Accordingly I should be well entitled to ask a favour in return, and this should be the permission for the use of the room for the concert and the permission for, and recommendation of, the participation of the Society in the performance of the *Passion*.

Felix could not deny that my two requests would not be turned down. I went on to say that if he would not despise me for a partner, with himself as the active member of the firm, the musical credit of the whole transaction, too, would be assured; and, finally, that if we devoted the proceeds to some charitable object, all cavillers would be silenced. So I concluded, saying: 'Herewith, then, I offer you this honest partnership, promising to take upon myself all the business cares, and to sing the part of Christ, while you are to conduct the forgotten treasure out into the world again.'

Felix still looked thoughtful; then he said: 'What pleases me most about the affair is that we are to do this together; that is nice, but believe me, Zelter will never give us his countenance. He, as well as others, has not been able to bring about a performance of the *Passion* and therefore he believes it cannot be done.'

I had more confidence in Zelter's upright nature and the strong sentiments latent in his rough character, but I was resolved, if the worst should happen, to appeal directly to the officers of the *Singakademie*, even in the face of Zelter's objection, and to force him to give in. Felix was most reluctant to take such extreme steps, considering them disrespectful; but I persuaded him that they would not be necessary, and thus, after long, drawn-out discussions, he finally agreed not to hold back from the enterprise.

His parents and Fanny approved my plan, which they considered the only one promising success. It pleased them, of course, that Felix, before taking his flight into the world, should accomplish a great and memorable task. The father was still somewhat worried about Zelter's opposition, but I was of good cheer.

Felix, whose attention was now thoroughly occupied by the idea, thought out a clever manner of procedure so as to avoid exposing himself and the enterprise. The choir rehearsals should be continued in the small hall of the Academy monthly with the members who were in the habit of assembling in his house – without the announcement of any further plan. This group should be slowly increased by members of the *Singakademie*, according to their inclination and desire (or, perhaps, curiosity). Thus he would gain a reliable nucleus and could, if everything went well, get the mass of singers to follow him; but if the study was not promising, or other obstacles turned up, the matter could be relinquished before the intended performance was even mentioned.

Thus prepared, we set out at once for Zelter's room, on the ground floor of the Academy. At the very door Felix said to me: 'If he grows abusive, I shall leave. I cannot squabble with him.' 'He is sure to be abusive,' said I, 'but I will take the squabbling in hand myself.'

We knocked. A loud, rough voice bid us come in. We found the old giant in a thick cloud of smoke, his long pipe in his mouth, sitting at his old two-manual harpsichord. The quill pen he used in writing was in his hand, a sheet of music paper before him; he wore drab-coloured, old-fashioned knee breeches, thick woollen stockings, and embroidered slippers. He raised his head, with its white hair combed back, turned his plain, yet impressive face towards us, and, recognising us through his spectacles, he said kindly in his broad manner: 'Why, how is this? Two such fine young fellows so early in the morning! Now what gives me the honour? Here, sit down.' He led us to a corner of the room, and sat down on a plain sofa; we took chairs.

Now I began my well-considered speech about our admiration of Bach's work, which we had first learnt to prize in his Friday group, and further studied at the Mendelssohns'; that we felt irresistibly impelled to make a trial of the work in public; and that we desired, by his leave, to ask the Academy to co-operate with us.

'Well,' he said, slowly putting up his chin, as he generally did when he was particularly emphatic, 'if it were only as easy as that! But more is needed than we have to offer nowadays.' He enlarged upon the demands and difficulties of the work: the choruses required resources such as existed in the Thomas-Schule when Bach himself was Cantor there; a double orchestra was needed; the violinists of today were no longer able to treat this music properly. All this had long and often been considered, and if the inherent obstacles could be so easily got over, not one but all four *Passions* of Bach would have been revived long ago.

He had become excited, rose, put aside his pipe, and began walking about the room. We, too, had risen; Felix pulled me by the sleeve, he thought nothing more could be done.

I replied that we, particularly Felix, considered the difficulties very great indeed, but had the courage not to imagine them insuperable. The *Singakademie* had become familiar with Bach through Zelter himself, and he had so splendidly schooled the choir that it could cope with any difficulty. Felix had acquired knowledge of the work through him, and had received from him the directions for his conducting. I was burning with the desire to sing the part of Christ in public. And we might hope that the same enthusiasm that moved us would take hold of the other participants and make the enterprise a success.

Zelter had become more and more angry. He had thrown in several doubtful and derogatory remarks during my last speech, which caused Felix to pull me again by the sleeve and then to draw near to the door. At last the old gentleman broke out: 'That one should have the patience to listen to all this! Quite different people have had to give up trying to do this very thing; and here is a pair of greenhorns who think it is all child's play.'

This rough sally he fired off with the utmost energy. I could scarcely help laughing. Zelter had the privilege of being as abusive as he pleased: for the sake of Bach we were ready to put up with more than this from our dear old master.

I looked round at Felix, who was at the door holding the handle; he looked somewhat pale and hurt and beckoned me to come away. I motioned to him that we must stay and recommenced my argument. I said that, though young, we were no longer wholly green, since he had entrusted to us many a difficult task; I pleaded that youth was the time to grapple with difficulties, and that it should please him if two of his pupils proposed to attempt the most difficult task he had shown them.

My arguments now began to take visible effect; the crisis was passed. 'We only want to see,' I continued, 'whether the enterprise can be carried through'; only this we asked him to permit and support; if it did not succeed, we could give it up, and that without shame.

'But how do you want to go at it?' he asked, standing still. 'You think of nothing. First there are the officers, who must consent – many heads and many minds, including feminine ones, by the way – they are not so easily brought into agreement.'

I replied that the officers were well-disposed towards me, and the principal ladies, as participants in the practice hours at Mendelssohn's house, were already won over; so I hoped to succeed in getting permission for use of the hall and co-operation from the members.

'Oh yes, the members,' Zelter exclaimed, 'that is where the real trouble starts. Today ten will come to rehearsal, and tomorrow twenty of them will stay away.'

We laughed heartily, with good reason, for we knew now that we had gained our point. Felix explained to the old man that he intended to hold the rehearsals at first in the small room, and discussed the arrangement of the orchestra, which was to be led by Eduard Rietz. Zelter, who finally had no more practical objections to make, said: 'Well, I don't want to cross you – I shall say a good word for you when it is needed. In God's name, go ahead; we shall see what will come of it.'

So we left our capital old bear with thankful feelings and as good friends. 'We came through,' I said, when we were in the hall. 'But listen,' replied Felix, 'you are really a d—— rascal, an arch-Jesuit.' 'Anything you like for the honour of God and Sebastian Bach!' and triumphantly, we stepped out into the keen winter air, now that the most important step had been a success.

Now everything went smoothly; the obstacles vanished as ghosts do when you approach them. The principals of the Academy consented without hesitation to all we asked; at our first rehearsal in the small hall twice as many attended as at Mendelssohn's, and the number increased on every occasion to such an extent that the copyist could not supply parts quickly enough. After our fifth practice we had to remove to the large concert hall. It should not be forgotten, however, that the many members of the Academy, attracted by the novelty of the undertaking, would, as Zelter had foretold, scarcely have returned had they not been won and fascinated at the very first meeting.

Felix, therefore, did not take up single pieces (for instance, the easy ones) first, but chose an entire section of the composition as the object of study; and so he continued in the first rehearsals. He worked out the choruses right away with inflexible exactness until the full expression was reached and then he transmitted to the singers a quite complete impression of the special quality of the work. His explanations and directions were clear, concise, full of meaning, and yet given in the manner of unpretentious youth.

Felix and I had several meetings to consider how the work could be shortened for performance. It could not be our purpose to give the work, which was influenced in many points by the taste of the period, in the entirety, but we had to convey the impression of its outstanding value. Most of the arias had to be omitted; of others only the introductions, the so-called symphonies (*Accompagnements*) could be given; even the part taken from the Gospel would have to be shorn of all that was not essential to the recital of the *Passion*. We often differed, for matters of conscience were involved; but what we finally determined upon seems to have been the right thing, for it has been adopted at most of the performances of the work.

It was now time to invite the solo singers, and we decided to make the rounds together. Felix was child enough to insist on our being dressed exactly alike on the occasion. We wore blue coats, white waistcoats, black neckties, black trousers, and yellow chamois gloves that were then fashionable. In this *Passion* uniform we started happily off on our way, after Therèse, to whom this was a solemn occasion, had offered us some festival chocolate, which Felix loved. We spoke of the strange chance that just a hundred years had to pass after the last Leipzig performance before this *Passion* would again see the light. 'And to think,' said Felix exuberantly, standing still in the middle of the Opern Platz, 'that it should be an actor and a Jew who give back to the people the greatest of Christian works.'

Felix on other occasions avoided all reference to his Jewish descent; but the striking truth of his observation and his joyful mood carried him away.

'You shall do the talking, and I will do the bowing,' said Felix at the first door where we had to call. We had little need of either; the four principal singers of our opera were ready and willing to help us. Their participation in the rehearsals, and the greater completeness the work assumed, gave a fresh impetus to our studies. Musicians and amateurs all thronged to the rehearsals, anxious to understand it better and better. All were amazed, not so much at its architectonic grandeur of structure, but at its abundance of melody, its wealth of expression and of passion, its peculiar declamation, and the power of its dramatic effects. No one indeed had ever suspected old Bach of all this.

But Felix's share in making these properties of the work felt and its wonderful structure known in full splendour is as memorable as the entire momentous undertaking itself. The ingenuity of comprehension with which he had taken hold of the work and made it his most sacred possession was only half his merit. His ability, energy, perseverance, and clever calculation of the resources at hand made the antiquated masterpiece modern, intelligible, and lifelike once more. Those who did not witness this can scarcely appreciate the magnificent talents and early maturity of this youth of twenty. In his entire life he has accomplished no other achievement of conducting like this, the first and perhaps the most difficult of all.

The authoritative presence of Zelter contributed to the rehearsals. As long as no orchestra took part, Felix had both to accompany and to conduct, a difficult matter with the rapid entrances of choral movements in ever-changing rhythms; here he had to achieve the feat of playing the entire accompaniment with the left hand, while with the right he wielded the baton.

When the orchestra had been added, the piano was placed, across the platform, between the two choirs; for it was then not yet considered decorous for the conductor to turn his back to the audience, which at the opera he had always been permitted to do. By this means, though the first choir was behind Felix, he faced at least the second and the orchestra. This latter consisted mainly of amateurs of the Philharmonic Society; only the leaders of the string instruments and the principal wind players belonged to the Royal orchestra. The wind instruments were placed at the back, above the semicircular platform, and extended toward the small concert room through three open doors. The task of steadying this wavering mass was attended to by Eduard Rietz.

Felix, the novice, was as calm and collected in his difficult post as though he had already conducted a dozen festivals. The quiet and simple way in which, by a look, a movement of the head or hand, he reminded us of the inflections of performance agreed upon, and thus ruled with gentle strength; the quiet confidence with which he would drop his baton in dress rehearsals and performance when longer pieces of steady tempo were well started, with a hardly noticeable nod as if to say, 'This will go very well without me', and listen with the radiant countenance that strangely transfigured him when he made music, occasionally glancing towards me, until he anticipated again that it would be necessary to use the baton – in all this he was as great as he was lovable.

We had had many discussions about musical conducting. The continued beating throughout a movement, that must necessarily become mechanical, vexed me, and does so still. Compositions are, as it were, whipped through by this process. It has always appeared to me that the conductor ought to beat time only when the difficulty of certain passages or a possible unsteadiness of the performers renders it necessary. Surely the aim of the conductor should be to make himself forgotten. Felix determined on this occasion to show me how far this could be done and in the performance of the *Passion* he succeeded to perfection.

I recall these circumstances with peculiar satisfaction, as of late years the extraordinary gesticulations of conductors have been made a primary attraction in musical performances.

Nothing less than the absolute success of the first resuscitation of Bach's masterpiece, on the 11th of March, 1829, could have initiated the revolutionary influence Bach was to win through the *Passion* on the music of modern times; and on this account the performance is memorable. The *Singakademie* achieved in these choral performances its most outstanding accomplishment and whoever heard the sound of these three to four hundred highly trained amateurs, whoever experienced with what fervent zeal great music could inspire them, will understand that, with perfect leadership, perfection was achieved.

Stümer sang the Evangelist with the most agreeable precision, entirely true to his rôle of Narrator, and without placing himself, in the expression of feeling in the Second Part, on an equal plane with the dramatic personages who speak for themselves. He also sang the aria, *I watch beside my Jesus* (*Ich will bei meinem Jesu wachen*), which was too high for Bader, who, in his unassuming willingness to help, sang the parts of Peter and Pilate. The ladies, too, achieved the full effect with their moving numbers: Madame Milder, with her ingratiating voice, particularly the accompanied recitative, *Thou dearest Saviour* (*Du lieber Heiland*), Miss von Schätzel, with her full-throated tone, the aria *Have mercy, Lord* (*Erbarme dich*). The latter was accompanied by Eduard Rietz, with his big and rich violin tone, in appropriate style and expression – an incomparable song of repentance.

So far as I was concerned, I knew that the impression of the entire work depended largely on that created by the presentation of the part of Jesus; here, too, everything is fashioned toward that end. It meant for me the greatest task a singer could be given. What gave me confidence was that the part lay well in my voice, and that I had long studied it with Felix and fully satisfied him. Carried along by the performance as a whole, I could thus sing with my whole soul, and I felt that the thrills of devotion that ran through me at the most impressive passages were also felt by the hearers, who listened in deadly silence.

Never have I felt a holier solemnity vested in a congregation than in the performers and audience that evening.

Our concert made an extraordinary sensation in the educated circles of Berlin. The resuscitation of the popular effect created by a half-forgotten genius was felt to be of epochal import. A second performance was called for, which took place on the 21st March, and was crowded like the first. There was yet one more, under Zelter, after Felix's departure, on Good Friday, the 17th April, in lieu of the usual *Tod Jesu* by Graun.

All the musical world of today knows how the sensation made by these performances caused other towns to make similar attempts; how the other *Passions* of Bach were taken in hand, especially that according to St John; how attention was then turned upon the instrumental productions of the old

master, how they were published, made into bravura pieces for concert use, etc. The worshippers of Bach, however, must not forget that this new cult of Bach dates from the 11th of March, 1829, and that it was Felix Mendelssohn who gave new vitality to the greatest and most profound of composers.
     THE BACH READER *(Eduard Devrient)*: *Hans T David and Arthur Mendel*

The Charity Children sing in St Paul's

I WAS INDEED in London during the first days of June last year, when a scrap of newspaper that had accidentally fallen into my hands informed me that the Anniversary Meeting of the Charity Children was going to take place in St Paul's Church. I at once went in quest of a ticket, which, after many letters and applications, I ended by securing through the courtesy of Mr Goss, chief organist of that cathedral. As early as ten o'clock in the morning the crowd blocked up the approaches to the church; I succeeded, not without trouble, in forcing my way through it. On arriving in the organ gallery reserved for the singers, men and boys, to the number of seventy, I received a bass part, which I was requested to sing with them, and a surplice, which I had to don, so as not to destroy, by my black frock-coat, the harmony of the white garb of the other choristers. Thus disguised as a churchman, I waited for what I was to hear, with a certain vague emotion brought about by what I saw. Nine almost vertical amphitheatres, each having sixteen rows of benches, had been erected in the centre of the building, under the cupola, and under the eastern row of arches in front of the organ, for the children. The six of the cupola formed a sort of hexagonal circus, opening east and west only. From the latter opening started an inclined plane extending to the top of the principal entrance door; it was already crowded by an immense audience, which could thus, even from the most distant benches, hear and see everything perfectly. To the left of the gallery that we occupied, in front of the organ, a platform awaited seven or eight trumpeters and kettle-drummers. On this platform a large mirror had been placed, so as to reflect, for the musicians, the movements of the precentor beating time in the distance, in a corner below the cupola, and dominating the entire choral mass. This mirror also served to guide the organist, whose back was turned to the choir. Banners placed all round the vast amphitheatre, of which the sixteenth row of benches almost reached to the capitals of the colonnade, indicated the places to be occupied by the various schools, and bore the name of the parishes or quarters of London to which they belonged.

    Just as the groups of children filed in, the compartments of the amphitheatres, as they filled up successively from top to bottom, presented a unique scene, recalling the spectacle presented in the microscopic world by the phenomenon of crystallisation. The needles of this crystal of human molecules, continually wending their way from the circumference to the centre, were of two colours, the dark-blue coats of the small boys on the upper benches, and the white gowns and caps of the little girls, who occupied the lower rows. Moreover, as the boys wore on their jackets some a plaque of polished copper, others a silver medal, their motions made the light reflected from these metallic ornaments glitter in such a way as to produce the effect of a thousand sparks being extinguished and relit at every instant on the dark background of the picture. The aspect of the platforms occupied by the girls was still more curious; the green and pink ribbons adorning the head and neck of these little maids in white made this section of the amphitheatres look exactly like a mountain covered with snow, through which blades of grass and flowers thrust themselves here and there. Add to this the variegated tints melting in the distance in the light and shade of the inclined plane where the audience sat, the pulpit of the Archbishop of Canterbury, hung with red cloth, the richly ornamented benches of the Lord Mayor and the British aristocracy on the floor below the dome, then at the further end, high up, the gilded pipes of the great organ; imagine this magnificent church of St Paul, the largest in the world after St Peter's, framing the entire scene, and you will still have but a poor picture of this incomparable spectacle. And in all directions an orderliness, a quietude, a serenity, that increased its magic twofold. The most admirable stage-setting that could be imagined could never approach the reality, which, it seems to me now, I must have seen in a dream. As the children, dressed in their new clothes, gradually occupied their seats with a sober joy, without the least touch of turbulence about it, but in which some little pride could be discerned, I could hear my English neighbours say among themselves: 'What a sight! What a sight!' and deep was my emotion when, the six thousand five hundred little singers being at last seated, the ceremony began.

Following a chord on the organ, there arose in a gigantic unison the first hymn sung by this extraordinary choir:

> *All people that on earth do dwell,*
> *Sing to the Lord with cheerful voice.*

It is useless for me to attempt to give you an idea of the musical effect; the strength and beauty were to those of the best choirs you have ever heard as St Paul's is to a village church, and then a hundredfold more. I must add that this broad and grand hymn is set to superb harmonies, with which the organ inundated it without ever submerging it.

In spite of the oppression and the tremors I was experiencing I managed to control them sufficiently to be able to take a part in the 'reading psalms', which the St Paul's choir had to perform next. The *Te Deum* of Boyce (written in 1760), a characterless work, also sung by the choir, finally restored my serenity. In the *Coronation Anthem* the children joined the small organ choir from time to time, but only with solemn ejaculations such as *God save the King!*', '*Long live the King!*', '*May the King live for ever!*', '*Amen, hallelujah!*', and again I was electrified. I began to count many pauses, in spite of the attentions of my neighbour, who was constantly pointing out to me in his part the bar we had reached, in the belief that I had lost my place. But when we came to the psalm in triple time by J Ganthaumy, an old English master (1774), sung by all the voices to the accompaniment of trumpets, kettle-drums, and organ, under the shattering effect of this glowing hymn, so grand in its harmony and of an expression as noble as touching, nature reasserted her right to be weak, and I had to make use of my music-copy, as Agamemnon did of his toga, to veil my face. Following this sublime piece, and while the Archbishop of Canterbury was delivering his sermon (which the distance prevented me hearing), one of the masters of ceremonies sought me out and led me, still in tears, to various places of the church, so that I might contemplate in all its aspects this picture, of which the eye could not, from any single point of vantage, take in all the grandeur. He then left me alone below, near the pulpit, among the fashionable world – that is to say, at the bottom of the crater of the vocal volcano – and when, for the final psalm, the eruption recommenced, I had to admit that here its power was twice as great as in any other part of the church. On leaving I met old Cramer, who, forgetting in his enthusiasm that he knows French to perfection, began shouting to me in Italian: '*Cosa stupenda! stupenda! la gloria dell' Inghilterra!*'

EVENINGS IN THE ORCHESTRA: *Hector Berlioz*

The village choir practice

'Now, WE'LL BEGIN,' interrupted Mr Torkingham, his mind returning to this world again on concluding his search for a hymn.

Thereupon, the racket of chair-legs on the floor signified that they were settling into their seats, – a disturbance which Swithin took advantage of by going on tiptoe across the floor above, and putting sheets of paper over knotholes in the boarding at points where carpet was lacking, that his lamp-light might not shine down. The absence of a ceiling beneath rendered his position virtually that of one suspended in the same apartment.

The parson announced the tune, and his voice burst forth with *Onward, Christian Soldiers!* in notes of rigid cheerfulness.

In this start, however, he was joined only by the girls and boys, the men furnishing but an accompaniment of ahas and hems. Mr Torkingham stopped, and Sammy Blore spoke, –

'Beg your pardon, sir, – if you'll deal mild with us a moment. What with the wind and walking, my throat's as rough as a grater; and not knowing you were going to hit up that minute, I hadn't hawked, and I don't think Hezzy and Nat had either, – had ye, souls?'

'I hadn't got thorough ready, that's true,' said Hezekiah.

'Quite right of you, then, to speak,' said Mr Torkingham. 'Don't mind explaining; we are here for practice. Now clear your throats, then, and at it again.'

There was a noise as of atmospheric hoes and scrapers, and the bass contingent at last got under way with a time of its own:

'*Honwerd, Christen sojers!*'

'Ah, that's where we are so defective – the pronunciation,' interrupted the parson. 'Now, repeat after me: "*On-ward, Christ-ian, sol-diers.*"'

The choir repeated like an exaggerative echo:

'On-wed, Christ-ing, sol-jaws!'

'Better!' said the parson, in the strenuously sanguine tones of a man who got his living by discovering a bright side in things where it was not very perceptible to other people. 'But it should not be given with quite so extreme an accent; or we may be called affected by other parishes. And, Nathaniel Chapman, there's a jauntiness in your manner of singing which is not quite becoming. Why don't you sing more earnestly?'

'My conscience won't let me, sir. They say every man for himself; but, thank God, I'm not so mean as to lessen old fokes' chances by being earnest at my time o' life, and they so much nearer the need o't.'

'It's bad reasoning, Nat, I fear. Now, perhaps we had better sol-fa the tune. Eyes on your books, please. Sol-sol! fa-fa! mi –'

'I can't sing like that, not I!' said Sammy Blore, with condemnatory astonishment. 'I can sing genuine music, like F and G; but not anything so much out of the order of nater as that.'

'Perhaps you've brought the wrong book, sir?' chimed in Haymoss, kindly. 'I've knowed music early in life and late, – in short, ever since Luke Sneap broke his new fiddle-bow in the wedding psalm, when Pa'son Wilton brought home his bride (you can mind the time, Sammy? – when we sung "*His wife, like a fair fertile vine, her lovely fruit shall bring*", when the young woman turned as red as a rose, not knowing 'twas coming). I've knowed music ever since then, I say, sir, and never heard the like o' that. Every martel note had his name of A, B, C, at that time.'

'Yes, yes, men; but this is a more recent system!'

'Still, you can't alter a old-established note that's A or B by nater,' rejoined Haymoss, with yet deeper conviction that Mr Torkingham was getting off his head. 'Now sound A, neighbour Sammy, and let's have a slap at Christen sojers again, and show the Pa'son the true way!'

Sammy produced a private tuning fork, black and grimy, which, being about seventy years of age, and wrought before pianoforte builders had sent up the pitch to make their instruments brilliant, was nearly a note flatter than the parson's. While an argument as to the true pitch was in progress, there came a knocking without.

'Somebody's at the door!' said a little treble girl.

'Thought I heard a knock before!' said the relieved choir.

The latch was lifted, and a man asked from the darkness, 'Is Mr Torkingham here?'

'Yes, Mills. What do you want?'

It was the parson's man.

'Oh, if you please,' said Mills, showing an advanced margin of himself round the door, 'Lady Constantine wants to see you very particular, sir, and could you call on her after dinner, if you ben't engaged with poor fokes? She's just had a letter, – so they say, – and it's about that, I believe.'

Finding, on looking at his watch, that it was necessary to start at once if he meant to see her that night, the parson cut short the practising, and, naming another night for meeting, he withdrew. All the singers assisted him on to his cob, and watched him till he disappeared over the edge of the Bottom.

TWO ON A TOWER: *Thomas Hardy*

Young Cardus alters the score

FOUR-PART SONGS were sung in school a half an hour or so a week, conducted by one of the corseted yellow faces; sometimes we had to read tonic-solfa at sight, not only from the blackboard but from various signs made by the teacher's hand. 'Doh' was a fist clasped strenuously; 'ray' was the right hand slightly aslant, as though in disapproval; and so on. The songs we sang included, *As pants the hart for cooling streams* and Balfe's *Excelsior*.

When the music was written in tonic-solfa on the blackboard, coloured chalks denoted the different voices, alto and treble. And when the singing-class was at an end the blackboard would be turned over and the reverse side used for other and more practical studies, such as long division. Once I was hauled out of class for some misdemeanour, and hidden out of the sight of my kind, girls as well as boys, segregated in two groups; and I was put behind this blackboard. The teacher left the class-room for a while, and I took some coloured chalks from her desk and altered at random the tonic-solfa notation, changing 'fahs' to 'rays', or 'tes' to 'lahs'. The following week, when the class sang *As pants the hart* at sight, empirical efforts in atonalism were heard for the first time in England. I was easily identified as the cause of the dissonances and I was – probably fairly and with justice for once in a way – prodigiously flogged.

SECOND INNINGS: *Neville Cardus*

On Conductors

Berlioz conducting a choral concert, by Gustave Dore, 1850

On Conductors

THE ART OF CONDUCTING is one of the most frequent topics of conversation among orchestral players. They spend their days being cajoled, bullied, abused, driven, flattered (seldom), exhorted; psychologists wishing to study the love-hate relationship could not find a better field to investigate, for there seems to be no consistent pattern on which the aspiring conductor can model his behaviour. It is not enough to know the score thoroughly; plenty of conductors do that and remain disliked. It is not enough to have a good stick technique; some of the greatest and most loved conductors have had a very poor one. It is not enough to be kind and considerate to the players, though it is certainly appreciated; it can easily lead to a loss of respect. It is not enough to be autocratic and ruthless; musicians are sensitive creatures, jealous of their rights and aware of their individual skills.

I was once asked to define the conductor's function, and my snap reply was, 'To be the orchestra's conscience.' It is not a comprehensive definition, but it's a good start. Every member of a professional orchestra knows in his heart how the music should go. He knows that this passage should be loud, that there should be a diminuendo here and that these notes are short and light. But it is very easy when one is surrounded by other musicians to feel that one's own contribution doesn't really matter. The good conductor makes every member of an orchestra really care; having achieved that, he then has to mould them to his way of thinking, so that they will accept that the tempo he has chosen is a convincing one even though it may be slower or faster than what they had previously regarded as ideal. He must respect the vanity of players and yet gain enough of their respect for them to be prepared to give way, not reluctantly, but with a sense of true understanding. Always he should look at the music from the players' point of view, considering their difficulties and appreciative of the contribution that their experience and skill can make. If it is his duty to teach them, he ought also to realise that he should never stop learning from them.

To conduct professionals demands an entirely different approach from conducting amateurs. An amateur choir or orchestra needs to be led far more positively; the conductor must be prepared by sheer force of personality to will the sopranos to reach the high B flat, to hypnotise the 'cellos into playing the run at which, without his presence, they would collectively quail. He must be patient with his first oboe, remembering that he has spent a day at the office, and probably hasn't practised since last Tuesday. Do not expect too much from amateurs, and they will give you more than you ask. Always ask more from professionals than they are at first prepared to give.

I have tried in my selection of passages about conducting which comprise this section to combine interest with instruction. The first extract, originally written in Latin by Johann Matthias Gesner (who appears in the sheer length of his sentences to have anticipated Henry James at his most prolix), is an example of working with amateurs at its finest. Bach appears to have identified himself with every member of the choir and orchestra, working heroically to get the performance under way. Festival adjudicators might knock a few marks off if the conductor continued to sing with the choir at the performance, but this apart, Bach seems to have learned a good deal about how to work with an amateur group.

Mozart's lesson in psychology is a different matter; here, he was working with a supposedly professional group, and his approach was designed to shake them out of their lethargy. It appears to have worked wonders. As to Spohr's lengthy description of the Beethoven fiasco, I have included this not only as a narrative about conducting, but for the insight that it gives us into Beethoven's social manner as well.

Conductors in those days must have had a difficult time; rehearsals were farcically inadequate, and I strongly suspect that the players were, with individual exceptions, barely up to the level of a student orchestra today. Berlioz and Wagner, perhaps more than anybody else, were responsible for elevating the status of the conductor, and this was largely because of the complexity of their own works. Wagner wrote a classic essay on conducting, a little too substantial to include in an anthology of this nature; it can be found easily enough in *Musicians on Music*, a collection edited by F Bonavia. I have preferred to quote a less-known passage from the Berlioz memoirs which is more human and less didactic. From all reports, Berlioz was a fine conductor, technically clear and yet emotionally inspiring. I cannot imagine that he was ever dull. But if you are looking for something more specific, the ten rules that Richard Strauss inscribed in a young conductor's album are remarkably sound, providing that they are taken with a grain of salt.

There follow two descriptions of conductors at work: Debussy's slightly sardonic comments on Nikisch and Richter.

Up to this point, all our observation of conductors has been as it were from the audience's view; I felt it only fair that the orchestral player should have the final word. For this I have turned to Bernard Shore's *The Orchestra Speaks*. Even if you do not know the score of *Heldenleben*, it is a fascinating revelation of how conductors really work; read between the lines and you can find something of the strange mixture of frustration and triumph that makes rehearsing an ever-renewing source of stimulation to the musician.

Bach's one-man band

IF YOU COULD see him, singing with one voice and playing his own parts, but watching over everything and bringing back to the rhythm and the beat, out of thirty or even forty musicians, the one with a nod, another by tapping with his foot, the third with a warning finger, giving the right note to one from the top of his voice, to another from the bottom, and to a third from the middle of it – all alone, in the midst of the greatest din made by all the participants, and, although he is executing the most difficult parts himself, noticing at once whenever and wherever a mistake occurs, holding everyone together, taking precautions everywhere, and repairing any unsteadiness, full of rhythm in every part of his body – this one man taking in all these harmonies with his keen ear and emitting with his voice alone the tone of all the voices. – *Bach Playing and Conducting – Johann Matthias Gesner to Marcus Fabius Quintilianus.*

THE BACH READER: *Hans T David and Arthur Mendel*

Mozart whips them up

A FEW DAYS BEFORE, Mozart had been persuaded to give a concert in the Gewandhaus. 'Mozart was wont to lament the "botching" of his compositions at public performances, chiefly by excessively rapid tempos', a memoirist wrote later on the basis of accounts of witnesses to this concert. ' "They think that is going to make it fiery," he would say. "But if the fire is not in the composition itself, racing through it will not put it in." He was therefore particularly dissatisfied with the majority of the newer Italian singers. "They race or trill and elaborate," he would say, "because they do not study hard and cannot hold a note!"

'The evening before the rehearsal of his public concert in Leipzig, I heard him declaiming with great ardour on this very point. When I went to the rehearsal next day, I heard to my astonishment that he took the first movement to be rehearsed – it was the allegro of one of his symphonies – very, very fast. No more than twenty measures had been played and – it was easy to foresee – the orchestra lagged behind the tempo, dragged along. Mozart called for a halt, pointed out to the men what was wrong, called, "Ancora!" and began again just as fast. The result was the same. He did everything he could to keep the tempo going; at one time he stamped the beat so forcefully that one of his beautifully worked steel shoe-buckles snapped to pieces. But it was all in vain. He laughed at the broken buckle, let the pieces lie, called "Ancora!" once more, and for the third time started in the same tempo. The musicians began to be angry at this deathly pale little man who was chivvying them so; they worked bitterly away, and at last achieved what was wanted. All that followed he took moderato.... After the rehearsal he said privately to several connoisseurs: "Do not be surprised. It was not caprice on my part. I saw that most of the musicians were rather advanced in age. There would have been no end of dragging if I had not whipped them up at the start and made them angry. Then they did their best out of sheer pique."

'As Mozart had never heard this orchestra play, I should say that this revealed no small knowledge of people. . . .'

MOZART AND HIS TIMES: Erich Schenk

Beethoven's tragi-comic concert

IMMEDIATELY on my arrival in Vienna I paid a visit to Beethoven, but not finding him at home I left my card. I hoped to meet him at some musical party but was informed that, when his deafness increased and he could not well hear music, he had become shy of society and had given up attending parties. I tried another visit but was again unsuccessful. Finally, I ran him to earth at the eating-house where I was in the habit of going with my wife. I had already given concerts which had been favourably commented upon by the Vienna Press and as I introduced myself, Beethoven, who must have heard of me, received me in an unusually gracious manner. We sat down at the same table and Beethoven became very talkative, surprising the other guests, for he was usually very taciturn. It was difficult to make him hear me and I was obliged to talk loudly enough to be heard a long distance off. We met again at the restaurant and he ended by visiting me at home. We thus became well-acquainted. He was a little blunt, not to say uncouth, in his manner, but there was a truthful eye under his bushy eyebrows. After my return from Gotha I met him at the Theater An der Wien where Count Palffy had given him a free seat behind the orchestra. After the opera he would accompany me to my house and spend the rest of the evening with us. He would then be very friendly with my wife and the children. He very seldom spoke of music. When he did, his opinions were very decided and he could not bear to be contradicted. He took no interest whatever in the work of others and I therefore had not the courage to show him my compositions. His favourite topic was criticism of the way Prince Lobkowitz and Count Palffy were running the theatres. He frequently abused the Count while we were still inside the theatre and in so loud a voice that the Count himself in his office could hear him. This embarrassed me greatly.

Beethoven's rough and even repulsive manner at the time arose partly from his deafness and partly from his poverty. He was a bad housekeeper and, moreover, was plundered by all those about him. In the early part of our acquaintance, not having seen him for several days, I asked him: 'I hope you were not sick?' He replied: 'I was not; but one of my shoes was; and as I have only one pair I was under "house arrest".' Sometime afterwards he was relieved by his friends in the following circumstances:

Fidelio, performed in unfavourable circumstances during the French occupation, had met with little success in 1805. Now the director of the Karthnerthor theatre produced it again for his benefit. Beethoven had been persuaded to write a new overture (in E) as well as a song for the jailer and the grand aria for *Fidelio* with horns *obbligati*. In this new form the opera had been a great success and kept its place for a long succession of crowded performances. His friends availed themselves of the favourable moment to give a concert for his benefit in the great Redouten-Saal where the most recent works of his were given. All who could fiddle, blow or sing were invited to assist and all the most celebrated artists in Vienna turned up, including myself and my orchestra. I then for the first time saw Beethoven conduct. His manner surprised me, although I had already heard a good deal about his behaviour on the rostrum. He indicated marks of expression to the orchestra with extraordinary motions of his body. The arms that were crossed on his breast were suddenly and violently thrust out when a *sforzando* occurred. When he wanted soft tones he would crouch down; when a *crescendo* was needed he raised himself by degrees, springing bolt upright when the *forte* was reached. If he wanted still louder sounds, he would shout to the orchestra without being actually aware of it.

On my expressing astonishment at this extraordinary method of conducting I was told the tragi-comical events that happened at Beethoven's last concert at the Theater An der Wien.

He was playing his new piano concerto, but at the very first *Tutti*, forgetting that he was the soloist, he began to conduct. When he came to the first *sforzando* he threw out his arms with such force that he knocked down the lights on the piano. The audience laughed and Beethoven, annoyed, stopped the orchestra and the concerto started again from the beginning. This time the leader took the precaution to order two choir boys to hold the lights for the pianist. When the *sforzando* was reached a second time, Beethoven acted as before, but instead of hitting the lights he hit one of the boys who, receiving a smart blow, dropped the light in terror. The other lad, guessing what was coming, had saved himself by suddenly bending and dodging the blow. If the public had laughed before, they now became hysterical and Beethoven, enraged, struck the piano with such force that at the very first chord six strings broke.

The concert got up by his friends was a great success. The new compositions were much applauded and the Seventh Symphony in particular made a deep impression, the second movement being encored. In spite of Beethoven's uncertain and, at times, laughable directions the execution was masterly.

It was easy to see that the poor deaf maestro could no longer hear his music. It was particularly noticeable in the second part of the first movement where occur two pauses in succession. The second is marked *pianissimo* and obviously Beethoven had overlooked it as he beat time before the orchestra had finished the pause. As usual with him he marked *crescendo* and *diminuendo* by crouching down and rising, but in this instance when he sprang up for the *forte* nothing happened. He looked round frightened and only recovered when he realized that the *forte* was on the way. Fortunately, this happened at the rehearsal. The hall being crowded for the concert, Beethoven's friends arranged for a repetition of the event and this realised an equally conspicuous sum so that Beethoven was relieved of financial worries for some time. But before his death he found himself once more in poverty and owing to the same cause.

As at the time I made Beethoven's acquaintance he had already given up playing in public I only had an opportunity to hear him when I accidentally dropped in during the rehearsal of a new trio (in D major). It was by no means an enjoyable experience. The piano was woefully out of tune – a fact which troubled him little since he could hear nothing – and of his excellence as a virtuoso there was hardly any evidence because of his deafness. In the *fortes* the poor deaf man hammered upon the keys in such a way that whole groups of notes became inaudible; the only way of knowing what was happening was to follow the performance on the score. I was deeply moved by so hard a fate. It is a sad thing for anyone to be afflicted with deafness; a musician cannot endure it without being driven to despair. The cause of Beethoven's continual melancholy was no longer a mystery to me.

MUSICIANS ON MUSIC (*Louis Spohr*): F Bonavia

The conducting of Hector Berlioz

BUT THE COMPOSER who, like myself, must travel to make his works known, has, on the contrary, to nerve himself to a task which is never-ending, still-beginning, and always unpleasant.

Who can imagine the tortures of the rehearsals? First he has to submit to the cold glances of the musicians, who are anything but pleased at all this unexpected upset on his account. 'What does this Frenchman want? Why doesn't he stay at home?' Each takes his place, but at the very first glance round the assembled orchestra, the author perceives important gaps. He requests an explanation from the Kapellmeister. 'The first clarinet is ill, the wife of the oboe has just been confined, the child of the first violin has the croup, the trombones are on parade – they forgot to ask for an exemption from their military duty for today; the kettle-drum has sprained his wrist, the harp will not come to the rehearsal because he needs time to study his part,' etc, etc. Still we begin. The notes are read after a fashion, at about half the right time – a dreadful trial to the composer. Little by little, however, his instinct gains the upper hand; as it warms, his blood carries him away; he insensibly quickens the time. Then, indeed, there is a nice mess, a fearful hubbub, distracting alike to mind and ear. He is forced to stop and resume the slow tempo, and bit by bit repeat those long phrases, the free and rapid course of which he has so often guided in other orchestras.

But, as if this were not enough, he is presently aware of sundry strange discords from some of the wind instruments. What can be the reason? 'Let me hear the trumpets alone. What are you doing? I ought to hear a third and you are playing a second. The second trumpet in C has a D; give me your D . . . very good. The first has a C which sounds F; give me your C. Fie! Horrible! you are playing E flat.'

'No, sir; I am playing what is written.'

'But I tell you no. You are a whole note wrong.'

'But I am sure that I am playing C.'

'In what key is your trumpet?'

'In E flat!'

'Well, there now, there's the mistake; you should have the F trumpet.'

'Ah, I had not noticed the signature; excuse me.'

Or again, I say, 'What the devil are you making that noise for over there, you kettle-drum?'

'Sir, I have a fortissimo.'

'Not a bit of it, it is a mezzo forte, there are not two f's, but m and f. Besides, you are using wooden sticks, and you ought to have them with sponge-heads. It is all the difference between black and white.'

'We don't know what you call "sponge-heads",' says the Kapellmeister. 'We have never seen them.'

'I guessed as much, so I brought some from Paris with me. Take the pair that I have put on that table. Now then, where are we? Good heavens! twenty times too loud. And the mutes, you have forgotten the mutes.'

'We haven't got them; the boy forgot to put them out. We shall have them tomorrow,' etc.

After three or four hours of such anti-harmonious skirmishes, not one single piece has been made intelligible. Everything is broken, inarticulate, out of tune, cold, commonplace, maddeningly discordant, hideous! and you have to send away sixty or eighty tired and discontented musicians under this impression, saying everywhere that they don't understand what it is all about, that it is 'an infernal, chaotic sort of music', and that they never tried anything of the sort before. The next day there is little if any progress; only on the third day does it begin to assume a definite shape.

Then at length the poor composer begins to breathe; the harmony becomes clear, the rhythms dart forth, the melodies smile and weep, and the whole mass gets compacted, and dashes boldly on. After its first stammering attempts, the orchestra walks, talks, becomes man! Acquaintance with the music restores courage to the astonished artists; the composer requests a fourth trial, his interpreters – taking them all round, they are the best people in the world – consent eagerly. This time, *fiat lux*. 'Attention to the lights and shades! You are not afraid now?' 'No, give us the real tempo!' *Via!* And light dawns, art appears, the thought flashes out, the work is understood, and the orchestra rises, applauding and saluting the composer, the Kapellmeister comes up and congratulates him, those inquisitive persons who had hitherto kept themselves hidden in the dark corners of the room now approach, get on the stage and exchange exclamations of surprise and pleasure with the musicians, at the same time casting astonished glances at the foreign master whom at first they had taken for a madman or barbarian. Now is the moment for rest. But let the unfortunate wretch beware before taking any. Far from it, he must now redouble his care and attention, and return before the concert to superintend the arrangement of the desks, and inspect the orchestral parts to be sure they are not mixed. He must go through the ranks, red pencil in hand, and mark the German names for the keys upon the music instead of those used in France for the wind instruments, such as C, D, Des, Es, and Fis, for ut, re, re bemol, mi bemol, and fa diese. He has to transpose a solo for the *cor anglais* for the oboe, because the orchestra does not possess the former instrument, and the performer is generally afraid to transpose it himself. He must rehearse the chorus and the solo singers separately, if they are not sure of themselves. But the room fills, the clock strikes, the composer appears at his desk, pale and exhausted with fatigue of body and mind, scarcely able to stand, uncertain, faint, and discouraged, until the applause of his audience, the spirit of the performers, and love for his own work shall transform him into an electrical machine, giving forth marvellous radiations, invisible indeed, but none the less real.

MEMOIRS OF HECTOR BERLIOZ: *Edited by Ernest Newman*

Ten golden rules inscribed in the album of a young conductor

1. Bear in mind that you are not making music for your own pleasure, but for the pleasure of your audience.
2. You must not perspire while conducting; only the public must get warm.
3. Direct *Salomé* and *Electra* as if they had been written by Mendelssohn: Elfin music.
4. Never encourage the brass, except with a curt glance, in order to give an important entrance cue.
5. On the contrary, never let the horns and woodwinds out of your sight; if you can hear them at all, they are too loud.

6. If you think that the brass is not blowing loud enough, mute it by a couple of degrees.

7. It is not enough that you yourself understand the singer's every word, which you know from memory; the public must be able to follow without effort. If the audience does not understand the text, it falls asleep.

8. Always accompany the singer so that he can sing without strain.

9. When you think that you have reached the most extreme *prestissimo*, take the tempo again as fast.

10. If you bear all this cheerfully in mind, you, with your beautiful talent and great knowledge, will ever be the untroubled delight of your listeners.

COMPOSERS ON MUSIC (Strauss): Sam Morgenstern

Nikisch and the sparrows

ON SUNDAY the Berlin Philharmonic Orchestra conducted by Nikisch gave its first concert. All the well-known and attentive ears that Paris boasts were there, and particularly the dear, wonderful ladies! This is the best kind of audience for one who knows how to make use of it. Almost all that is required to rouse its enthusiasm is a graceful attitude or a romantically waved lock of hair. Nikisch has the pose and the lock but, fortunately, he has also more solid qualities. Moreover, he has his orchestra marvellously in hand and one seems to be in the presence of men whose sole aim is the serious production of music; they are poised and unaffected like the figures in a primitive fresco – quite a touching novelty.

Nikisch is a unique virtuoso, so much so that his virtuosity seems to make him forget the claims of good taste! I would take as an example his performance of the *Tannhäuser overture*, in which he forces the trombones to a *portamento* suitable at best to the stout lady responsible for sentimental ditties in the Casino de Suresnes, and in which he stresses the horns at points where there is no particular reason for bringing them into prominence. These are effects without any appreciable causes, amazing in a musician as experienced as Nikisch shows himself to be at other times. Earlier, he had given evidence of unique gifts in Richard Strauss's *The Merry Pranks of Till Eulenspiegel*. This piece might be called 'An hour of original music in a lunatic asylum'. The clarinets leap in frenzied curves, the trumpets everlastingly choke, and the horns, forestalling a latent sneeze, hasten to rejoin: 'God bless you!' while a big drum goes boom, boom! apparently emphasising the antics of the clowns. One wants to shout with laughter or else to shriek with pain. Then follows the startling discovery that everything is in the right place; for, if the doublebasses blew down their bow or the trombones fiddled on their brass tubes with an imaginary bow, or if Nikisch perched himself on the knee of a programme seller, it would not be in the least surprising. Meanwhile, there is no gainsaying that genius is shown at times in this work, above all in the amazing orchestral assurance, the mad rhythm that sweeps us along from beginning to end and forces us to share in all the hero's merry pranks. Nikisch conducted this orchestral tumult with outstanding coolness and the ovation which greeted both his orchestra and himself was eminently justified.

During the performance of Schubert's *Unfinished Symphony* a flock of sparrows fluttered to the windows and twittered pleasantly. Nikisch had the grace not to demand the expulsion of these impertinent melomaniacs who were probably drunk with the ether or perhaps were merely innocent critics of a symphony which cannot decide once and for all to remain unfinished.

MUSICIANS ON MUSIC (Claude Debussy): F Bonavia

Richter omnipotent

IF RICHTER looks like a prophet, when he conducts the orchestra he is the Almighty: and you may be sure that God Himself would have asked Richter for some hints before embarking on such an adventure. While his right hand, armed with a small, unpretentious baton, secures precision of rhythm, his left hand, multiplied a hundredfold, directs the performance of each individual. This left hand is 'undulating and diverse', its suppleness unbelievable! Then, when it seems that there is really no possibility of obtaining a greater wealth of sound, up go his two arms, and the orchestra leaps through the music with so furious an onset as to sweep the most stubborn indifference before it like a straw. Yet all this pantomime is unobtrusive and never distracts the attention unpleasantly or comes between the music and the audience.

MUSICIANS ON MUSIC (Claude Debussy): F Bonavia

The orchestra speaks

MENGELBERG'S GREAT EXPERIENCE enables him to solve every orchestral problem. In a difficult work like *Heldenleben* he hears everything and sees at the same time; instantly puts his finger on a weak spot, and proceeds to clear it up without losing his temper; and never resorts to sarcasm, or the time-honoured remark that every other orchestra 'plays this easily'.

Not the least part of his success in getting results is due to the scrupulously marked parts he brings with him. Detailed as possible in bowing, phrasing, and breathing instructions, they are all admirably practical and there is a definite purpose behind every mark.

As far as the strings are concerned, he is very definite that solo playing and orchestral playing require two different styles, and the bowing is marked accordingly. Knowing to the finest point what will sound clear to the farthest member of the audience, he is not content with apparent clarity on the rostrum. He knows that a string passage which, played in a certain way, would be perfectly satisfactory on a solo violin, may when played by a group of twenty, sound muddy at the end of the hall. He knows exactly the kind of bow to be used with the greatest effect. He mostly avoids too much *legato* in the strings, for, he says, definition tends to be blurred – 'it will sound quite *legato* enough if there is air between the strokes of the bow'.

This brings us to his favourite manner of expressing blurred playing. In a very scornful and powerful voice he will exclaim '*Ter-der!*' with the accent on the first syllable, and at the same time he makes a horrible scraping on his desk with his baton. The correct sound he wants is then indicated by his rapping out sharply with the butt end of his stick. '*Ti-ta-to!*' is his opposite exclamation to '*Ter-der!*' standing for clear, incisive playing and attack. The orchestra soon gets used to this dreary '*Ter-der!*' and takes all possible pains to avoid its recurrence. The exclamation, with the attendant nerve-racking scrape, is inclined to put the players on edge – which is precisely what he wants.

Mengelberg's rehearsals all point to the concert – he does not rehearse for rehearsing's sake, though he may talk for talking's sake. His unremitting attention to technical details of every kind, as they arise, results in magnificent and confident playing, which it is doubtful whether any conductor can surpass. The orchestra is completely and always confident in him, for he appears never to do anything different on the night from what he has previously shown at rehearsals. There are conductors who ignore points they have repeatedly made at rehearsal and who may give a different beat in a place where the orchestra is expecting an especially clear lead. Mengelberg is not one of them. He is the complete master in every way, and leaves no doubt whatever of his intentions even in playing an unfamiliar and unrehearsed work – which is most unusual, for the conductor who is accustomed to adequate rehearsal is seldom at his ease when playing 'on his verve'.

A virtuoso conductor, on his first appearance in front of a strange orchestra, generally says 'Impossible!' and straightway proceeds to completely change the whole lay-out. Mengelberg, however, does not always alter everything.

When he conducted the BBC Orchestra for the first time, he bowed to the exigencies of broadcasting, and only grumbled a little at having his basses and 'celli separated. He also likes his principal wood-wind in the centre, and the four horns the other way about to the usual procedure in this country, with his first horn in the centre of the orchestra. One or two minor changes were made in the brass, but nothing serious. He began by talking of the wonderful experiences he has had all over the world conducting every orchestra of note, for nearly fifty years, finishing with the remark, 'And, you see, ther ees nothing I don't know! – Zo' (with a benignant 'God help you' grin) 'give me now the A, Mr Oboe!'

Tuning with him is a ceremony that may take anything from five minutes to (in extreme cases) two hours. The first violins are directed to take the A only from the oboe, followed by the seconds, violas, 'celli and basses. The rest of the orchestra then tunes, starting with the flutes and ending with the tuba.

Not until the whole orchestra has the A are the strings allowed to tune their other strings. The oboe officiates like a High Priest, and has to stand and turn in the direction of the department concerned, for the benefit of those far away, while Mengelberg, sitting like a Buddha on the rostrum, criticises the slightest deviation in pitch. On the first occasion this tuning took twenty-five minutes, and gave rise to his first dissertation:

'Eet has taken twenty-five minutes to tune – it should take two minutes! Der rehearsal, it begin wid tuning – eet ees no good, unless you are in tune! You may be first-class orchestra, but if you play not in tune? – It is difficult now for musicians – fifty years ago it did not matter so much perhaps; but now, it is necessary to haf full haus, and if you play not in tune, vell? Der haus, it will be empty! Der feerst oboe, feerst clarinet moost help deir colleagues, like a mutter her children; and, you, Mr Oboe, moost make the face, if someone play bad A! – You moost vatch, like der cat der mouse. – There – dat leetle double bass, you hear heem behind there?'

Tuning eventually comes down to a matter of five or six minutes. If he is starting the programme with *A Midsummer Night's Dream*, he will have all the wood-wind chords played to him at the last moment, before going on the platform.

Usually, he likes five rehearsals for a symphony concert; two for the wind, two for the strings, and the final rehearsal together. He does not find it necessary to have more than one general rehearsal, for he says that if sufficient detailed work is put in by the two halves of the orchestra, he has no difficulty in joining them up.

Mostly he rehearses from memory.

The whole of his first rehearsal with the BBC Orchestra was devoted to the opening portion of *Heldenleben* as far as the entry of the solo violin.

Thoroughly characteristic of his methods was the way in which he tackled the great opening phrase. Each note of the arpeggio had to be detached, in spite of the composer's direction, because, he said, the audience should hear every note, 'and if they are all slurred by the strings, there will be no definition, and the passage will only sound like a chord of E flat', whereas he wants it to make the effect of a brilliantly clear arpeggio. The first two notes after the tied minim are invariably lost in performance, consequently he puts a rest or comma in place of the tie. For the same reason he places another in the 2nd bar, after the dotted minim C, to ensure an incisive attack on the last beat of the bar, and the strings are directed to hit the E flat with the point of the bow. However, the next phrase is played *legatissimo* to the last beat of bar 4, in front of which a breathmark allows for another attack leading to the two heavily accented minims.

Four bars before Fig 1, he again cuts out the ties and inserts rests. This may, on paper, seem very drastic, but the effect in playing is brilliant; and the sharp contrast of *sostenuto* and *staccato* stands out with the greatest effect. Not only is this opening passage typical of his genius for producing superb playing, but it also shows his attitude to the composition he is interpreting. Nothing will induce him to obey blindly the composer's directions if his own experience tells him that they could be made more effective by a slight alteration. In his own words: 'Beethoven, like many other composers, sometimes made changements in his scores, even after publication, and then he also was deaf. So vy not the conductor also, who often knows mooch better than the composer? I vos de best pupil of Svhidler, who vos the best pupil of Beethoven, zo I know vat Beethoven meant. Zo, in dis verk of Strauss; I haf been great friend of Richard Strauss since I vos a boy, and I know joost what he wants and ve vill make some changements also!'

He rehearses the opening as far as Fig 2 at great length, first of all taking the violas, 'celli and horns, until there is complete unanimity in ensemble, phrasing, intonation, and style, and all trace of untidiness at these inserted breath-gaps is removed. He arrives at the episode of the *Critics* (1st bars before Fig 14) after two hours' work, and makes the flute play his subject, *staccatissimo*, and as spitefully as he can, and the counter-subject in the oboe drawled and wooden, with each entry of the other wood-wind almost overblown in the anxiety to be heard. The celebrated fifths of the two tubas are considerably broadened with a big *crescendo* and *diminuendo* to the held note. So much are they elongated that the rest of the orchestra has to adjust its playing to them.

He spent a long time at each rehearsal over this tuba motif. 'Zis motif represents one of Strauss's most hated critics, M Quentin, und eet moost sound like MONSIEUR QUENTIN. Play it to me! – No, it is not together! Boot you don't give me the *crescendo* to the second beat and then *diminuendo*! Now fur der last time!'

He rehearses all the first part of this section until all the contrapuntal parts are clear in every detail, and the utmost character portrayed in the different themes. At the end of this episode for wind he finds the accompaniment too heavy at the *pianissimo* syncopated chords in bassoons and horns, and later in the strings as well, so it gives him another opportunity to discourse on the playing of 'accompaniments generally'.

'You moost play with joost the right amount of tone, neither too mooch, nor too little, if you play an accompaniment too soft, then it ees joost as wrong as playing too loud. Listen to the soloist. Then, if you arhe der soloist, you moost be heard, even if der mark es *pianissimo*. Zo, not forgotten dat if you are accompanying, play less than vhat you haf, und when you arhe de soloist, play a leetle more. Eet moost be a hundred per cent and not joost seventy-five per cent!'

At *Festes Zeitmass*, two bars before Fig 22, he plays the four-bar passage six or seven times until the rhythm is sufficiently accurate and *staccato*; with frequent interjections of 'Ter-der!!' The unfortunate solo violin does not get an opportunity to set out on his difficult solo until well into the middle of the second rehearsal – a very trying experience – for each time the conductor arrives at his entry he stops him in mid-air, on his first C sharp, and returns to a figure some way back. Much the same thing happened in Brahms's B flat piano concerto. He would let the pianist play one chord in his opening solo, and then stop and start again, working at considerable length over the first *tutti*, stopping the pianist each time in his first stride.

The ensuing passage in *Heldenleben* contains many difficulties for the orchestra as well as the exacting solo for the violin. The first one crops up in the 'celli, basses and bassoons at the end of the fifth bar of Fig 23, and continues much in evidence throughout the whole of the accompaniment to the violin. This is the elusive semiquaver which always precedes the principal subject of this section. 'TER-DER, I don't hier dhat sixteenth note – vhat do you call it – semiquaver! Put der bow on the string and separate the note from der next bar. Give me furst der 'celli – zo – now der double basses – it is difficult! Better! Now, der 1st and 2nd horn. You will haf to play louder, 2nd horn! – Now, 'celli, basses, mit 1st and 2nd horn. Ah ha! I begin to hear it at last, eet is no longer Ter-der and nearly eighty per cent. 'Celli and bass, use mo-ore *glissando!*'

About ten bars further on he practises the *pizzicato* chords in the 2nd violins for ensemble and intonation, both times the passage occurs, demanding a clear but quiet plucking of the string at right angles for a dry sound, and not along the string for a more sustained sound. At the end of the solo violin passage at Fig 32, he has further trouble with the 'semiquaver' and does not continue until 'celli, basses, oboes, clarinets and bassoons articulate the note distinctly before the great G flat chord.

The next section might almost be labelled the 'left hand of the strings', so frequently does he demand the utmost warmth and life in the vibrato, as much as in great breadth of bowing. He continues to take all those playing the same phrases in unisons and octaves separately, and often one department at a time, aiming at a rich and glowing sound where perfect intonation and ensemble increase the volume. Not until he obtains the right volume given him by these two matters – 'one hundred per cent – and not joost seventy per cent!' – does he turn to the balancing of the parts.

Four bars after Fig 38, he makes the utmost of the 1st and 2nd violin passage in octaves, by getting both departments to take the same amount of bow in exactly the same style and position, stopping instantly if any player is taking obviously too much or playing in the wrong part of the bow. 'It ees no goot, dhat long bow in de orchester, it looks well, yes in der front, but de notes are not dhere! A soloist may do it perhaps, but eet ees no goot in der orchester.'

At the trumpet call at Fig 42 he insists on the absolute clarity of the first two notes of each part, even if it means making them longer than demi-semi-quavers; clear articulation is more important than anything else here. Also the balance between the three trumpets must be equal. Immediately after this figure, he asks the basses and 'celli almost to 'crush' the *sforza* on the B flat. 'It is bad to crush ze tone, perhaps, boot hiere it is an exception! Yes, – I want it brutal' (and makes a fearful grimace).

He does not spend much time on the battle scene, and only insists that those tunes which stand out from the general din be clearly and accurately handled.

The insistent rhythm which appears on the strings and side-drum at the *Festes Zeitmass* after Fig 49 is hammered out as hard as possible, with short little jabbing strokes of the bow, near the heel; and the drum and strings have to clear up a ragged ensemble, the side-drum being a long distance away. At the climax, two bars after 75 he again insists on the perfect articulation of the quaver-two semiquaver figure.

The tuba figure again fails to satisfy him before Fig 85, but the violas and 2nd clarinet fortunately get over their shaky bridge at Fig 85 without disaster. A typical stroke of Mengelberg's comes out in the 'celli, a few bars further on, their last sextolet being drawn out in a *molto allargando* and *diminuendo*, making an exquisite sound with the bows just brushing the string before falling at length on the G major chord.

He touches upon the various quotations from Strauss's earlier works in the next episode, particularly demanding a special effort from the horns in their *Don Juan* motif. After Fig 94, in the semiquaver passages, he makes a terrific effect from the strings, by forbidding too much bow, as near the heel as possible, so that he gets articulation and *staccato*, even at high speed. Should any player forget himself and let his bow trickle to the point, he shouts, 'Vy do you play dhere? It is no goot; I haf tolt you, you are not playing as soloist – you are in der orchester.' The player is then eyed for a few moments: 'Now we moost do it again.'

For the last time, he makes sure of getting every semiquaver clearly played after the tied notes, between Figs 95 and 96, and at the end of the episode he takes the great descending quintuplet in two beats, making groups of two and three.

In the concluding scene, a Mengelberg of extreme gentleness appears, capable of exquisite tenderness; and the lovely interjectory phrases on the first and second violins, during the *cor anglais* solo, are made to sound as if there was all humanity in them. The left hand of the violins is singled out for his medium of expression, the bows held well in control to avoid over-emphasis. The violin solo to the end is made to tell on every note, and the player is able to play with complete freedom, both in expression and delicacy, with the rest of the orchestra hushed to an extreme *pianissimo* which is yet alive – the colour of a moving part just coming to the surface now and again.

With all his dictatorial grip of his players, he seems to need a similar grip on the part of his soloists in the orchestra. If he senses that responsive grip his hand becomes like velvet and at the performance he will himself respond to the players' expression and bring it to full bloom. But if he cannot obtain what he wants from an artist, he will be hard as iron and may seem to oppose rather than aid. He has the true virtuoso's intolerance of inadequate playing; he expects to be able to start his rehearsing from scratch, without having to nurse any weakness amongst his players. His ear detects everything. His particular genius is for hearing from the point of view of the man at the back of the hall. Besides satisfying him, this redoubles the clarity for the rest of the audience.

His interpretations, intensely personal and vivid, have his great conviction behind them. Though he may depart from the directions of the composer, audience and orchestra alike are carried away by the grip and mastery of it all. He holds everyone close, and a whole department of strings will think that his eye is compelling each man individually.

An orchestra that is proud of its work and is without passengers can look forward to working with Mengelberg, as a student to a lesson with a great master. Each man knows that he will be able to put forth all his own skill and power to the utmost advantage under him, and enjoy the exhilaration of taking part in magnificent playing. It is good for an orchestra sometimes to show off all its skill for its own sake, and Mengelberg knows as much as any conductor living how to make this possible. Long dissertations at rehearsals may be more trying, but there is always some truth in what he says, and though the time-table may go wrong, his rehearsals really are rehearsals.

Mengelberg inspires an orchestra to its utmost power, and to sit under him is to sit at the feet of a great virtuoso. As he says, and it is most true, 'There ees nothing I do not know about der orchester.' An orchestra, having finished a rough passage with him, will have humming in their ears, like the sound of the sea in a shell: 'Ter-der – hoondered per cent; Ter-der – hoondered per cent – always hoondered per cent.'

THE ORCHESTRA SPEAKS: *Bernard Shore*

Opera

(Italian=work: the same as the Latin and originally used in the same sense.) A musical work for the stage of varying type, originating in the first years of the seventeenth century in Italy. The dramatic foundation of it is a Libretto, which is set to music in various ways.

A sketch by Chaliapin (*Mephistopheles*)

Opera

'I WOULD quite like opera if it wasn't for the singing....' This profound statement was made to me by a young girl in ATS uniform, after I had delivered a lecture on opera to some troops at an anti-aircraft gunsite on the Dover cliffs during the war. It represents an understandable point of view; she liked the spectacle, the colour, the sense of occasion, the surge of orchestral sound, possibly even the acting, although this is not normally of a standard to stir the emotions very deeply. She just found the convention of singing everyday dialogue hard to take – and I can sympathise with her. A convincing marriage of words and music is a problem which has given much concern to composers. One of the best arguments for singing opera in a language the audience doesn't understand is that they are less likely to be embarrassed by the infelicities of the dialogue. For myself, I prefer, in principle, to have the opera performed in the language of the country, even if it means having to translate *Peter Grimes* into Finnish for a performance in Helsinki. I realise that Wagner suffers particularly for being sung in any other language than German, but fortunately in his case, the action moves slowly enough for one to be able to pass the time working out what happened during the last twenty minutes. Strongly though I may defend translations, I stipulate, needless to say, that they should be good translations. Lines like the classic 'Thou the dust slave abject biting on the throne while I find room' should have had their day by now.

My selection of operatic writings is of two kinds, representing as one might say Opera Seria and Opera Buffa. Beginning with Jean-Jacques Rousseau's description of opera in Paris in 1760, we learn of some of the abuses which Gluck was so anxious to cure, and which his famous preface to *Alceste* also enumerates. The musical artificiality of opera in the early part of the eighteenth century was largely due to the extraordinary vanity of the singers, whose petty jealousies could only be mollified if each was given an equal share of the glory.

'The number and order of the songs were strictly regulated, each principal character had to have so many, in various styles and the secondary characters fewer, perhaps two each. At the end of a song, the singer invariably left the stage.' (I quote from Professor Dent's admirable little history of opera.) Conventions of this nature were utterly stultifying: even in Mozart's time, the finale of each act was supposed to introduce all the main characters in a certain order, regardless of dramatic necessity. The extent to which Mozart exercised his mind on this matter is illustrated by the long letter to his father about *L'oca del Cairo*, or *The Cairo Goose*, an opera that we today only know as an unfinished work. In subsequent years, the Mozart operas were to be subjected to all kinds of vandalism, especially in Paris. One production of *The Magic Flute* given in 1820 under the title of '*Les mystères d'Isis*' was referred to as '*Les Misères d'ici*' by a Mozart-lover. Things seem to have been little better in Russia, to judge from Tolstoy's graphic description of an opera rehearsal.

The remaining excerpts are less serious in tone; Chaliapin, the perfectionist, and Caruso, the irreverent, show opposite sides of the same coin; Neville Cardus tells an entertaining Beecham story, and commemorates Frank Mullings in a splendid piece of critical writing at its most perceptive. I included this to give the lie to the myth that the British cannot produce world-class singers. I was driving past the San Francisco Opera House one day when I saw the names of Richard Lewis and Geraint Evans billed in huge letters outside. I felt very proud at that moment; poor Mullings lived at a time when our singers were not for export. His inclusion in this book may be a source of satisfaction to those who saw him when he was in his prime.

Opera in Paris, 1760

IMAGINE A CRATE about fifteen feet long and proportionately wide: that is the stage. On each side are placed a row of screens on which the settings of the acts to be played are crudely painted. The back-drop is a big curtain, similarly daubed and almost always torn, which may represent caverns on earth or holes in the sky, depending on the perspective. Everyone who walks across the stage behind this curtain produces a sort of tremor in it which is rather attractive. The sky is represented by some bluish rags that hang from rods or ropes like laundry on a line. The sun, which is occasionally to be seen, is a torch inside a lantern. The chariot for the gods and goddesses is made of two-by-fours hung like a swing within a frame, the god sitting on a transverse board in front of which is bunched some tinted cloth – the cloud appropriate to the god's magnificence. Near the bottom of the machine stand two or three stinking candles, which, while the illuminated personage waves and shrieks in his little swing, smoke him up to his heart's content – incense worthy of the god.

Since chariots form the most important part of the Opera's equipment, you can from these infer the rest. The troubled sea consists of long structures of blue cloth or cardboard mounted on parallel rods and turned by urchins. Thunder is a heavy cart drawn across the beams – by no means the least touching instrument of this delightful band. Lightning is achieved by throwing handfuls of resinous pitch on a lighted torch; but a real bolt calls for a fuse and rocket.

The stage is provided with little square trap-doors which on being opened signify that demons are coming up from the cellar. Should they need to rise into the air, they are cleverly replaced by straw demons of brown buckram, or sometimes by actual chimney sweeps who majestically vanish into the aforementioned blue rags. But what is really tragic is when the ropes jam or break, for then the infernal spirits or immortal gods fall and break their legs, and are sometimes killed. To all this you must add the monsters used to lend excitement to certain scenes (such as dragons, lizards, tortoises, crocodiles, or large toads), which, by perambulating the stage in a menacing way, permit us to witness the Temptations of Saint Anthony. Each of these characters is animated by a lout of a Savoyard who actually hasn't sense enough to act the dumb beast.

But what you cannot imagine is the frightful cries, the prolonged bellowings, which fill the theatre during the performance. You see actresses virtually in convulsions as they rend from their lungs the most violent ululations; both fists clenched against the breast, the head thrown back, cheeks aflame, veins bursting, and diaphragm heaving. It is impossible to say which is the more unpleasantly assailed, the eye or the ear; these motions cause as much pain to those who look as the singing to those who listen, but what is still more astonishing is that the howls and cries are almost the only thing applauded by the audience. From the handclapping you might suppose a company of deaf-mutes in a frenzy of delight at catching here and there a few piercing sounds, and eager to encourage their repetition. For my part, I am convinced that people applaud a prima donna as they do the feats of the strong man at a fair. The sensations are painfully disagreeable, hard to endure, but one is so glad when it is all over that one cannot help rejoicing.

PLEASURES OF MUSIC (*Jean-Jacques Rousseau*): *Jacques Barzun*

Mozart on opera, to his father

Now LET US TALK of something else. I have only three more arias to compose and then the first act of my opera will be finished. I can really say that I am quite satisfied with the aria buffa, the quartet and the finale and am looking forward to their performance. I should therefore be sorry to have written this music to no purpose, I mean, if we do not secure what is absolutely necessary. Neither you nor Abbate Varesco nor I have noticed that it will have a very bad effect and even cause the entire failure of the opera if neither of the two principal female singers appear on the stage until the very last moment, but keep on walking about on the bastions or on the ramparts of the fortress. The patience of the audience might hold out for one act, but certainly not for a second one – that is quite out of the question. This first occurred to me at Linz, and it seems to me that the only solution is to contrive that some of the scenes in the second act shall take place in the fortress – *camera della fortezza*. The scene could be so arranged that when Don Pippo gives orders for the goose to be brought into the fortress, the stage should represent a room where Celidora and Lavina are. Pantea comes in with the goose and Biondello slips out. They hear Don Pippo coming and Biondello again becomes a goose. At this point a good quintet would be very suitable, which would be the more comic as the goose would be singing along with the others. I must tell you, however, that my only reason for not objecting to this goose story altogether was because two people of greater insight and judgement than myself have not disapproved of it, I mean yourself and Varesco. But there is still time to think of other arrangements. Biondello has vowed to make his own way into the tower; how he manages to do so, whether in the form of a goose or by some other ruse, does not really matter. I should have thought that effects far more natural and amusing might be produced, if he were to remain in human form. For example, the news that in despair at not being able to make his way into the fortress he has thrown himself into the sea, could be brought in at the very beginning of Act II. He might then disguise himself as a Turk or anyone he chose and bring Pantea with him as a slave (a Moorish girl, of course). Don Pippo is willing to purchase the slave for his bride. Therefore, the slave-dealer and the Moorish girl must enter the fortress in order to be inspected. In this way Pantea has an opportunity of bullying her husband and addressing all sorts of impertinent remarks to him, which would greatly improve her part, for the more comic an Italian opera is the better. Well, I entreat you to expound my views very clearly to Abbate Varesco and to tell him that I implore him to go ahead. I have worked hard enough in this short time. Why, I should have finished the whole of Act I, if I did not require some alterations in the words of some of the arias. *But say nothing of this to him at present.* My German opera, *Die Entführung aus dem Serail*, has been performed both in Prague and Leipzig excellently and with the greatest applause. I have heard both these facts from people who saw the performances.

THE LETTERS OF MOZART & HIS FAMILY: *Emily Anderson*

Tolstoy witnesses a rehearsal

I ARRIVED when the first act had already commenced. To reach the auditorium I had to pass through the stage entrance. By dark entrances and passages, past immense machines for changing the scenery and lighting the stage and the theatre, I was led through the vaults of an enormous building; and there in the gloom and dust I saw workmen busily engaged. One of these men – pale, haggard, in a dirty blouse, with dirty, work-worn hands and cramped fingers, evidently tired and out of humour – went past me, angrily scolding another man. Ascending by a dark stair, I came out on the boards behind the scenes. Amid various poles and rings and scattered scenery, decorations, and curtains, stood and moved dozens, if not hundreds, of painted and dressed-up men in costumes fitting tight to their thighs and calves, and also women, who were, as usual, as nearly nude as might be. These were all singers, or members of the chorus, or ballet dancers, awaiting their turns. My guide led me across the stage and, by means of a bridge of boards, across the orchestra, in which perhaps a hundred musicians of all kinds, from kettle-drum to flute and harp, were seated, to the dark pit stalls.

On an elevation, between two lamps with reflectors and in an armchair placed before a music stand, sat the director of the musical part, baton in hand, managing the orchestra and singers, and in general the production of the whole opera.

The performance had already commenced, and on the stage was being represented a procession of Indians who had brought home a bride. Besides men and women in costume, two other men in ordinary clothes bustled and ran about on the stage: one was the director of the dramatic part, and the other, who stepped about in soft shoes and ran from place to place with unusual agility, was the dancing master, whose salary per month exceeded what ten labourers earn in a year.

These three directors arranged the singing, the orchestra, and the procession. The procession, as usual, was enacted by men and women in couples with tinfoil halberds on their shoulders. They all came from one place and walked round and round again and then stopped. The procession took a long time to arrange: first the Indians with halberds came on too late, then too soon; then at the right time but crowded together at the exit; then they did not crowd but arranged themselves badly at the sides of the stage – and each time the whole performance was stopped and recommenced from the beginning. The procession is preceded by a recitative, delivered by a man dressed up like some variety of Turk, who, opening his mouth in a curious way, sings, '*Home I bring the bri-i-ide*'. He sings, and waves his arm (which is of course bare) from under his mantle. The procession commences. But here the French horn, in the accompaniment of the recitative, does something wrong; and the director, with a shudder as if some catastrophe had occurred, raps with his stick on the stand. All is stopped, and the director, turning to the orchestra, attacks the French horn, scolding him in the rudest terms – as cabmen abuse one another – for taking the wrong note. And again the whole thing recommences. The Indians with their halberds again come on, treading softly in their extraordinary boots; again the singer sings, '*Home I bring the bri-i-ide*'. But here the pairs get too close together. More raps with the stick, more scolding, and a recommencement. Again, '*Home I bring the bri-i-ide*', and again the same gesticulation with the bare arm from under the mantle; and again the couples, treading softly with halberds on their shoulders, some with sad and serious faces, some talking and smiling, arrange themselves in a circle and begin to sing. All seems to be going well, but again the stick raps and the director in a distressed and angry voice begins to scold the men and women of the chorus. It appears that when singing they had omitted to raise their hands from time to time in sign of animation. 'Are you all dead, or what? What oxen you are! Are you corpses, that you can't move?' Again they recommence, '*Home I bring the bri-i-ide*', and again, with sorrowful faces, the chorus women sing, first one and then another of them raising their hands. But two chorus girls speak to each other – again a more vehement rapping with the stick. 'Have you come here to talk? Can't you gossip at home? You there in red breeches, come nearer. Look at me! Begin again!' Again, '*Home I bring the bri-i-ide*'. And so it goes on for one, two, three hours. The whole of such a rehearsal lasts six hours on end. Raps with the stick, repetitions, placings, corrections of the singers, of the orchestra, of the procession, of the dancers – all seasoned with angry scolding. I heard the words, 'asses', 'fools', 'idiots', 'swine', addressed to the musicians and singers at least forty times in the course of one hour. And the unhappy individual to whom the abuse is addressed – flautist, horn-blower, or singer – physically and mentally demoralised, does not reply, and does what is demanded of him. Twenty times is repeated the one phrase, '*Home I bring the bri-i-ide*', and twenty times the striding about in yellow shoes with a halberd over the shoulder. The conductor knows that these people are so demoralised that they are no longer fit for anything but to blow trumpets and walk about with halberds and in yellow shoes, and that they are also so accustomed to dainty easy living that they will put up with anything rather than lose their luxurious life. He therefore gives free vent to his churlishness, especially as he has seen the same thing done in Paris and Vienna, and knows that this is the way the best conductors behave, and that it is a musical tradition of great artists to be so carried away by the great business of their art that they cannot pause to consider the feelings of other artists.

PLEASURES OF MUSIC (*Leo Tolstoy*): *Jacques Barzun*

Chaliapin the perfectionist

THE NEXT SEASON I presented a *Boris* of my own of which I was forgivably proud. That was in Chicago, where I was offering the Russian Opera Company in a full season of Russian opera, the first such season in America.

It was the only performance of *Boris* to be given in this country all in Russian; at the Metropolitan Chaliapin sang in Russian and the rest of the cast in Italian. With Chaliapin supervising the settings, the costumes, the music, it was as authentic a production, as faithful to Mussorgsky's music and to the Russia which nourished him and Chaliapin, as could be achieved.

The settings were designed by Anchutin, whose pretty daughter Leda grew up to become a ballerina and to marry the fine dancer Andre Eglevsky. I bought a handsome Persian chair for the Coronation Scene.

And as a special touch of sentiment, the entire Russian Opera Company gathered on the stage after the first-act curtain and presented Chaliapin with the bread and salt of welcome in the ancient Russian ceremony; the bread on a silver tray wrapped in a hand-sewn white napkin.

The performance was quite late in starting, because Chaliapin had to go over every detail once more. And the second-act curtain did not go up for so long a time that it seemed forever.

From my favourite spot at the back of the house I became aware of the growing restlessness of the audience. They had gone out and smoked their cigarettes in the lobby and exchanged greetings with their friends, and had come back and settled themselves in their seats, and still the curtain did not rise on the second act. I looked at my watch. The intermission was already thirty-five minutes long.

I hurried back-stage.

'What's the matter with you? Why doesn't the curtain go up? The audience ...'

Without a word the stage-manager led me onto the stage. There stood Chaliapin on the set, pen-knife in hand, laboriously carving out designs in the window for great authenticity.

When the next intermission stretched to twenty-five minutes, to thirty minutes, I went back-stage again. This time I found him kneeling on the stage, the handsome Persian throne lying ignominiously on its back, while with a saw he had borrowed from the stage carpenter he sawed an inch off each of its legs. The chair was too high, he explained, industriously sawing away.

And as he sawed, I could literally feel the money running out of my pocket. For in the theatre the witching hour of eleven-thirty changes everything. Stagehands, musicians must be paid overtime. And with those intermissions, the great opera, long to begin with, ran on well past midnight.

Chaliapin's fanaticism for detail had already put the entire opera season hopelessly in the red before the curtain had ever gone up. Rehearsal time stretched on interminably, and the bill for the orchestra grew heavier and heavier, while he corrected the conductor in his tempi, the artists in their every inflexion.

Over our bottle of wine one night after a performance I asked him why he did this. 'Why is every word so important to you, Fe'd'r Ivanitch? Why must you demand from every artist such perfection in every detail? Will you never be satisfied?'

'No,' he roared. 'Because on one word may hang the meaning of a whole character, or of a whole mood. Why, if I say a speech in this way, the audience will think the man I speak of is alive, while if I say it another way, they will be sure he is dead! No, Salomon, an artist who does not insist on perfection is no artist!'

IMPRESARIO: *S Hurok in collaboration with Ruth Goode*

Caruso the irreverent

IT MAY BE a surprise to those who have thought of Caruso merely as the fierce temperamental artist to learn that he was full of practical jokes, and that his bubbling sense of humour was so irrepressible that he would make fun even in the middle of the most poignant of scenes, such as the last Act in *La Bohème* where Mimi is dying on the bed. Never shall I forget one night at Monte Carlo, before an immense audience 'thick' with Grand Dukes and Princesses and Marquesas, how I was suddenly startled in the middle of the death scene by a strange squeaking noise which seemed to come from Caruso as he bent over me. I went on singing, but I could not help wondering at the time if Caruso was ill, for his face was drawn and solemn, and every time he bent down there was this same extraordinary noise of squeaking. And then with a gulp which almost made me forget my part, I realised that he had a little rubber toy in his hand, which at the most pathetic phrases he was pressing in my ear. You know how difficult it is to stop laughing when you are supposed to be solemn; but when you are supposed to be dying the temptation is almost too much to be borne.

MELODIES AND MEMORIES: *Nellie Melba*

The magnificent Mullings

NOT ALL the finest artists become known to the world at large. Many circumstances, which have nothing to do with art, are frequently needed to make extraordinary talent and subtlety of imagination known to the many. In the days of theBeecham opera we in Manchester knew that one of the greatest living actors in opera was Frank Mullings; I call him an actor because his voice, a tenor, was often strangled by unnatural production, yet it was the most histrionic voice I have heard amongst all the tenors known or suffered by me; and as a creator of character, or rather, as an artist with power to incarnate a dramatic conception, I have known only one in opera who was his superior, and that Chaliapin. He was a noble towering presence as Othello. When he told the quarrellers to put up their swords, with superb implication of his shame for them, what loftiness and unselfconscious dignity of carriage! When he appeared in the closing scene, to kill Desdemona, his intense silence – he could fill the theatre with intense silence – the torment of his awareness to what he was about to do, the sense that he knew he was caught in the snare of his own blood and passion; it was all much more than great art. This was 'the pity of it'; we were taken up into a realisation of the tragically entangled texture of being. I have been told that when he entered the bedroom of Desdemona with a quietness that was as a sleep-walker's, the artist playing Desdemona often was really apprehensive that Mullings might forget himself and stray beyond histrionics into actuality. His collapse to the earth at the end of the scene in the hall of the castle was a subsidence in nature; we had seen simple manliness and trustfulness suffer corruption. Mullings never let us forget that Othello was compact of primitive stuffs not easily jealous but, being wrought, perplex'd in the extreme. Mullings, in fact, was the only artist I have known who, throughout the opera, kept us constantly reminded that Othello, after all, is Shakespeare's and not Verdi's creation.

So with his Tristan, never heard of in Bayreuth or the Metropolitan. Much of quality in the world does indeed go by and the crowd never hears of it. I have seen most of the celebrated Tristans of the last thirty years. I have heard the music sung with a vocal splendour far beyond the best in Mullings's command; but nobody has by voice and presence made me feel, with the intensity of Mullings, the inmost heart and mind of Tristan, and, much more important, the tragic doom that invisibly follows him about. At his entrance in Act I, when Tristan at the request of Isolde comes through the curtain of Isolde's parlour on the deck of the ship, he brought with him poignantly tragic foreknowledge; he was the music embodied. The *lento* theme in the strings, with the heavy and bodeful accents, has never been so 'lived up to' as when Mullings stood facing Isolde, and in tones achingly toneless said, 'Demand, lady, what you will.'

In the second act, during the love-duet, his voice actually lent tragic eloquence to the music by very reason of its hint of uncertainty of pitch; the strict ear was sometimes lacerated but somehow it was absolutely right. I once whispered to Langford in the darkened theatre, 'He's out of tune, worse than ever', and Langford grunted back, 'So's Wagner!' The fever and delirium of Act III consumed him; Mullings was an enormous man in physique, yet as we saw this Tristan raving and heaving on his pallet, we could swear he was being wasted before our very eyes. Nobody has melted, as Mullings melted, when Tristan, full to overflowing in the heart, clasped the old servitor and cried out, '*O Kurwenal, du trauter Freund!*' As Parsifal he stood watching the ritual of the unfolding of the Grail as nobody else. Other tenors might as well leave the stage; perhaps they most of them do leave it – I have never, so to say,'checked-up' on them. Mullings did not allow us to forget his presence, though he was concealed in the darkness. By some power of histrionic suggestion we could see through the eyes of Parsifal as well as through our own; and so the drama was heightened to a spiritual dualism; we suffered the agony of Amfortas; and at the same time we were moved by the innocence of Parsifal.

Mullings ennobled everything; the second-rate assumed a sense of imaginative largeness and dignity if Mullings touched it. Even in the dreadful opera of Saint-Saëns, heroic pathos stood before us when Mullings was led into the temple, the blind Samson, by the little boy. When he stood between two pillars (obvious 'props') and outstretched his arms, we could feel the gathering of enormous power in a deliberate weighing of effort; the theatre entire might well have come crashing down. In the experience and vision of art it did.

SECOND INNINGS: *Neville Cardus*

Pot-pourri

(*French – literally 'rotten pot'.*) A medley of preserves, identical with the Spanish *olla podrida*, the name of which is applied to selections of themes from various works, especially operas or operettas, dished up for piano or other instruments... as a light and easy entertainment and to awaken memories of works previously heard in their entirety.

Beethoven: An imaginary portrait by R Farnsworth, taken from a photograph of a rare sculpture, now destroyed

Pot-pourri

INTRIGUING THOUGH the prospect of fitting the items of this anthology into musical forms was, it was inevitable that there would be some gems that would be virtually impossible to classify. Some, like Mendelssohn's visit to Buckingham Palace, were substantial enough to claim an entire section for themselves; the remainder have been herded into this penultimate category where they mingle uneasily under the pejorative title of Pot-pourri.

For years I have been told of Schumann's famous article, saluting Chopin's appearance with the phrase, 'Hats off gentlemen, a genius!'; but it has always been difficult to track down the complete passage. Since it is a classic of musical criticism, I have given it first place in this section. Too much may have been made of the psychological implications of Schumann's decision to write his articles in the form of a dialogue between the imaginary characters of Florestan and Eusebius. Certainly, they represent two opposing attributes of his musical personality; but the question-and-answer method was a reasonably well-worn device of musical criticism, and nobody has suggested that Thomas Morley and Berlioz were schizophrenic because they used it. People have sometimes complimented me on the way in which I draw the unsuspecting listener into a broadcast so that he does not realise until he is well and truly hooked that I am going to discuss a work by a composer whom he thoroughly dislikes. Schumann was using a similar technique; at the time, few members of the public knew Chopin's name, but the article is so readable that they are drawn into it in spite of themselves.

You may feel that there has been enough of Mozart already in this anthology, but I can never have enough of him myself. I have chosen two oddments that seem to me to have more than personal interest, for they both concern audience reaction. We have become very high-minded about applause nowadays, to such a degree that we even receive a movement like the *March to the Scaffold* from the *Fantastic Symphony* in complete silence. Berlioz would probably have committed suicide if he had been treated so chillingly during his lifetime. Similarly, it seems to me ludicrous that we shouldn't applaud the brilliant march in Tchaikovsky's sixth symphony, or the first movement of either of the Brahms piano concertos. It is surely a matter of common-sense to judge when a composer invites applause or forbids it.

As Hugo Wolf said:

> Let people continue to clap, but only when the work itself in some measure calls for it, when it concludes brilliantly and loud, when its character is festive, gay, warlike or heroic. Would anyone deny that the close of the *Coriolan* overture affects the soul in a different way from the close of *Egmont*?

In an ideal society, there would be occasions when to receive a work in silence would be a greater testament of approval than to dispel the atmosphere by clapping furiously. This is not to say that I would defend the customs of Mozart's day when, apparently outbursts of applause *during* a movement were not only commonplace, but acceptable to the composer – or so it would seem. It is my firm conviction that the reason why Mozart seldom gave the pianist anything to play after the cadenza in the first movement of a concerto was that he knew perfectly well that the final bars would be drowned by applause. Audience participation was certainly regarded in a very different light in Mozart's day and the description of his spontaneous improvisation suggests something nearer to a jazz concert than anything that we normally experience.

I sincerely hope that one of the functions that this book will fulfil is to pull down some of the great musicians from those distant niches into which we tend to put them and make them come to life as human beings. The rooms at the Royal College of Music where I teach are well-lined with pictures, and there one sees the placid expressions of Meyerbeer and Moscheles, Mozart, Mendelssohn or Macpherson all gazing with equal indifference on the aspiring students who stumble their way through scales or sonatas alike. It is all so impersonal. 'No interpretation without identification' should be the cry, identification with the composer, with the period in which he lived, with his state of mind, with everything that conspired to make him what he was. We all know of Chopin's winter in Majorca with George Sand; but clad as it is in a romantic veil, we tend to think of the incident almost as something that happened in a novel. The ludicrous rulings of the authorities about the composer's piano make us realise that life was real and very earnest at the time.

Paderewski's parrot, Cocky Roberts, sounds such a lovable character that I felt he couldn't be left out. I know many musicians who are devoted to their pets, but there is surprisingly little literature about them; perhaps it is more of a twentieth-century phenomenon than we imagine. Busoni had an enormous St Bernard called Giotto; on one occasion, when Busoni was waiting in a station restaurant, the dog knocked down the sword of a Swiss officer. 'Please excuse him,' said the pianist; 'he is anti-militarist.' There is a shortage of such stories, however, and I felt that Cocky Roberts should stand in for all the unrecorded pets who have inspired affection in their owners.

Mendelssohn was a prolific and engaging letter-writer, and it was a temptation to include many of his vivid descriptions of everyday events. As a sample of his style I have chosen a reference to the holiday in Scotland which was immortalised in the Hebrides overture. It's interesting to note that one of his letters at this time contains a sketch of the opening bars of the overture, virtually as it stands today – a genuine and rare instance of spontaneous inspiration. He was a good amateur artist too, and often decorated his letters with little sketches, showing a view from a hotel window, substitutes for the colour slides which we now collect for our friends' benefit when we travel.

Lastly, as a demonstration of the high emotional level at which nineteenth-century life seems to have been lived, we have the tale of Liszt and the Countess. It is a scenario writer's dream, though were we to see it reproduced in a film we should doubtless deplore the introduction of so melodramatic a scene into the unblemished respectability of a Great Composer's Life. Strictly speaking, it has nothing to do with music, except insofar as Liszt was the object of the lady's anger; but as an incident it is sufficiently entertaining to warrant inclusion in this bag of odds and ends.

A classic of criticism

EUSEBIUS dropped by one evening, not long ago. He entered quietly, his pale features brightened by that enigmatic smile with which he likes to excite curiosity. Florestan and I were seated at the piano. He, as you know, is one of those rare musical persons who seem to anticipate everything that is new, of the future and extraordinary. This time, however, there was a surprise in store even for him. With the words, 'Hats off, gentlemen, a genius!' Eusebius spread out before us a piece of music.

We were not allowed to see the title. I turned the pages idly; there is something magical about this secret enjoyment of music unheard. It seems to me, moreover, that every composer has his own musical handwriting. Beethoven looks different on paper from Mozart, just as Jean Paul's prose differs from Goethe's. Here, however, it was as if I were being stared at oddly by strange eyes – eyes of flowers, basilisks, peacocks, maidens. In certain places it became clearer – I thought I could discern Mozart's *La ci darem la mano* being woven through a hundred chords, Leporello winking at me, and Don Giovanni hurrying by in a white cloak.

'Well, let's hear it,' said Florestan. Eusebius obliged, while we listened, pressed against each other in the embrasure of a window. He played as if possessed, conjuring up countless figures of the most vivid actuality. It was as if the enthusiasm of the moment had given to his fingers a dexterity far beyond their normal endowment. Florestan's applause, to be sure, not counting a serene smile, consisted of nothing more than a statement that the variations could have been by Beethoven or Schubert, had either of them been a great piano virtuoso. But then he looked at the title and read: *La ci darem la mano, varié pour le Pianoforte par Frédéric Chopin, Œuvre 2*, and we both exclaimed incredulously, 'An Opus 2!'

We all started talking at once, our faces flushed with excitement. The general tenor was: 'Something decent, at last – Chopin, never heard of him! – Who can he be? – A genius in any case! – Was that not Zerlina laughing, or Leporello?'

The scene was quite beyond description. Drunk with wine, Chopin and conversation, we dashed off to Master Raro. He laughed sceptically and said:

'Oh, I know you and all your new discoveries. But anyway, bring this Chopin round.' We promised to oblige next day. Eusebius soon took his leave, quietly as always. I stayed behind for a while with Master Raro. Florestan, who has no home for the moment, fled through the moonlit streets to my house. I found him there in my room after midnight, stretched out on the sofa, his eyes closed.

'Chopin's variations,' he began, as if talking in his sleep, 'keep going through my head. Certainly it's all dramatic, and it's all Chopin. The introduction – as complete in itself as it is – (do you remember Leporello's skips in thirds?) – strikes me as the least appropriate to the whole. But the theme (I wonder why he chose B flat), the variations, the concluding episode and the Adagio – genius peeks out at you from every bar. Of course, dear Julius, the characters are Don Giovanni, Zerlina, Leporello and Masetto. Zerlina's answer in the theme is amorously enough defined. The first variation might be described, perhaps, as aristocratic and coquettish – the Spanish grandee flirting amiably with the peasant girl. This becomes self-evident in the second variation, which is more intimate, more comical and more contentious, just as if two lovers were chasing each other and laughing rather more than usual. How it all changes in the third variation! Here is moonlight and fairy-magic, with Masetto standing apart and cursing roundly – and Don Giovanni unperturbed. Now about the fourth, what do you think of it? (Eusebius played it very cleanly, by the way.) Is it not pert and wanton and straight to the point? The Adagio is in B flat minor, to be sure, but I can think of nothing more appropriate. It seems to imply a moral admonition to the Don. It's naughty, of course, but also delightful that Leporello should be eavesdropping – laughing and mocking from behind the bushes; that oboes and clarinets should pour forth their charming seduction, and that B flat major, in full bloom, should signal the first amorous kiss. But all that is nothing compared with the last movement – is there wine left, Julius? That is the whole Mozart finale, complete with popping champagne corks and clinking glasses – with Leporello's voice intruding, and the vengeful, pursuing shades, and Don Giovanni in full flight! And then the ending – reassuring and conclusive.'

Only in Switzerland, he concluded, had he ever experienced such sensations as in hearing this finale (on one of those lovely days when the evening sun reaches higher and higher to the tips of the highest mountains and disappears with one final ray of light, and one senses that the white giants of the alps have closed their eyes, and one feels that he has been vouchsafed a heavenly vision). 'Now, Julius,' he said, 'how about alerting yourself to some new dreams and going to sleep!'

'Dearest Florestan,' I replied, 'these private feelings may well be praiseworthy, if rather subjective; but, obvious as Chopin's genius may be, I, too, bow my head to such inspiration, such high endeavour, such mastery!'

On this we slept.

THE MUSICAL WORLD OF ROBERT SCHUMANN: *Henry Pleasants*

All right on the night

I HAVE HAD TO COMPOSE a symphony for the opening of the Concerts Spirituels. On Corpus Christi Day it was performed, and won great applause. I hear that a notice of it was carried in the *Courière de l'Europe* – so it was exceptionally well liked. At the rehearsal I was terribly worried, for in all my life I have never heard anything worse. You cannot imagine how they stumbled and scraped through the symphony twice in succession. I was really alarmed. I would have liked another rehearsal, but because they had so many things to rehearse there was no time. So I had to go to bed with fear in my heart and anger and dissatisfaction in my mind. Next day I decided not to go to the concert at all. But the weather turned fine in the evening, and I finally went, resolving that if the performance went as badly as the rehearsal I would rush into the orchestra, snatch the violin from the hand of Monsieur Laboussaye, the first violin, and conduct it myself. I prayed to God that it would go well, for all is to His greater honour and glory. And – *ecce!* – the symphony began, Raaff stood up, and right in the first allegro was a passage which I was sure would please. The whole audience was carried away by it, and there was great applause. Because I knew as I wrote it what an effect it would produce, I had brought the passage in once more at the close, and there was the same enthusiasm for the repeat. The andante was also well received, and the last allegro particularly so. Because I had heard that here all final allegros start out, like the first, with all instruments playing together and usually in unison, I began with two violins alone, piano for eight measures. Then came a sudden forte. The audience, as I expected, whispered 'Sh' at the piano. Then the forte crashed in. They clapped immediately. I was so pleased that after the symphony I went straight to the Palais Royal, had a good sherbet, said the rosary as I had vowed, and went home.

Mozart improvises

BY GENERAL REQUEST Mozart then performed on the pianoforte at a grand concert in the opera house. Never before had the theatre been so crowded as it was on this occasion; never before had there been such overwhelming and unanimous ecstasy as his divine playing aroused. We truly did not know which we ought to admire the more, the extraordinary compositions or the extraordinary playing. Both together produced a total effect upon our souls which resembled a sweet enchantment. At the end of the concert, when Mozart improvised alone for more than half-an-hour, and our rapture reached its highest degree, the spell dissolved in a thunderous outpouring of applause. And in truth this improvisation surpassed all that anyone could imagine possible in the art of clavier playing, for the pinnacle of the art of composition was here united with sublime skill in performance. As a result of the storm of applause, he felt compelled to sit down at the clavier once more. The torrent of this new improvisation had an even more powerful effect, and the consequence was that he was overwhelmed for the third time by the ardent audience. Once more Mozart re-appeared. Sincere gratification at the enthusiastic appreciation for his artistic achievements radiated from his countenance. He began for the third time with still higher inspiration, performed feats that had never been performed before. Suddenly, out of the prevailing utter silence, a loud voice in the parterre cried: 'From *Figaro*!' Whereupon Mozart introduced the theme of that favourite aria *Non piu andrai farfallone* . . . and produced impromptu a dozen of the most fascinating and artful variations, and thus, amid roars of jubilation, concluded this remarkable exhibition of his art, which for him was certainly the most glorious in his life, and for the Bohemians, who were intoxicated with rapture, was surely the most enjoyable.

MOZART AND HIS TIMES: *Erich Schenk*

Plus ça change. . . .

FOR A PIANO which we had sent from France, we were asked to pay seven hundred francs import duty, which was practically the value of the instrument. We tried to send it back, but this was forbidden; to leave it at the port until further notice was equally forbidden; to have it moved out of the town (we were then living in the country) and thereby avoid at least the harbour dues, which differ from the customs dues, was illegal; to leave it in the town, and thereby avoid the exit dues, which are different from the entrance dues, was impossible; all that we had the right to do was throw it in the sea.

WINTER IN MAJORCA: *George Sand*

Paderewski's parrot

COCKY ROBERTS stayed with us during the Australian and New Zealand tours, and throughout the whole American tour, and afterwards he lived with us for some six or seven years. He was here, at Morges, an important member of the family. He was an excellent traveller, though he did not like rough weather on board ship; quite especially when we were travelling from New Zealand to Tasmania on that famous Tasmanian Sea, which is the roughest in the world. The ship, a very small one, was rolling all the time and sometimes pitching in a dreadful way. Cocky Roberts's cage was moving constantly from one corner of the cabin to the other, and the poor parrot did not understand what was the matter with it. He was in a state of fury. 'Oh, you wretches, you wretches,' he would scream. 'Go to hell!'

Cocky Roberts was a beautiful, lovable bird. But such a voice, especially when he was angry! A voice so shrieking, so penetrating that I could not stand it. But in spite of his voice, I loved that parrot and he loved me. I could do anything with him. He always came to have his neck scratched and he was delighted when I touched him. He used to come regularly to my room when I was practising. I tried to avoid him and would close the doors. When this happened he would knock sharply with his beak. At first I would keep very quiet. Then he would knock again, a little harder, and I would call out through the door, 'Who is there? Who is it?' Then an angry voice would answer, 'Cocky Roberts.' 'Who?' I would say, pretending not to understand, and then that angry shrill little voice would come again, 'Cocky Roberts! Cocky Roberts!'

Of course, I had to let him in after that and he would walk straight to the piano and perch there on my foot for hours while I practised, and the pedalling (and my pedalling is very strenuous as you know) did not seem to disturb him in the least. He would sit perfectly still on top of my foot. And then from time to time he would say in a very loving and scratchy voice, 'Oh, Lord, how beautiful! How beautiful!' Ah, it was touching.

When I stopped and got up, as I generally did once during my practice, he understood perfectly that there would be no more playing for some little time, and then he would walk about the room and amuse himself. But he would not leave me; he stayed close beside me until I began to play again. When I had really finished, then he could be persuaded to go to his own little room, and there he would sit on his perch and was very quiet. But whenever I played, he felt it was his duty to watch me and that his place was by my side, and there he would stay as long as I practised.

THE PADEREWSKI MEMOIRS: *Ignace Jan Paderewski and Mary Lawton*

Mendelssohn's Scottish lament

... THIS THEN is the end of our Highland journey and the last of our joint letters. We have been happy together, we have led a merry life, and roved about the country as gaily as if the storm and rain which all newspapers reported (by this time perhaps even those in Berlin) had not existed. But they did exist. We had weather that made the trees and rocks crash. The day before yesterday on Loch Lomond we were sitting in deep twilight in a small row-boat and were going to cross to the opposite shore, invited by a gleaming light, when there came a sudden tremendous gust of wind from the mountains; the boat began to rock so fearfully that I caught up my cloak and got ready to swim. All our things were thrown topsy-turvy and Klingemann anxiously called to me, 'Look sharp, look sharp!' But with our usual good luck we got through it safely. When on shore, we had to live in a room with a cursing young Englishman, who was half-sportsman, half-peasant, half-gentleman, and altogether insufferable, and with three other individuals of the same calibre. We were obliged to sleep in the next house close to the roof, so that from sitting-room to bedroom we walked with umbrellas, cloak and cap. To describe the wretchedness and comfortless, inhospitable solitude of the country, time and space do not allow; we wandered ten days without meeting a single traveller; what are marked on the map as towns, or at least villages, are just a few sheds huddled together, with one and the same hole for door, window and chimney, for the entrance and the exit of men, animals, light and smoke. To all questions you get a dry 'No', brandy is the only beverage known, there is no church, no street, no garden, the rooms are pitch-dark in broad daylight, children and fowls lie in the same straw, many huts are without roofs altogether, many are unfinished, with crumbling walls, or just ruins of burnt houses, and even such inhabited spots are but sparingly scattered over the country. Long before you arrive at a place you hear it talked of; the rest is heath with red or brown heather, withered fir branches and white stones between, or black moors where they shoot grouse. Now and then you find beautiful but empty parks, broad lakes, but without boats, and the roads are deserted. And over all this is the brilliance of the rich sunshine which changes the heath into a thousand colours, all so divinely gay and warmly lighted and the cloud shadows chasing hither and thither! It is no wonder that the Highlands have been called melancholy. But two fellows have wandered gaily through them, laughed at every opportunity, rhymed and sketched together, growled at one another and at the world when they happened to be vexed or found nothing to eat, devoured everything edible when they did find it, and slept twelve hours every night; those two were we, and we will not forget it as long as we live.

MENDELSSOHN LETTERS: G Selden-Goth

Don't shoot the pianist!

ONE OF HIS PUPILS, a Cossack lady, had followed him amongst others, when he left Rome. She was a Countess, still fairly young, but painfully thin. She had a pale, intelligent face, large, black eyes, pleasing manners, and was altogether very '*comme il faut*'.

She read Kant and Schopenhauer, and to amuse herself had studied the microscope and vivisection, and now she wanted at any price to become a pianist. We found out, afterwards, that she had had relations with the master for several years.

Liszt was living in a delightful suite of rooms in the house of his friend, the Curé Schwendtner. Every Sunday afternoon all the fashionable world of Budapest went there to visit him. At one of these matinées the Countess played Chopin's *Grande Ballade in G minor*, and she played it with such bravura and fire that the master publicly congratulated her.

She had promised to play at a charity concert which was to take place shortly, and we all advised her to play this *Ballade* which she played so admirably. But we none of us knew that we were giving her the worst kind of advice.

On the evening of the concert a brilliant audience assembled. The Countess arrived, on the arm of Liszt, wearing a violet velvet dress buttoned up to her throat. He got her a seat in the little drawing-room with open colonnades facing the audience, which was reserved for the artists.

When her turn came she was very graciously received, and she commenced her *Ballade*, of course playing by heart. All went well until the sixth page, when she hesitates and gets confused. In desperation, she begins again, encouraged by indulgent applause. But, at the very same passage, her overwrought nerves betray her again. Pale as a sheet she rises. Then the master, thoroughly irritated, stamps his foot, and calls out from where he is sitting: 'Stop where you are.' She sits down again, and, in the midst of a sickening silence, she begins the wretched piece for the third time. Again her obstinate memory deserts her. She makes a desperate effort to remember the final passage, and at last finishes the fatal piece with a clatter of awful discords.

I was never present at a more painful scene. Going out, the master upbraided her more than angrily, as she clung to his arm. He had been severely tried, and he at last lost all patience with the freaks of his pupil. And, this breakdown confirming, as it did, his oft-expressed opinion that she was not of the stuff that artists are made of, he no longer spared her.

The Countess went home, took a dose of laudanum, and slept for forty-eight hours. They thought she was dead, but she woke up again.

After letters had passed between them, the master insisted on her leaving Budapest immediately. They say she went to his apartments, one morning, with a revolver. She deliberately took aim at him. 'Fire,' said Liszt, advancing towards her. The unhappy woman dropped her hand, and fell at his feet, but all her entreaties were in vain. Liszt was inexorable, and she was obliged to leave Budapest.

LISZT: *Sacheverell Sitwell*

Requiem

The Mass for the Dead in the Roman Catholic church service, used generally on All Souls' Day (2nd November) and specifically at funeral services at any time. It may be sung to plainsong or in more or less elaborate musical settings. Some of the greatest settings, although originally written to order (Mozart) or intended for a special religious occasion (Berlioz, Verdi), are now fit mainly or solely for concert use, and some were actually written for that purpose (eg Dvorak).

The death of Mozart, by O'Neill

Requiem

'THOSE WHOM THE GODS LOVE DIE YOUNG'. . . . Young in spirit or in body? The old proverb retains its enigma; but in music, death has been impartial. We may bewail the premature loss of Mozart and Schubert, but we must also be grateful for the astonishing late flowering of Verdi's genius, and acknowledge that Bach, Handel and Haydn all outlived many of their immediate contemporaries. The expectation of life was short; at least Mozart and Schubert wrote within the brief span of their lives as much as would satisfy the demands of any reasonable being. Perhaps they simply burned themselves out. Composers of such genius are consumed by an inner daemon; look at their complete works, handsomely bound in the library shelves, and who can fail to be amazed by the fantastic industry which led them to write unceasingly from one year's end to the next. Handel finished one opera on Christmas Eve, played in Church on Christmas Day and started another opera on Boxing Day. Schubert would break off a song in mid-phrase, go to bed (sometimes still wearing his spectacles) and continue the following morning as if there had been no interruption.

It is easy to speculate about what might have been if medical science had been more advanced in the nineteenth century. How many more creative years might Mozart or Beethoven have been given; in what direction might they have turned had they lived even another decade? But death came, often painfully and messily, and to read about it is perhaps a way, paradoxical though it may seem, of bringing these men to life more vividly in our minds. When I think of the last agonising months of Beethoven's life, it hurts me more when I play the slow movement of the *Hammerklavier* or Op 110, and that is as it should be. Afflicted with dropsy, he was tapped four times by the surgeons, and as the water spurted from his body he said to the doctor, 'Professor, you remind me of Moses striking the rock with his staff.' On another occasion he pointed to the fluid that seeped from him, and growled,

'Better from my belly than my pen.' I have spared you most of the gory details, but you may find them in Thayer's *Life of Beethoven* if you wish.

I include in this rather harrowing section a brief description of Bach's death, in which his momentary regaining of sight suggests that his blindness may have been diabetic; a long narration by Mozart's sister-in-law Sophie which comes from that inexhaustible treasure-trove, the collected letters of Mozart and his family, so lovingly and ably translated by Emily Anderson. Normally, one would not expect to be moved by an article in a dictionary, but the earlier editions of Grove contained an article on Schubert which actually brought tears into my eyes when I first read it. The phrase about 'turning his poor tired hands to the wall' has haunted me ever since; you will not find it in the current edition of Grove, since such romanticism is alien to present-day scholarship. I include it partly as a tribute to Sir George Grove, whose book on Beethoven's symphonies has given me more pleasure than any other analytical writings, with the exception of Tovey's essays.

Lastly, we hear from Brahms of Schumann's death in a letter to a friend. I have already commented on the conflict of emotions he must have experienced at this time.

REQUIEM AETERNAM DONA EIS

BACH

THE INDEFATIGABLE diligence with which, particularly in his younger years, he had frequently passed days and nights, without intermission, in the study of his art, had weakened his sight. This weakness continually increased in his latter years till at length it brought on a very painful disorder in the eyes. By the advice of some friends who placed great confidence in the ability of an oculist who had arrived at Leipzig from England, he ventured to submit to an operation, which twice failed. Not only was his sight now wholly lost, but his constitution, which had been hitherto so vigorous, was quite undermined by the use of perhaps noxious medicines in connection with the operation. He continued to decline for full half a year till he expired on the evening of the 30th of July, 1750, in the sixty-sixth year of his age. On the morning of the tenth day before his death, he was all at once able to see again and to bear the light. But a few hours afterwards he was seized with an apoplectic fit; this was followed by a high fever, which his enfeebled frame, notwithstanding all possible medical aid, was unable to resist.

THE BACH READER (*Forkel on Bach Life and Works*): Hans T David and
Arthur Mendel

MOZART

NOW I MUST TELL YOU about Mozart's last days. Well, Mozart became fonder and fonder of our dear departed mother and she of him. Indeed, he often came running along in great haste to the Wieden (where she and I were lodging at the Goldner Pflug), carrying under his arm a little bag containing coffee and sugar, which he would hand to our good mother, saying, 'Here, mother dear, now you can have a little *Jause*.'[1] She used to be as delighted as a child. He did this very often. In short, Mozart in the end never came to see us without bringing something.

Now when Mozart fell ill, we both made him a night-jacket which he could put on frontways, since on account of his swollen condition he was unable to turn in bed. Then, as we didn't know how seriously ill he was, we also made him a quilted dressing-gown (though indeed his dear wife, my sister, had given us the materials for both garments), so that when he got up he should have everything he needed. We often visited him and he seemed to be really looking forward to wearing his dressing-gown. I used to go into town every day to see him. Well, one Saturday when I was with him, Mozart said to me: 'Dear Sophie, do tell Mamma that I am fairly well and that I shall be able to go and congratulate her on the octave of her name-day.' Who could have been more delighted than I to bring such cheerful news to my mother, who was ever anxious to hear how he was? I hurried home therefore to comfort her, the more so as he himself really seemed to be bright and happy. The following day was a Sunday. I was young then and rather vain, I confess, and liked to dress up. But I never cared to go out walking from our suburb into town in my fine clothes, and I had no money for a drive. So I said to our good mother: 'Dear Mamma, I'm not going to see Mozart today. He was so well yesterday that surely he will be much better this morning, and one day more or less won't make much difference.' Well, my mother said: 'Listen to this. Make me a bowl of coffee and then I'll tell you what you ought to do.' She was rather inclined to keep me at home; and, indeed, my sister knows how much I had to be with her. I went into the kitchen. The fire was out. I had to light the lamp and make a fire. All the time I was thinking of Mozart. I had made the coffee and the lamp was still burning. Then I noticed how wasteful I had been with my lamp, I mean, that I had burned so much oil. It was still burning brightly. I stared into the flame and thought to myself, 'How I should love to know how Mozart is.' While I was thinking and gazing at the flame, it went out, as completely as if the lamp had never been burning. Not a spark remained on the main wick and yet there wasn't the slightest draught – that I can swear to. A horrible feeling came over me. I ran to our mother and told her all. She said: 'Well, take off your fine clothes and go into town and bring me back news of him at once. But be sure not to delay.' I hurried along as fast as I could. Alas, how frightened I was when my sister, who was almost despairing and yet trying to keep calm, came out to me saying: 'Thank God that you have come, dear Sophie. Last night he was so ill that I thought he would not be alive this morning. Do stay with me today, for if he has another bad turn, he will pass away tonight. Go in to him for a little while and see how he is.' I tried to control myself and went to his bedside. He immediately called me to him and said: 'Ah, dear Sophie, how glad I am that you have come. You must stay here tonight and see me die.' I tried hard to be brave and to persuade him to the contrary. But to all my attempts he only replied: 'Why, I

[1] *Afternoon coffee*

am already tasting death. And, if you do not stay, who will support my dearest Constanze when I am gone?' 'Yes, yes, dear Mozart,' I assured him, 'but I must first go back to our mother and tell her that you would like me to stay with you today. Otherwise she will think that some misfortune has befallen you.' 'Yes, do so,' said Mozart, 'but be sure and come back soon.' Good God, how distressed I felt! My poor sister followed me to the door and begged me for Heaven's sake to go to the priests at St Peter's and implore one of them to come to Mozart – a chance call, as it were. I did so, but for a long time they refused to come and I had a great deal of trouble to persuade one of those heartless people to go to him. Then I ran off to my mother who was anxiously awaiting me. It was already dark. Poor soul, how shocked she was! I persuaded her to go and spend the night with her eldest daughter, the late Josefa Hofer. I then ran back as fast as I could to my distracted sister. Süssmayr was at Mozart's bedside. The well-known *Requiem* lay on the quilt and Mozart was explaining to him how, in his opinion, he ought to finish it, when he was gone. Further, he urged his wife to keep his death a secret until she should have informed Albrechtsberger, who was in charge of all the services. A long search was made for Dr Closset, who was found at the theatre, but who had to wait for the end of the play. He came and ordered cold poultices to be placed on Mozart's burning head, which, however, affected him to such an extent that he became unconscious and remained so until he died. His last movement was an attempt to express with his mouth the drum passages in the *Requiem*. That I can still hear. Müller from the Art Gallery came and took a cast of his pale, dead face. Words fail me, dearest brother, to describe how his devoted wife in her utter misery threw herself on her knees and implored the Almighty for His aid. She simply could not tear herself away from Mozart, however much I begged her to do so. If it was possible to increase her sorrow, this was done on the day after that distressing night, when crowds of people walked past his corpse and wept and mourned for him. All my life I have never seen Mozart in a temper, still less, angry.

THE LETTERS OF MOZART & HIS FAMILY: *Emily Anderson*

BEETHOVEN

THROUGH A SPACIOUS anteroom in which high cabinets were piled with thick, tied-up parcels of music we reached – how my heart beat! – Beethoven's living-room, and were not a little astonished to find the master sitting in apparent comfort at the window. He wore a long, grey sleeping-robe, open at the time, and high boots reaching to his knees. Emaciated by long and severe illness he seemed to me, when he arose, of tall stature; he was unshaven, his thick, half-grey hair fell in disorder over his temples. The expression of his features heightened when he caught sight of Hummel, and he seemed extraordinarily glad to meet him. The two men embraced each other most cordially. Hummel introduced me. Beethoven showed himself extremely kind and I was permitted to sit opposite him at the window. It is known that conversation with Beethoven was carried on in part in writing; he spoke, but those with whom he conversed had to write their questions and answers. For this purpose thick sheets of ordinary writing-paper in quarto form and lead-pencils always lay near him. How painful it must have been for the animated, easily impatient man to be obliged to wait for every answer, to make a pause in every moment of conversation, during which, as it were, thought was condemned to come to a standstill! He always followed the hand of the writer with hungry eyes and comprehended what was written at a glance instead of reading it. The liveliness of the conversation naturally interfered with the continual writing of the visitor. I can scarcely blame myself, much as I regret it, for not taking down more extended notes than I did; indeed, I rejoice that a lad of fifteen years who found himself in a great city for the first time, was self-possessed enough to regard any details. I can vouch with the best conscience for the perfect accuracy of all that I am able to repeat.

The conversation at first turned, as is usual, on domestic affairs, – the journey and sojourn, my relations with Hummel and matters of that kind. Beethoven asked about Goethe's health with extraordinary solicitude and we were able to make the best of reports, since only a few days before the great poet had written in my album. Concerning his own state, poor Beethoven complained much. 'Here I have been lying for four months,' he cried out, 'one must at last lose patience!' Other things in Vienna did not seem to be to his liking and he spoke with the utmost severity of 'the present taste in art', and 'the dilettantism which is ruining everything'. Nor did he spare the government, up to the most exalted regions. 'Write a volume of penitential hymns and dedicate it to the Empress,' he remarked with a gloomy smile to Hummel, who, however, made no use of the well-meant advice. Hummel, who was a practical man, took advantage of Beethoven's condition to ask his attention to a matter which occupied a long time. It was about the theft of one of Hummel's concertos, which had been printed illicitly before it had been brought out by the lawful publisher. Hummel wanted to appeal to the Bundestag against this wretched business, and to this end desired to have Beethoven's signature, which seemed to him of great value. He sat down to explain the matter in writing and meanwhile I was permitted to carry on the conversation with Beethoven. I did my best, and the master continued to give free rein to his moody and passionate utterances in the most confidential manner. In part, they referred to his nephew, whom he had loved greatly, who, as is known, caused him much trouble and at that time, because of a few trifles (thus Beethoven at least seemed to consider them), had gotten into trouble with the officials. 'Little thieves are hanged, but big ones are allowed to go free!' he exclaimed ill-humouredly. He asked me about my studies and, encouraging me, said: 'Art must be propagated ceaselessly,' and when I spoke of the exclusive interest in Italian opera which then prevailed in Vienna, he gave utterance to the memorable words: 'It is said *vox populi, vox dei*. I never believed it.'

On March 13 Hummel took me with him a second time to Beethoven. We found his condition to be materially worse. He lay in bed, seemed to suffer great pains, and at intervals groaned deeply despite the fact that he spoke much and animatedly. Now he seemed to take it much to heart that he had not married. Already at our first visit he had joked about it with Hummel, whose wife he had known as a young and beautiful maiden. 'You are a lucky man,' he said to him now smilingly, 'you have a wife who takes care of you, who is in love with you – but poor me!' and he sighed heavily. He also begged of Hummel to bring his wife to see him, she not having been able to persuade herself to see in his present state the man whom she had known at the zenith of his powers. A short time before he had received a present of a picture of the house in which Haydn was born. He kept it close at hand and showed it to us. 'It gave me a childish pleasure,' he said, 'the cradle of so great a man!' Then he appealed to Hummel in behalf of Schindler, of whom so much was spoken afterwards. 'He is a good man,' he said, 'who has taken a great deal of trouble on my account. He is to give a concert soon at which I promised my co-operation. But now nothing is likely to come of that. Now I should like you to do me the favour of playing. We must always help poor artists.' As a matter of course, Hummel consented. The concert took place – ten days after Beethoven's death – in the Josephstadt-Theater. Hummel improvised in an obviously exalted mood on the *Allegretto of the A major Symphony*; the public knew why he participated and the performance and its reception formed a truly inspiring incident.

Shortly after our second visit the report spread throughout Vienna that the Philharmonic Society of London had sent Beethoven one hundred pounds in order to ease his sick-bed. It was added that this surprise had made so great an impression on the great poor man that it had also brought physical relief. When we stood again at his bedside, on the 20th, we could deduce from his utterances how greatly he had been rejoiced by this altruism; but he was very weak and spoke only in faint and disconnected phrases. 'I shall, no doubt, soon be going above,' he whispered after our first greeting. Similar remarks recurred frequently. In the intervals, however, he spoke of projects and hopes which were destined not to be realised. Speaking of the noble conduct of the Philharmonic Society and in praise of the English people, he expressed the intention, as soon as matters were better with him, to undertake the journey to London. 'I will compose a grand overture for them and a grand symphony.' Then, too, he would visit Madame Hummel (she had come along with her husband), and go to I do not know how many places. It did not occur to us to write anything for him. His eyes, which were still lively when we saw him last, dropped and closed today and it was difficult from time to time for him to raise himself. It was no longer possible to deceive one's self – the worst was to be feared.

Hopeless was the picture presented by the extraordinary man when we sought him again on March 23rd. It was to be the last time. He lay, weak and miserable, sighing deeply at intervals. Not a word fell from his lips; sweat stood upon his forehead. His handkerchief not being conveniently at hand, Hummel's wife took her fine cambric handkerchief and dried his face several times. Never shall I forget the grateful glance with which his broken eye looked upon her. On March 26, while we were with a merry company in the art-loving house of Herr von Liebenberg (who had formerly been a pupil of Hummel's), we were surprised by a severe storm between five and six o'clock. A thick snow-flurry was accompanied by loud peals of thunder and flashes of lightning, which lighted up the room. A few hours later guests arrived with the intelligence that Ludwig van Beethoven was no more – he had died at 4.45 o'clock.

THE LIFE OF LUDWIG VAN BEETHOVEN: *Alexander Wheelock Thayer*

SCHUBERT

ON SUNDAY THE 16TH NOV. the doctors had a consultation; they predicted a nervous fever, but they still had hopes of their patient. On the afternoon of Monday, Bauernfeld saw him for the last time. He was in very bad spirits, and complained of great weakness, and of heat in his head, but his mind was still clear, and there was no sign of wandering; he spoke of his earnest wish for a good opera-book. Later in the day, however, when the doctor arrived, he was quite delirious, and typhus had unmistakably broken out. The next day, Tuesday, he was very restless throughout, trying continually to get out of bed, and constantly fancying himself in a strange room. That evening he called Ferdinand on to the bed, made him put his ear close to his mouth, and whispered mysteriously, 'What are they doing with me?' 'Dear Franz,' was the reply, 'they are doing all they can to get you well again, and the doctor assures us you will soon be right, only you must do your best to stay in bed.' He returned to the idea in his wandering – 'I implore you to put me in my own room, and not to leave me in this corner under the earth; don't I deserve a place above ground?' 'Dear Franz,' said the agonised brother, 'be calm; trust your brother Ferdinand, whom you have always trusted, and who loves you so dearly. You are in the room which you always had, and lying on your own bed.' 'No,' said the dying man, 'that's not true; Beethoven is not here.' So strongly had the great composer taken possession of him! An hour or two later the doctor came, and spoke to him in the same style. Schubert looked him full in the face and made no answer; but turning round, clutched at the wall with his poor tired hands, and said in a slow earnest voice, 'Here, here is my end.' At three in the afternoon of Wednesday the 19th November 1828 he breathed his last, and his simple earnest soul took its flight from the world. He was thirty-one years, nine months, and nineteen days old. There never has been one like him, and there never will be another.

GROVE'S DICTIONARY OF MUSIC AND MUSICIANS

SCHUMANN

To Julius Otto Grimm

MY DEAR JULIUS,

What must you think of me for not answering? Don't be angry! Had you been bright and a little more —— and written to Frau Klara (Schumann), you wouldn't have had to wait.

Rather than make excuses and so on, I'll give you some particulars about those days.

I had spent Schumann's birthday with him – June 8th – and found him remarkably changed, suddenly, compared with the previous time. Then Frau Klara came back from England, and just as she arrived, so did worse news from Endenich. A week before his death, on the Wednesday, we had a telegraphic dispatch. I barely read, it said roughly this: 'If you wish to see your husband while he still lives, come at once. His appearance is frightful to behold.'

We drove over. He had had an attack which the doctors thought would be fatal. I don't know the right name – an asthmatic seizure? I went to him, saw him in fact in an attack, and so greatly agitated that I, and the doctors too, dissuaded Frau Schumann from going to him and urged her to make the return trip.

Schumann just lay, taking nothing but an occasional spoonful of wine and jelly. Frau Schumann's misery was so great all this while that on Saturday evening I *had* to suggest that she come back again and see him.

Now we give thanks to God that it happened so, for it is now absolutely indispensable for her peace of mind. She saw him again on Sunday, Monday, and early Tuesday. He died in the afternoon about four o'clock.

I cannot ever again experience anything so touching as the reunion of Robert and Klara.

At first he lay a long time with closed eyes, and she kneeled in front of him, more quietly than one would have thought possible. But he recognised her and again on the following days. Once he desired clearly to embrace her and threw his arms around her.

Of course he was no longer able to speak; one could only make out single words (perhaps imagine them), but even that must have pleased her. He often refused the wine that was offered him, but took it eagerly from her finger, for so long at a time and so ravenously, that one was convinced he recognised the finger.

Tuesday noon Joachim from Heidelberg, which held us up a while in Bonn, otherwise we would have arrived before his death, but we were half an hour too late. He died as easily as you read these words. We should have breathed more freely once he had been released but could hardly believe it.

His death was so gentle that it almost passed unnoticed. His body looked calm, as if all were for the best. It would have been impossible for a woman to stand it much longer.

They buried him Thursday afternoon. I carried the wreath before the coffin, with Joachim and Dietrich. The members of a choral society were pall bearers. There was trumpeting and singing.

The town had prepared ahead of time a beautiful spot for the event and had it decorated with five plane trees. Madame Klara found another kind of consolation in the institution itself. It set at rest all the evil rumours which had come to her ears about things – for example through Bettina —. I might and could write it all to you – somehow – but it wouldn't do. You can imagine for yourself on the strength of these bare facts, how sad, how beautiful, how moving this death was.

We (Joachim, Klara, and I) have put in order the papers that Schumann left: and that includes all he ever wrote! One comes to love and honour the man more and more as one has these closer dealings with him.

I shall delve deeper and deeper into all this.

Farewell. Forgive the hurried scrawl: there is no peace here for a peaceful letter. We are now in Heidelberg, after a few weeks on Lake Vierwaldstätter.

If you write to Frau Schumann and me, address us at Düsseldorf, to which we are returning very soon.

But still here for another week!

My next one will be longer and calmer. Regards to your dear wife. And don't be angry with me.

       Affectionately yours,
        J BRAHMS
    PLEASURES OF MUSIC: *Jacques Barzun*

Acknowledgements

I gratefully acknowledge the co-operation of:

Martin Secker and Warburg Limited, for *Mozart and his Times* by Eric Schenk; and for *If it Die* by André Gide.

John Farquharson Limited and Victor Gollancz Limited for *The Great Pianists* by Harold Schonberg and *The Musical World of Robert Schumann* by Henry Pleasants.

Thames and Hudson Limited for *Beethoven: Letters, Journals and Conversations* by Michael Hamburger.

Edward Arnold Limited for *Charles Villiers Stanford* by Harry Plunkett-Greene; and *Howard's End* by E M Forster.

Elek Books Limited for *Mendelssohn Letters* by G Selden-Goth.

Siegfried Sassoon and Faber and Faber Limited for *The Old Century and Seven More Years* by Siegfried Sassoon.

Faber and Faber Limited and Random House Inc, for *Composers on Music* by Sam Morgenstern.

Faber and Faber Limited and David Higham Associates for *British Composers in Interview* by B Murray Schafer.

Kistner and Siegel and Co for *Chopin's Teaching Methods* by Carl Mikuli.

Angus and Robertson Limited for *Duet for Three Hands* by Cyril Smith.

Collins Publishers for *Paderewski's Memoirs* by P and M Lawton and *Second Innings* and *Sir Thomas Beecham* by Neville Cardus.

Thornton Butterworth, Publishers for *Memories and Melodies* by Nellie Melba.

Chatto and Windus Limited for *Swann's Way* by Marcel Proust, translated by C Scott Moncrieff.

Wesleyan University Press for *Silence* by John Cage.

Paul Hamlyn Publishers for *The Composer in Love* by Cyril Clarke.

William Heinemann Limited for *Selected Correspondence of Frédéric Chopin* by Bronislaw Edward Sydow, translated by Arthur Hedley.

Calder and Boyars Limited for *Arnold Schoenberg* by H H Stuckenschmidt, and *Alban Berg: The Man and his Music* by H F Redlich.

The Psychic Book Club and the Spiritualist Press for *Talks with Great Composers* by Arthur Abell.

Icon Books Limited for *Delius as I Knew Him* by Eric Fenby.

Arthur Barker Limited for *Words by Request* by Christopher Hassall.

Eyre and Spottiswoode Limited for Psalm 150, Crown copyright.

Viking Press Inc for *The Pleasures of Music* by Jacques Barzun.

Laurence Pollinger Limited, T Werner Laurie Limited and Simon and Schuster Inc for *Enrico Caruso* by Dorothy Caruso.

Longmans Green Limited for *The Orchestra Speaks* by Bernard Shore.

David Higham Associates and Faber and Faber Limited for *Liszt* by Sacheverell Sitwell.

Centaur Press Limited for *Life of Ludwig van Beethoven* by Alexander Thayer.

Routledge and Kegan Paul Limited for *Wings of Song* by Lotte Lehmann; *The Art of the Prima Donna* by Frederick H Martens; and David Higham Associates and Routledge and Kegan Paul Limited for *Musicians on Music* by F Bonnavia.

Cassell and Company Limited for *My Life of Song* by Madame Tetrazzini.

Peter Davies Limited for *Master Musicians* by J Cuthbert Hadden.

Harvard University Press for *A Composer's World, Horizons and Limitations* by Paul Hindemith and *Poetics of Music* by Igor Stravinsky.

Macmillan and Company Limited for *Letters of Mozart and His Family* translated by Emily Anderson; *Groves' Dictionary of Music* and *Two on a Tower* by Thomas Hardy (Trustees of the Hardy Estate).

J M Dent and Company Limited for *Beethoven's Pianoforte Sonatas Discussed* by Eric Blom; *Everyman's Dictionary of Music*; *Schubert's Documents* by Otto Erich Deutsch and *The Bach Reader* by David and Mendel (with W W Norton Inc).

The Daily Telegraph for *Yehudi Menuhin's Genius* by Robin H Legge and *Britten Looking Back*.

Oxford University Press Limited for *Beethoven: Essays and Lectures in Music* by Donald Francis Tovey, *The Language of Music* by Deryck Cooke and *Gustav Holst* by Imogen Holst.

Mr Marziale Sisca for the drawing of Caruso from *Enrico Caruso* by Dorothy Caruso.

The late Mr Gerard Hoffnung and Dennis Dobson for the illustration from *The Hoffnung Companion to Music*.

Mr Eric Fenby and Icon Books for the sketch of Delius from *Delius as I Knew Him*.

I have made every endeavour to trace the owners of all copyright material included in this book, in a few instances without success. I would like to take this opportunity to apologise and express sincere regret if I have unintentionally transgressed by omitting a proper acknowledgement where due.

A H

Music and Books published by Travis & Emery Music Bookshop:
Anon.: Hymnarium Sarisburiense, cum Rubricis et Notis Musicis.
Anon.: Säcularfeier des Geburtstages von Ludwig van Beethoven
Agricola, Johann Friedrich from Tosi: Anleitung zur Singkunst.
Bach, C.P.E.: edited W. Emery: Nekrolog or Obituary Notice of J.S. Bach.
Bateson, Naomi Judith: Alcock of Salisbury
Bathe, William: A Briefe Introduction to the Skill of Song
Bax, Arnold: Symphony #5, Arranged for Piano Four Hands by Walter Emery
Burney, Charles: The Present State of Music in France and Italy
Burney, Charles: The Present State of Music in Germany, The Netherlands …
Burney, Charles: An Account of the Musical Performances … Handel
Burney, Karl: Nachricht von Georg Friedrich Handel's Lebensumstanden.
Burns, Robert: The Caledonian Musical Museum ..The Best Scotch Songs. (1810)
Cobbett, W.W.: Cobbett's Cyclopedic Survey of Chamber Music. (2 vols.)
Corrette, Michel: Le Maitre de Clavecin
Crimp, Bryan: Dear Mr. Rosenthal … Dear Mr. Gaisberg …
Crimp, Bryan: Solo: The Biography of Solomon
Crotch, William: Substance of Several Courses of Lectures on Music
d'Indy, Vincent: Beethoven: Biographie Critique
d'Indy, Vincent: Beethoven: A Critical Biography
d'Indy, Vincent: César Franck (in French)
Fischhof, Joseph: Versuch einer Geschichte des Clavierbaues. (Faksimile 1853).
Frescobaldi, Girolamo: D'Arie Musicali per Cantarsi. Primo & Secondo Libro.
Geminiani, Francesco: The Art of Playing the Violin.
Handel; Purcell; Boyce; Geene et al: Calliope or English Harmony: Volume First.
Häuser: Musikalisches Lexikon. 2 vols in one.
Hawkins, John: A General History of the Science and Practice of Music (5 vols.)
Herbert-Caesari, Edgar: The Science and Sensations of Vocal Tone
Herbert-Caesari, Edgar: Vocal Truth
Hopkins, Antony: The Concertgoer's Companion - Bach to Haydn.
Hopkins, Antony: The Concertgoer's Companion – Holst to Webern.
Hopkins, Antony: Music All Around Me
Hopkins, Antony: Sounds of Music / Sounds of the Orchestra
Hopkins, Antony: Understanding Music
Hopkins, Edward and Rimboult, Edward: The Organ. Its History & Construction.
Hunt, John: - see separate list of discographies at the end of these titles
Isaacs, Lewis: Hänsel and Gretel. A Guide to Humperdinck's Opera.
Isaacs, Lewis: Königskinder (Royal Children) A Guide to Humperdinck's Opera.
Kastner: Manuel Général de Musique Militaire
Lacassagne, M. l'Abbé Joseph : Traité Général des élémens du Chant.
Lascelles (née Catley), Anne: The Life of Miss Anne Catley.
Mainwaring, John: Memoirs of the Life of the Late George Frederic Handel
Malcolm, Alexander: A Treaty of Music: Speculative, Practical and Historical
Marx, Adolph Bernhard: Die Kunst des Gesanges, Theoretisch-Practisch
May, Florence: The Life of Brahms
May, Florence: The Girlhood Of Clara Schumann: Clara Wieck And Her Time.
Mellers, Wilfrid: Angels of the Night: Popular Female Singers of Our Time
Mellers, Wilfrid: Bach and the Dance of God

Music and Books published by Travis & Emery Music Bookshop:
Mellers, Wilfrid: Beethoven and the Voice of God
Mellers, Wilfrid: Caliban Reborn - Renewal in Twentieth Century Music
Mellers, Wilfrid: Darker Shade of Pale, A Backdrop to Bob Dylan
Mellers, Wilfrid: François Couperin and the French Classical Tradition
Mellers, Wilfrid: Harmonious Meeting
Mellers, Wilfrid: Le Jardin Retrouvé, The Music of Frederic Mompou
Mellers, Wilfrid: Music and Society, England and the European Tradition
Mellers, Wilfrid: Music in a New Found Land: ... ... American Music
Mellers, Wilfrid: Romanticism and the Twentieth Century (from 1800)
Mellers, Wilfrid: The Masks of Orpheus: ...... the Story of European Music.
Mellers, Wilfrid: The Sonata Principle (from c. 1750)
Mellers, Wilfrid: Vaughan Williams and the Vision of Albion
Panchianio, Cattuffio: Rutzvanscad Il Giovine
Pearce, Charles: Sims Reeves, Fifty Years of Music in England.
Pettitt, Stephen: Philharmonia Orchestra: A Record of Achievement, 1948-1985
Pettitt, Stephen (ed. Hunt): Philharmonia Orchestra: Complete Discography 1945-1987
Playford, John: An Introduction to the Skill of Musick.
Purcell, Henry et al: Harmonia Sacra ... The First Book, (1726)
Purcell, Henry et al: Harmonia Sacra ... Book II (1726)
Quantz, Johann: Versuch einer Anweisung die Flöte trave rsiere zu spielen.
Rameau, Jean-Philippe: Code de Musique Pratique, ou Methodes.
Rameau, Jean-Philippe: Erreurs sur La Musique dans l'Encyclopédie
Rastall, Richard: The Notation of Western Music.
Rimbault, Edward: The Pianoforte, Its Origins, Progress, and Construction.
Rousseau, Jean Jacques: Dictionnaire de Musique
Rubinstein, Anton : Guide to the proper use of the Pianoforte Pedals.
Sainsbury, John S.: Dictionary of Musicians. (1825). 2 vols.
Serré de Rieux, Jean de : Les dons des Enfans de Latone
Simpson, Christopher: A Compendium of Practical Musick in Five Parts
Spohr, Louis: Autobiography
Spohr, Louis: Grand Violin School
Tans'ur, William: A New Musical Grammar; or The Harmonical Spectator
Terry, Charles Sanford: Bach's Chorals – Parts 1, 2 and 3.
Terry, Charles Sanford: John Christian Bach
Terry, Charles Sanford: J.S. Bach's Original Hymn-Tunes for Congregational Use.
Terry, Charles Sanford: Four-Part Chorals of J.S. Bach. (German & English)
Terry, Charles Sanford: Joh. Seb. Bach, Cantata Texts, Sacred and Secular.
Terry, Charles Sanford: The Origins of the Family of Bach Musicians.
Tosi, Pierfrancesco: Opinioni de' Cantori Antichi, e Moderni
Tosi, Pierfrancesco: Observations on the Florid Song.
Van der Straeten, Edmund: History of the Violoncello, The Viol da Gamba ...
Van der Straeten, Edmund: History of the Violin, Its Ancestors... (2 vols.)
Walther, J. G. [Waltern]: Musicalisches Lexikon [Musikalisches Lexicon]
Wagner, Richard: Beethoven (Leipzig 1870)
Wagner, Richard: Lebens-Bericht (Leipzig 1884)
Wagner, Richard: The Musaic of the Future (Translated by E. Dannreuther).
Zwirn, Gerald: Stranded Stories From The Operas

Discographies by John Hunt.

3 Italian Conductors and 7 Viennese Sopranos: 10 Discographies: Arturo Toscanini, Guido Cantelli, Carlo Maria Giulini, Elisabeth Schwarzkopf, Irmgard Seefried, Elisabeth Gruemmer, Sena Jurinac, Hilde Gueden, Lisa Della Casa, Rita Streich.

A Gallic Trio: 3 Discographies: Charles Muench, Paul Paray, Pierre Monteux.

A Notable Quartet: 4 Discographies: Gundula Janowitz, Christa Ludwig, Nicolai Gedda, Dietrich Fischer-Dieskau.

American Classics: The Discographies of Leonard Bernstein and Eugene Ormand

Antal Dorati 1906-1988: Discography and Concert Register.

Back From The Shadows: 4 Discographies: Willem Mengelberg, Dimitri Mitropoulos, Hermann Abendroth, Eduard Van Beinum.

Carlo Maria Giulini: Discography and Concert Register.

Columbia 33CX Label Discography.

Concert Hall Discography: Concert Hall Society and Concert Hall Record Club

Conductors On The Yellow Label: 8 Discographies: Fritz Lehmann, Ferdinand Leitner, Ferenc Fricsay, Eugen Jochum, Leopold Ludwig, Artur Rother, Franz Konwitschny, Igor Markevitch.

Dirigenten der DDR: Conductors of the German Democratic Republic

From Adam to Webern: the Recordings of von Karajan.

Giants of the Keyboard: 6 Discographies: Wilhelm Kempff, Walter Gieseking, Edwin Fischer, Clara Haskil, Wilhelm Backhaus, Artur Schnabel.

Gramophone Stalwarts: 3 Separate Discographies: Bruno Walter, Erich Leinsdorf, Georg Solti.

Great Violinists: 3 Discographies: David Oistrakh, Wolfgang Schneiderhan, Arthur Grumiaux.

Hans Knappertsbusch: Kna: Concert Register and Discography of Hans Knappertsbusch, 1888-1965. Second Edition.

Her Master's Voice: Concert Register and Discography of Dame Elisabeth Schwarzkopf [Third Edition].

Hungarians in Exile: 3 Discographies: Fritz Reiner, Antal Dorati, George Szell.

Leopold Stokowski (1882-1977): Discography and Concert Register

Leopold Stokowski: Discography and Concert Listing.

Leopold Stokowski: Second Edition of the Discography.

Makers of the Philharmonia: 11 Discographies Alceo Galliera, Walter Susskind, Paul Kletzki, Nicolai Malko, Issay Dobrowen, Lovro Von Matacic, Efrem Kurtz, Otto Ackermann, Anatole Fistoulari, George Weldon, Robert Irving.

Makers of the Philharmonia: 11 Discographies: Alceo Galliera, Walter Susskind, Paul Kletzki, Nicolai Malko, Issay Dobrowen, Lovro Von Matacic, Efrem Kurtz, Otto Ackermann, Anatole Fistoulari, George Weldon, Robert Irving.

Metropolitan Sopranos: 4 Discographies: Rosa Ponselle, Eleanor Steber, Zinka Milanov, Leontyne Price.

Mezzo and Contraltos: 5 Discographies: Janet Baker, Margarete Klose, Kathleen Ferrier, Giulietta Simionato, Elisabeth Hoengen.

Mid-Century Conductors and More Viennese Singers: 10 Discographies: Karl Boehm, Victor De Sabata, Hans Knappertsbusch, Tullio Serafin, Clemens Krauss, Anton Dermota, Leonie Rysanek, Eberhard Waechter, Maria Reining, Erich Kunz.

More 20th Century Conductors: 7 Discographies: Eugen Jochum, Ferenc Fricsay, Carl Schuricht, Felix Weingartner, Josef Krips, Otto Klemperer, Erich Kleiber.

More Giants of the Keyboard: 5 Discographies: Claudio Arrau, Gyorgy Cziffra, Vladimir Horowitz, Dinu Lipatti, Artur Rubinstein.

More Musical Knights: 4 Discographies: Hamilton Harty, Charles Mackerras, Simon Rattle, John Pritchard.

Musical Knights: 6 Discographies: Henry Wood, Thomas Beecham, Adrian Boult, John Barbirolli, Reginald Goodall, Malcolm Sargent.

Philharmonic Autocrat 1: Discography of: Herbert Von Karajan [Third Edition]

Philharmonic Autocrat 2: Concert Register of Herbert Von Karajan Second Ed.

Philips Minigroove: Second Extended Version of the European Discography.

Pianists For The Connoisseur: 6 Discographies: Arturo Benedetti Michelangeli, Alfred Cortot, Alexis Weissenberg, Clifford Curzon, Solomon, Elly Ney.

Sächsische Staatskapelle Dresden: Complete Discography.

Singers of the Third Reich: 5 Discographies: Helge Roswaenge, Tiana Lemnitz, Franz Voelker, Maria Mueller, Max Lorenz.

Singers on the Yellow Label: 7 Discographies: Maria Stader, Elfriede Troetschel, Annelies Kupper, Wolfgang Windgassen, Ernst Haefliger, Josef Greindl, Kim Borg

Six Wagnerian Sopranos: 6 Discographies: Frieda Leider, Kirsten Flagstad, Astrid Varnay, Martha Moedl, Birgit Nilsson, Gwyneth Jones.

Sviatoslav Richter: Pianist of the Century: Discography.

Teachers and Pupils: 7 Discographies: Elisabeth Schwarzkopf, Maria Ivoguen, Maria Cebotari, Meta Seinemeyer, Ljuba Welitsch, Rita Streich, Erna Berger

Tenors in a Lyric Tradition: 3 Discographies: Peter Anders, Walther Ludwig, Fritz Wunderlich.

The Art of the Diva: 3 Discographies: Claudia Muzio, Maria Callas, Magda Olivero.

The Furtwaengler Sound Sixth Edition: Discography and Concert Listing.

The Great Dictators: 3 Discographies: Evgeny Mravinsky, Artur Rodzinski, Sergiu Celibidache.

The Lyric Baritone: 5 Discographies: Hans Reinmar, Gerhard Huesch, Josef Metternich, Hermann Uhde, Eberhard Waechter.

The Post-War German Tradition: 5 Discographies: Rudolf Kempe, Joseph Keilberth, Wolfgang Sawallisch, Rafael Kubelik, Andre Cluytens.

Wagner Im Festspielhaus: Discography of the Bayreuth Festival.

Wiener Philharmoniker 1 - Vienna Philharmonic and Vienna State Opera Orchestras: Discography Part 1 1905-1954.

Wiener Philharmoniker 2 - Vienna Philharmonic and Vienna State Opera Orchestras: Discography Part 2 1954-1989.

Available from: Travis & Emery at 17 Cecil Court, London, UK. (+44) 20 7 240 2129. email on sales@travis-and-emery.com .

© Travis & Emery 2011

www.ingramcontent.com/pod-product-compliance
Lightning Source LLC
Chambersburg PA
CBHW071703160426
43195CB00012B/1563